Confessions of an Eco-Shopper

The true story of one woman's mission to go green

Kate Lock

HODDER

For Isis, the best daughter in the universe.
Because it's your generation that will inherit this earth.

First published in Great Britain in 2008 by Hodder & Stoughton
An Hachette Livre UK company

First published in paperback in 2009

1

The ... of ... the Author f
the ... has been asserted by her in accordance ... ...
... Copyright ... Act 1988.

All ... this fashion. No part of this publication may
repro... st... ... trieval ... ... in
any for... ... ... w... ... ... ssion
of the pu... ... nor be ... ise circulat of in any form ... binding
or co... other than ... ... which ... is ... ... and w... out
a simila... ... ... aser.

A CIP cata... ... ... ord for this title is ... from the Br... h Library

ISBN 978 0340 954713

Typeset in Optima by Hewer Text UK Ltd, Edinburgh

Printed and bound by CPI Mackays, Chatham ME5 8TD

Hodder & Stoughton policy is to use papers that are natural, renewable
and recyclable products and made from wood grown in sustainable
forests. The logging and manufacturing processes are expected to
conform to the environmental regulations of the country of origin.

Hodder & Stoughton Ltd
338 Euston Road
London NW1 3BH

www.hodder.co.uk

Contents

Introduction   1

AISLE 1 – Fresh Challenges: *Fruit and Vegetables*

Challenge 1: Can you do without supermarkets?   7

Challenge 2: The vege box: getting to grips with mystery greens   13

Challenge 3: The organic moral maze and the land of local produce 18

Challenge 4: Does it taste any better? 'Organic vs Ordinary'   23

Challenge 5: Can you grow your own?   27

AISLE 2 – Homemade Challenges: *Dinners, Dairy, Baking, Preserves and Soup*

Challenge 6: Ready meals vs proper dinners   31

Challenge 7: Back to basics: can one woman make her own?   38

AISLE 3 – Chiller Challenges: *Milk, Meat and Fish*

Challenge 8: The quest to find the mystery milkman   48

Challenge 9: Going veggie: the one-week challenge   52

Challenge 10: Fishing for . . . anything that isn't cod   56

AISLE 4 – *Household Challenges:*
Cleaning, Washing, Wiping and Wrapping

Challenge 11: Domestic cleaning without chemicals   63
Challenge 12: Green washing: laundry the eco way   72
Challenge 13: Does recycled toilet roll pass the test? 78
Challenge 14: Can a girl live without clingfilm!?   82

AISLE 5 – *Healthy Challenges 1: Beauty Products*

Challenge 15: Staying lovely without chemicals   85
Challenge 16: Can you make your own skincare stuff at home? 99

AISLE 6 – *Healthy Challenges 2: Personal Care Products*

Challenge 17: Do natural deodorants really work?   106
Challenge 18: Sunscreens: what's the safety factor?   109
Challenge 19: Girl talk: the gory details on sanitary protection 116

AISLE 7 – *Liquid Challenges 1: Hot Drinks*

Challenge 20: Does Fairtrade tea make the best brew?   123
Challenge 21: Does ethical coffee hit the spot?   131

AISLE 8 – *Liquid Challenges 2: Cold Drinks*

Challenge 22: Does organic booze beat the hangover?   138
Challenge 23: Juicy fruit: squashing your own   144
Challenge 24: Water: what's the best?   150

AISLE 9 – *Baby Challenges: Nappies, Milk and Toys*

Challenge 25: Do real nappies do the business?   157
Challenge 26: Mother's milk or formula?   169
Challenge 27: Which toys pass the toddler test?   174

AISLE 10 – *Material Challenges: Clothes, Cotton, Swapping and Shoes*
Challenge 28: Can a girl be eco-smart and still be stylish?   181
Challenge 29: Can you find out where your fabrics come from?   191
Challenge 30: Handmade and hand-me-downs   197
Challenge 31: Shoes and handbags: can a girl ever have enough?   203

AISLE 11 – *Checkout Challenges: Bags, Packaging and Recycling*
Challenge 32: Kicking the plastic bag habit   209
Challenge 33: Packaging: can we get radical?   215
Challenge 34: Can the `Three Rs' solve the rubbish crisis?   222

AISLE 12 – *Rubbish Challenges:*
Composting, Wormeries and Magic Microbes
Challenge 35: Is composting the answer?   229
Challenge 36: Worms: charming or alarming?   236
Challenge 37: Do Bokashis and magic microbes do the business?   241

Conclusion   248

Acknowledgements   257
Web Directory   259

Introduction

Doing the weekly shop used to be pretty straightforward, didn't it? We came, we shopped, we conquered. Then we lugged it all home. We didn't worry about where the stuff we bought came from. After all, when it's on the shelf in front of you, it's already done the hard part. All we had to do was pick it up and pop it in the trolley. Shop 'n' go, no questions asked. Why would you? If the supermarket's selling it, it must be OK, right?

I'm trying to remember back to that time of blissful ignorance when asparagus flown in from Peru was considered a delicacy, not an act of environmental delinquency, and baby sweetcorn from the River Kwai wasn't a bridge too far in a stir-fry. There was none of this angst-ing in the aisles about farmed salmon or whether coffee growers were being exploited. We simply got on with it, glad of the convenience, and bought free-range eggs over the bog-standard ones if we were feeling conscientious.

To be fair, we didn't know then what we know now. It took writers like Joanna Blythman, George Monbiot and Felicity Lawrence, investigative programmes like *Panorama*, campaigning organisations like the Soil Association and pressure groups like

Friends of the Earth to make us aware that there was a back story to all of these products that we took for granted. We didn't know, but then we didn't think to ask, either.

Still, there's no point in beating ourselves up any more than we do already. The weekly shopping trip is enough of a guilt trip as it is. Locally produced pesticides or far-flung organic? In-season swede or unseasonal sweetcorn? Cheap whole chicken or two organic drumsticks? Cadbury's hot chocolate (daughter likes it) or that Fairtrade brand she never drinks? The kitchen roll that soaks up spills or the recycled stuff that dissolves? Small pack of environmentally friendly dishwasher tabs or the large box of polluting ones on special offer? How much sugar? Too much salt. Bad fats. No GM. Nut traces. Aspartame or tooth-rot? Danish bacon or save the British kind? Economy brand crap or branded rip-off? Three for two or buy one get one half-price? Bulk buy? Bargain! Save! Indulge! Excuse me while my head explodes.

Shopping for food has become an ethical, environmental and nutritional minefield, and that's before you factor in the time it takes, whether you've got small children in tow and the not insignificant matter of cost.

The economic downturn that began in 2008, after I wrote this book, has since become a full-on recession, inevitably affecting priorities. While food retailing is one of the few sectors of the market that hasn't been too badly hit – we don't need luxury goods but we do need to eat – consumers are cutting back. At such a time, arguing that we ought to be prepared to pay more for goods that are responsibly and sustainably produced is a tough case to make. If it's a choice between ethics or economising, what do you do? Can eco-shopping survive the credit crunch, or will people put their purse-strings above their principles?

There are two issues at the heart of this. The first is that eco-shopping tends to be perceived as more expensive, an indulgence of the well-heeled who can afford to pay higher prices. And, to the extent that products such as ethical washing powder, for example, command a premium, this is true. Even though there's been a boom in sales of organic produce, ethical brands are still regarded as 'niche' within the grocery market and are less likely to go into the trolleys of 'value' shoppers. So are such brands likely to survive in these increasingly straitened times?

Hearteningly, the reports are that ethical shopping can weather the financial storm. Ethical consumers care about more than price and tend to have deeper ties to their favoured brands, according to a report in *Ethical Corporation* magazine (5th March 2008). It helps that there's been a trend for supermarkets to narrow their margins on ethical products, particularly Fairtrade. However, judging by the fact that the eco-agenda, so prominent in 2007, virtually disappeared from the media in 2008, one can't be blasé about ethical brands being 'recession-proof'. Consumers that have already made the decision to shop conscientiously are more likely to carry on, perhaps becoming more inventive and resourceful with cooking and sourcing food. (According to a report in *The Times*, 14th October 2008, one in ten shoppers is now growing their own vegetables, described as 'the biggest change in shopping habits in a decade'.) Having said that, the bottom line is always going to be cost. If you're on a restricted budget, dilemmas such as the cheap-whole-chicken-or-two-organic-drumsticks become a no-brainer. Or so you'd think . . .

Then again, maybe not. As I show throughout this book, the concept of eco-shopping is much broader than that. Taking an ethical approach to the weekly shop means making lifestyle choices rather than just buying different stuff. Much of it is about finding alternative ways to do things, producing things yourself and, radical as it may sound, not shopping at all. It is, if you like, 'eco shopping around' rather than 'eco-shopping' with the emphasis on the 'eco' rather than the shopping. And, as importantly, it will pay you to do so. I've added some new research to Aisle 1 that I conducted myself to show you that supermarkets, despite their much-touted price wars, aren't necessarily the cheapest places to do your food shopping. By making changes and sourcing your ingredients more sustainably you can not only go green but save money, too.

People are waking up to this now. Witness the success of WRAP's 'Love Food, Hate Waste' campaign, which has encouraged canny shoppers to return to home-cooked meals and be creative with leftovers. The fact that it's also reduced the amount of food waste sent to landfill, meaning there's less of the powerful greenhouse gas methane going into the atmosphere, isn't the priority for most folk. It's simply that it's cheaper. Going green is common sense because it makes the most effective use of our resources. Doesn't matter if you've come to it because you're economising rather than taking an ethical stance. We are all in this together. If ever there was a time to be an eco-shopper it is now.

I've focused on supermarkets because you can get anything and everything at a supermarket these days, from fashion to flu jabs, holidays to takeaways, photo-printing to pet insurance, dinner to diet clubs. You can even register the birth of your baby. Supermarkets would like to be all things to all men (and, especially, to all women) so you never need go anywhere else. They work hard at customer loyalty and they've been very successful – 92 per cent of the population of the UK uses them* – but whatever inducements they offer, the only mutual feeling I've ever identified among supermarket shoppers is a common desire to get the shopping done and get out again as quickly as possible.

I don't hate supermarkets. They have their uses, and I can't see how we would manage without them now, but they've become too big, too dominant, too powerful. With the products arrayed

*Oxfam Survey for Fairtrade Fortnight, 2 March 2007

in those endless aisles, they are soulless places for production-line purchasing and offer no connection with what we buy, whether it is a £2.50 chicken or jeans for a tenner. We've given the decisions over to them and, as a result, they've been allowed to ride roughshod over farmers and producers, to pillage and plunder the environment and to set their own agenda. That's why we need to be 'eco-smart', to gen up on the story behind the scenes and use our ecological intelligence. And that's what this book is all about.

I started this project almost four years ago, when I began trying to reform my own eco-sluttish habits and wrote about it in my column in *The Press* (my local paper in York). The column grew into a blog and the book grew out of that. If it helps, that's great. If it makes you laugh as well, that's even better. If it makes you dump your excess packaging at the till, I'll be delighted. If you start making your own yoghurt you'll be doing better than me. If you've got your own goat to make said yoghurt then there's probably nothing I can teach you. Enjoy the book and give it to a friend, preferably one who claims not to be into 'all that green stuff', and tell them it isn't a guide or a 'how to' book. If my experiences of cocking up composting, making jam and scouring the loo with bicarbonate of soda are good for anything, it's probably as a 'how not to' book.

There is quite enough eco-advice about how to 'save the planet' coming at us from the media, from the Government, from environmental groups, online and, of course, from other books. This eco-bombardment, while commendable, isn't always helpful: people feel overwhelmed by the global scale of the problem and helpless in the face of it, which leads to inertia rather than change. A survey report, *Be Good Guilt*, commissioned by Norwich Union in August 2007, revealed that, although people want to live ethically, many do not know how to go about it and end up anxious and guilt-ridden. Half of the 1500 individuals questioned said that they were too confused or had too little time to make their lifestyles greener and many people confessed to telling 'little green lies' to cover their environmental inaction. If the net result of all this pressure is that people get turned off, give up or never even make an attempt to start reducing their carbon footprint, then a more user-friendly approach is needed, something that tells it like it is. Can you really make a difference? How easy/hard is it to do? Does it involve huge sacrifices? Is it a lot of extra work? Is it more expensive? Can you live your life as a full-on eco-shopper, or is that just unrealistic? And what the hell does it mean, anyway?

As a novice greenie, encountering various pitfalls, problems and dilemmas with living an ethical low-carbon lifestyle, it struck me that, rather than telling people what to do, it would be more constructive to tell people how I got on trying to do it myself. To that end, I set myself a series of 'eco-challenges', actions that I had to take to test these things out. Some are a bit kooky, some are substantial projects but all are centred around the kind of dilemmas that would-be eco-shoppers find themselves facing on a regular basis (hence the idea of structuring the book around a weekly supermarket shop). Some I succeeded in, others I failed at, but the main thing was that I learned something useful and important from every one of them. Some of the challenges were long-term commitments that have now become a way of life; others I tried once – and once was enough!

It's been a big undertaking and there were some things that I couldn't do myself so I roped in my friends, family, colleagues and even a few strangers to help me out. I tested coffee on teachers, got academics drunk in the name of science, persuaded a group of new mums to swap disposable nappies for real ones, got my girlfriends swishing and put some environmentalists on the spot over organic food. For my own part, I've become an anti-plastic-bag lady, made my own moisturisers, practised worm charming in high heels and dance-tested natural deodorant at a salsa class, to name just a few of my many and varied challenges.

In the course of all this, I became aware that being 'eco-smart' isn't just to do with reducing carbon emissions, although, of course, that tends to be the primary definition. Switching to a low-carbon lifestyle is vital if we are to have any hope of preventing runaway climate change and that means national and international action as well as accepting personal responsibility ourselves. I'm not going to go into the politics of climate change here; the overwhelming scientific consensus is that it's real and that it's already happening (there's more about this on my blog, www.klockworks.co.uk, including links to other websites on the subject).

There is, of course, a difference between what's strictly 'eco' – i.e. to do with protecting the environment – and what's ethical, that is, to do with how we ought to treat people or animals. Sometimes, eco and ethical priorities can conflict, as we'll see, but I've come to the conclusion that the two overlap so much that it's almost impossible to consider them separately. Not that I'd want to. I believe that being eco-smart refers to how we treat the world around us – not just the environment and animals but other people, too – and, ironically, how other people, particularly the large corporations, treat us. These issues are rarely clear-cut and interests sometimes collide, which is what makes those shopping dilemmas such a headache. There's the ideal world, where we'd all have enough money and time to be year-round perfect eco-shoppers, and the real world, where we muddle along, counting and compromising and trying to do our best. I'm not claiming I've got all the answers but it's been an enlightening journey and it's certainly produced some surprising results. I've come across contradictions, confusions and things one might be forgiven for thinking of as cover-ups, given the degree of stonewalling I've encountered from some companies and organisations. And all this from simply asking questions as an ordinary consumer. It just goes to make you think.

Well, I hope it does, anyway. But don't take my word for it. Try these challenges for yourself. If I can do it, you can, too.

AISLE 1

Fresh Challenges:
Fruit and Vegetables

Challenge 1:
Can you do without supermarkets?

Supermarket shopping has been a feature of my life ever since I was little. I still remember my parents rationing out the trolley rides. Mum and Dad went to Sainsbury's every Thursday night (not Tesco; it was considered 'common' then) and it's a pattern of shopping that's remained with me – especially since becoming a parent myself – until fairly recently. The only differences were that I didn't limit myself to Thursdays, especially since twenty-four-hour shopping came in, and I was much more promiscuous with my customer loyalties and far less snobby about Tesco.

Until a couple of years ago, I never questioned that routine. It was simple, straightforward, everything was under one roof and you could get it all done in one fell swoop and not have to worry about it for another week. It was also time-consuming, exhausting and expensive, no matter how many bargains I bought. Few of us can resist a bit of impulse shopping – I certainly can't – which meant my excursions (a good supermarket shop is an outing in itself, particularly when you factor in coffee and a Danish and a wander round the clothing section) were inevitably tinged with a nasty tug of guilt, renewed when the Visa bill came in.

Quite apart from the fact that it fed my shopaholic tendencies, it wasn't just the overspending that made me feel bad. I would look at the stuff I'd got piled up in the trolley and realise, with a sinking heart, that I'd bought too much and there would inevitably be slimy courgettes and a black lettuce at the back of the fridge two weeks later. Then there was all the packaging to dispose of – much of it wasn't recyclable – not to mention all the food miles involved.

Why not just cut back? Well, when I saw the light – the green light, that is – I realised that the way of life encouraged by super-market shopping isn't good for the planet. Yes, the 'Big Four' (Tesco, Sainsbury's, Asda and Morrisons) have belatedly jumped aboard the green bandwagon, citing their eco-friendly credentials and, in some cases, doling out recycled carrier bags. There's Marks & Spencer's Plan A ('Because there is no Plan B'); Sainsbury's has compostable packaging and Tesco is investing £500m into driving what it calls 'a green consumer revolution'. Welcome to the carbon-neutral, biodegradable, oh-so-right-on future. It's a win-win situation, surely?

I'd like to think so. However, I'm not convinced. Even if super-markets reinvent themselves as palaces of ethical shopping, they'll still be out there monopolising the market and mopping up the land (which they've already 'banked'). They may be touting themselves as the new green giants but however they pitch it they're strangling local shops and businesses with the same old ruthlessness, bullying farmers and promulgating a carbon-guzzling global food supply chain. In February 2008, the Competition Commission announced that it was appointing an ombudsman to resolve disputes between supermarkets and their suppliers and introducing a new Grocery Supply Code of Practice: good news at last for hard-pressed suppliers, but there was no cheer for small retailers. A new 'competition test' might sound like a benefit for smaller shopkeepers, but it's designed to stop any one supermarket (eg Tesco) dominating and to give the others a chance. Indeed, rather than taking measures to curb supermarket growth, the Commission recommended that more should be opened. Competition from out-of-town superstores, which have the advantage of free parking and heavily discounted prices, is already forcing small shops to close at a rate of 2000 a year, but the supermarkets are now mopping up in metropolitan areas as well, killing off corner shops with Tesco Express and Sainsbury's Local stores.

Eradicating the competition is at the heart of the supermarket business model and that makes it no friend of the earth. Supermarkets are premised on a car-based lifestyle and over-consumption. What they want is for us to buy, buy, buy and pack our car boots with more expensive green goods instead. The good news is that this gives eco-shoppers real power. If enough of us want it, they will sell it, whether it's low-energy light bulbs, locally sourced milk or free-range chicken.

It seemed only right that the first eco-challenge on my list should be breaking my supermarket dependence. You might think that this doesn't sound too onerous, but believe me, it's harder than it sounds. The first day I started it, I had planned to do a round trip of the local shops but it was chucking it down with rain, I had a great long list of sundries to get and not enough cash on me to buy them with. The ATM by the video shop charges you £1.50 per transaction, whereas at Sainsbury's I could draw cash without a charge, stay dry and grab a cappuccino before I got started. I capitulated, went to Sainsbury's and spent over £100. Don't ask me how. I am ashamed to even admit it. I suspect I may have a teeny, tiny little shopping problem. In my defence, I did make it last for about a month afterwards. But, as you can tell, my resolve, when tempted by the call to shop, is pretty weak.

What eventually forced me to go cold turkey was that Yorkshire

Water decided to sink a massive new sewage pipe outside our local shops, necessitating the road's closure and creating an exclusion zone that added a minimum fifteen-minute diversion to just about any car journey. The tailbacks were such a hassle that I picked up my jute shopper and a few old Tesco bags and headed for the (now blissfully traffic-free) shops.

I bought locally produced sausages from the butcher, veggies and Yorkshire-made ice-cream from the greengrocer, bread and cheese from the delicatessen, toiletries from the pharmacy and donated some jumpers to a charity shop, where I conducted a shouted conversation over the noise of the diggers. I trotted home thinking, 'I could get used to this'. And, you know what? I have.

It's taken a while but these days I have totally broken my reliance on supermarkets. We are fortunate in having great local shops, so I pick up bits and pieces on my way back from dropping my daughter off at school and do a bigger shop on Saturdays. I enjoy chatting to people in the queue in the butcher's shop. He sells the best-tasting chicken I've ever had – it's organic and he'll joint it for me if I ask. All the meat is fully traceable and the lamb is reared on their own farm. The two greengrocers' shops have both diversified and between them offer dairy products, local preserves, freshly squeezed orange juice and Eastern and Mediterranean ingredients; the deli not only sells fantastic cheeses and hot soup but the whole Ecover range and the hardware shop sells everything from pet food to plates and light bulbs to lawn feed.

When I began this challenge I wrote down assiduously everything I spent for the first month (November 2006) so that I could do a proper price comparison. Averaging out what I used to spend on the weekly shop in my supermarket days it represented an overall reduction at the end of the month of £138.63. After that, Christmas kind of distorted the figures and by January I'd got out of the habit of noting it all down and so this practice petered out.

It's difficult to make any hard-and-fast claims but I'm definitely spending less, largely because I'm buying strictly according to need and not impulse shopping, but also for the entirely pragmatic reason that I am limited to what I can physically carry.

According to figures from the Office for National Statistics' report *Family Spending 2008* (which covers the calendar year for 2007, the latest for which a full breakdown is currently available), the average spending on food and non-alcoholic drinks in the UK was £48.10 per week, with people spending just £3.70 on fresh vegetables and £3.00 on fresh fruit. Price hikes driven by inflation and global food shortages have driven the price of a basket of supermarket goods up steeply since then, making basics such as meat, dairy produce, eggs, juice and vegetables much more expensive and the household budget even harder to prioritise. Our family spends around £10–12 a week on vegetables and £6 on fruit, but since vegetables now form the mainstay of many of our meals we buy much less meat. We don't buy alcohol, which accounts for a further spend of £14.60 per week by the average UK family.

Shopping locally inevitably means that you spend more on some items. Small businesses stand no chance of competing with supermarkets on price and however much you want to support them, when you're feeling the squeeze financially it can be difficult to justify the extra expense, especially when you know you can get stuff cheaper at Asda. (Or, increasingly, budget chains such as Aldi, Netto and Lidl, which have seen their popularity soar.) I have stuck to my principles and I haven't abandoned my local shops, but we struggle with our bills, too, and food inflation has forced me to redefine what I once regarded as 'necessities'. For example, a whole free-range chicken is a once- or occasionally twice-a-month luxury. We eat well but simply, with the emphasis on seasonal produce, and we buy less.

These days, the weekly supermarket shop is a thing of the past. We still pick up bits and bobs from the small 'local' store down the road but I haven't done one of my 'supermarket sweeps' in three months now, preferring to spread my custom. It fits well with my freelance lifestyle but I realise it's not easy if you work full time, in which case a weekend sortie to your local shops supplemented by online shopping might be a compromise. Online shopping is also a boon for bulk-buying dry goods like washing powder and baked beans if you're doing a once-a-month restock and it's greener than making the trip yourself because one van delivers to multiple customers. You can now choose to decline plastic carrier bags if you shop online at Tesco, while Sainsbury's has started to introduce battery-powered electric vans powered by renewable energy and with zero emissions.

Given the fact that supermarkets are now falling over themselves to promote their squeaky-green credentials, you might ask what's wrong with doing all your shopping at them, especially since they're usually (but not always) cheaper. To which I would reply, supermarkets are useful, of course, but they're not the be-all and end-all. However much they reinvent themselves, it will not change this central truth: if we don't diversify the way we shop, if we don't support local retailers and farmers, if we don't encourage competition and variety and small-scale, specialist producers, then we will not only lose out, we will lose more than we ever dreamed of. We will lose a whole way of life.

Challenge 2:
The vege box: Getting to grips with mystery greens

Why would you buy a load of muddy, misshapen, boring organic vegetables jumbled up in a rooty-smelling box when you can pluck polystyrene trays of nice, clean, regularly sized, shrink-wrapped, topped and tailed, ready-to-cook veggies from anywhere in the world off the supermarket shelf? I used to belong to the mange-tout set and nothing I'd heard about vegeboxes convinced me they were a better way to shop since (a) I like to choose things myself, (b) the selection would restrict what I wanted to cook and (c) when-ever I inspected anyone else's vegebox, the contents looked distinctly uninspiring. However, the new eco-Kate was up for a challenge.

From an eco-shopper's viewpoint, the advantages of vegeboxes and fruit boxes – a box or sack of produce that's delivered to your door – are that they're run mostly on a local or regional basis, which means that food miles are cut down, the local economy benefits, the food is fresher and there's minimal packaging involved. Nation-wide box schemes also exist and some supermarkets are now doing their own, but I decided to go for a local supplier to keep food miles to a minimum (though most box schemes have to import some produce to cater for customers' tastes and because the UK struggles to produce enough organic food to meet demand). Having done some online research – you can find a box delivery near you by going to the organic directory on the Soil Association's website, www.soilassociation.org/directory – I placed an order for an extra-large vegebox and a medium fruit box. These days you can usually customise your order and even buy stuff like bread and tinned goods and dairy products too, but I chose not to, preferring to see what surprises the standard boxes would bring.

Unpacking it all was great fun, just like Christmas, but without all the packaging (hooray!). The fruit box, a cardboard crate in which the fruit was loose and unwrapped, contained black grapes (seeded), English plums, apples, pears, kiwis, oranges, a lime and a grapefruit. I went for an extra-large vegebox, which actually turned out to be a two-thirds-full potato sack and was, even for us, way too much. The entire haul comprised lettuce, watercress, spring onions, chillies, runner beans, a bag of alfalfa and radish sprouts, sweetcorn, peppers, a cabbage, a cauliflower, courgettes, cucumber, onions, potatoes, beetroot (quite a lot of that) and three mystery vegetables that I could not, for the life of me, identify. Surprisingly, there were no carrots.

The mystery veggies were pinkish coloured and about the size of hand grenades and one of them looked like two bottoms stuck together. I canvassed my friends, including quizzing one of York's top chefs over the phone, and after taking it round to my neighbour Yvonne we eventually discovered they were bizarrely shaped sweet potatoes. Lesson number one: organic produce does not grow to supermarket specifications. It's not unusual to get celeriac the size of a child's head and spring onions the size of leeks. I once got a red pepper so large it made soup for four.

Regardless of their odd appearance, the sweet potatoes were jolly nice mashed with regular potatoes on top of a cottage pie and when I served up our first vegebox meal both father and daughter had seconds. In fact, they ate almost all of their veg (I had the alfalfa sprouts later that week in a salad; one can't expect miracles) and my husband even ate his cabbage, which he normally tries to hide under his fork. Until, that is, I told him about the organic slug I'd washed off it earlier, which did put him off a bit.

I don't mind scrubbing off mud and removing 'critters' if it gets the family eating healthily (and washing an organic lettuce can sometimes be more educational than an organised minibeast hunt). A proper veg brush is essential for this. I got a wooden one like an oval-backed scrubbing brush but it went black with mould and had to be relegated to cleaning out the guinea pigs' cage. Then I found a Japanese 'Turtle' brush, which does the job far better and doesn't rot. Known in Japan as *tawashi*, they are made from palm fibres tightly bound into a loop with thick wire and can be hung up so that they drip dry, which is much more hygienic.

I discovered that it's important to sort out the contents of your vegebox as soon as possible, otherwise your lettuce will go limp and your watercress will wilt. I refrigerate what I can, but I try to avoid storing stuff in plastic freezer bags because they take about 500 years to break down in landfill. Vegetables like potatoes and onions, and roots such as swedes and parsnips, just need to be stored somewhere cool and out of the light. And don't clean the carrots before you need them; in my experience, even if you put them in the fridge afterwards, they go black and manky. I've come to the conclusion, after a lot of trial and error, that it's best to gently rub off the worst of the dirt with your fingers or a piece of newspaper and keep them in a paper bag in the fridge. I put the other veg in the salad crisper, either loose or in mesh bags such as the 'Weigh and Store' bags you can get from Lakeland (www.lakeland.co.uk).

What you get in your vegebox changes with the seasons, which is one of the things I love about it. There's a downside – I've had to stipulate 'no kohl rabi' after a glut of those in the winter – but on the plus side at least I know what kohl rabi is now. When it first arrived, looking like a pale green alien spaceship with those strange long stalks sticking out of the top, I didn't have a clue (it's basically like a turnip only larger and tastes less harsh, almost sweet). It's nice grated in a salad or put in soup or cooked and mashed with other root veg, but I'm done with it for a while.

I've also been introduced to other vegetables that I hadn't tried before: cavolo nero, a dark green cabbage with long, long leaves, various sprouted seeds and both kinds of artichokes (Jerusalem at Christmas, globe in early summer), neither of which I've had before and neither of which I've discovered I like, so my box now says 'no 'choke' as well as 'no kohl'.

The low-to-no-packaging aspect of the box scheme (I return the crate and sack when the driver comes the following week) is especially appealing, but there are drawbacks to buying your fruit and vegetables this way and I appreciate that it won't appeal to everyone. For starters, it helps to be a creative, confident cook because when you're faced with a box of raw and occasionally mysterious veggies that require cooking from scratch it can be a bit daunting. Having said that, it's the perfect opportunity to learn and improve your culinary skills. Some schemes supply recipe suggestions with their boxes, which is a great idea. I also think it would be helpful if they listed exactly what's in your box and where it comes from.

It is also, inevitably, more time-consuming to have to clean and prepare your veggies and I won't deny that it's a faff when you're trying to get the tea ready in a hurry. Also, your meal choices are dictated by what comes in your box, which will need using up before the next delivery arrives and within order of perishability. The most frequent complaint about vegeboxes is that organic fruit and veg go off more quickly, which is true. The trick is to assess the perishables and eat them up in the first two or three days, saving the keepers for later in the week. If you've stored them properly, they should be fine. And if things start to look past their best, make soup (more of which in Aisle 2).

My experience of box schemes is that they're really good value financially (we've downsized to a large vegebox and medium fruit-box – our total order now comes to £16 – but you can get a basic box for as little as £3). In fact, organic vegeboxes can work out cheaper than buying even non-organic vegetables from major supermarkets. I discovered this by conducting my own research after this book was first published in August 2008.

I unpacked the contents of my vegebox and fruit box; sorted, counted and weighed all the produce, then priced up an equivalent shop at two major supermarkets. Out of interest, I priced both organic and non-organic versions of the same fruit and vegetables to compare the price differential. I also went to our local green-grocer and priced the equivalent fruit and veg, then went to York's outdoor market and did the same. All the prices were taken in the same period (28 August–1 September 2008) but the produce from the greengrocer and the market stall wasn't organic.

The results of my snapshot survey amazed me. The contents of my £10 organic vegebox worked out cheaper than all the other retailers, with the exception of the market stall, which was cheapest of all. Supermarket organic prices were considerably higher: by almost 65 per cent in Sainsbury's (£16.42) and 44 per cent in Tesco (£14.37). Even their loose, unpackaged, non-organic veggies were more costly, particularly Tesco's, which came to £11.44, almost 15 per cent more. And the pattern was repeated with the £6 organic fruit box. The local greengrocer's shop did pretty well, considering, coming out at a consistent nine to ten per cent higher than the organic box scheme but still cheaper than at least one of the two major supermarkets each time compared with their non-organic fruit and veg. As for Gordon and Jane's stall in Newgate Market, that was the runaway winner, undercutting the vegebox by 73p and the fruit box by 61p and trouncing the same basket of non-organic vegetables in Tesco by more than £2.00.

Going by these findings, the last place you should go for value for money for fruit and vegetables is the major supermarkets. With food inflation running so high every penny counts. More importantly perhaps, it's forcing my family to eat healthily. Even my daughter, who is very fussy about eating her greens, is continuing to make limited progress, though she still turns her nose up at cabbage, peppers and courgettes – oh, and aubergines and mushrooms and celery and runner beans. What she doesn't know is that I roast them, puree them and put them in her pasta sauce. I'm much more creative these days; getting a vegebox has definitely increased my range of dishes and the fridge no longer harbours mouldy courgettes and yucky lettuces. We've been getting a vegebox for two years now and I'm a total convert, plus I swear I'm healthier, too. I almost never get a cold these days, though whether that's because I'm eating my 'five a day' (and sometimes more) or because I'm not consuming pesticide residues and other such toxins, I don't know. If it's the latter, then that really is food for thought.

Challenge 3:
The organic moral maze and the land of local produce

My friend Pauline had an apple on her desk at work that remained shiny and unblemished in a warm office for four weeks. Despite its lustre, she didn't fancy eating it. 'What chemicals must it have been sprayed with for it to stay perfect for so long?' she asked me.

Pauline is right to be concerned. An average Cox's apple can be sprayed up to sixteen times with thirty-six different pesticides*, many of which won't be removed by washing with water (or at all; even if you peel off the skin there are still residues in the flesh). She went to Tesco to try to find organic English apples and came back empty-handed. 'They only had organic apples from New Zealand. I don't want fruit that's got that many food miles.'

It's a dilemma that most conscientious shoppers find themselves facing, and there is no easy answer. British organic apple growers can't produce the volume a supermarket chain requires and, besides, the inbuilt inequality in the supermarket supply chain is responsible for drastically reducing apple growing in the UK anyway. Supermarkets are saying they want to source more organic English apples

*Soil Association

but, despite that, they're still selling apples from the southern hemi-sphere when apples are in season here (October to December).

Even organic box schemes deliver apples from New Zealand, though usually only in the spring and summer when they're not available here. Like Pauline, I find it hard to reconcile myself to this, but we can't have it both ways. If you want apples all year round, that's the environmental price you pay. So should we be giving them up out of season? Food miles, considered the main indicator of sustainability, went up by 31 per cent in 2006**, creating a 5 per cent increase in UK carbon emissions. The case for transporting apples from the southern hemisphere does not look good. However, New Zealand growers argue that food miles are a 'soft target' and that their fresh apples shipped to the UK clock up lower carbon emissions than UK-grown apples kept in electricity-consuming cold storage over winter.

It's true that a product's carbon footprint is more complex than just the number of food miles it travels: methods of production and mode of transport need to be taken into account, too. For example, tomatoes grown in a field in Spain and trucked to the UK may result in lower carbon dioxide (CO_2) emission levels than hothouse tomatoes grown locally. Trying to calculate the greenest option is enough to give even the keenest of eco-shoppers a headache but supermarkets are working with the Carbon Trust and Defra on a more accurate carbon labelling system and M&S and Tesco are already stickering air-freighted produce.

If you're in a quandary about apples, the advice is to grow and store your own. This isn't terribly practical for most of us. Personally, I waver on the apple issue. At one point I thought it better to eat conventional, that is, 'non-organic', apples grown in Kent and just wash them well or peel them, but now I'm not so sure. Pesticide

**Defra (Department for Environment, Food and Rural Affairs)

residues get taken up throughout the fruit: a report by Friends of the Earth has revealed that children could be exposed to residue levels in excess of internationally accepted safety levels by eating a single apple.* Detectable levels of hormone disrupting chemicals such as Carbendazim and Chlorpyrifos have been found in 12 per cent and 20 per cent of pear and apple samples respectively,** yet the Government deems these levels acceptable. Hmm . . . call me sceptical if you like, but these days I stick with organic whenever I can, English for preference.

Even though we get the box delivery, I still use local shops to 'top up' on vegetables. Both of our greengrocers have cottoned on to the value customers put on local produce and one of them has taken the initiative to sell herbs from a nearby organic nursery and broad beans from local allotments. However, most of the vegetables available locally aren't organic, so I wash them with 'Veggi-Wash', a patented product that claims to 'neutralise harmful chemicals and rapidly assist in the removal of toxic grime and insects', particularly those that can't be removed with water alone. It foams like washing-up liquid, which makes it a bit disconcerting when your spuds disappear in suds, and it needs to be rinsed off thoroughly. There's no aftertaste and I do feel that it makes things like grapes (which can be high in pesticide residue) safer to eat although ultimately it's only removing surface residues. I also use it on some organic produce, particularly lettuces, which are often pretty dirty and crawling with bugs.

Sticking with the local theme, I also love going to the farm shop, though I make my visits an occasional treat because it is about five or six miles away and you have to drive there. Since you can pick your own fruit and veg, as well as buy

*Children's Exposure to Pesticides in Apples and Pears, August 2004
**Soil Association: What's Your Poison?

local meats and dairy products, I'm confident it cancels out the car journey. I also walk to farmers' markets when they're on in town, which are a great alternative to supermarket shopping, though I'd offer a word of caution. Just because something's local, it doesn't necessarily make it good quality and it certainly doesn't make it organic, unless it specifically says so (check for Soil Association certification). Make sure you compare prices – stalls at the end of the rows can sometimes charge more – and ask where the produce has come from. There are over 550 farmers' markets nation-wide but FARMA, the National Farmers' Retail and Markets Association, only certifies 170 or so of them. Under FARMA rules, produce must typically be sourced within a thirty- to fifty-mile radius of the market but a *Times* investigation in April 2007 revealed that stallholders at some farmers' markets are 'topping up' with wholesale produce from other parts of the UK and even Europe. FARMA certification should ensure that the produce you buy is genuinely local; if a market doesn't have it, use your common sense. Just because the vegetables are dirty, they may not be the real deal.

Can supermarkets play a positive role in promoting local produce? Absolutely. They don't like being seen as the bad guys and all the stories about how British farmers and producers are suffering at their hands have started to hit home. The Church of England has accused the supermarkets of 'invisible and pernicious practices' towards farmers and says in a report to the Church's Ethical Investment Advisory Group (November 2007) that they are threatening farmers' livelihoods through unfair methods of which consumers are largely unaware. It's true that we don't know about grade-outs (when an entire crop of leeks gets rejected, for example, because they are too long) and other such unsalubrious goings-on, but shoppers' awareness of air miles and our appetite for fresh, seasonal, local produce has grown hugely and that has had a knock-on effect. Tesco and Sainsbury's are now actively wooing small- and medium-scale producers through regional food groups and at regional roadshows and events, offering them help and support and the chance to grow their businesses by supplying to them. That speaks volumes about consumer power and how our purchasing decisions can make a difference. Of course, supermarkets will be taking their cut, so the decision to go with them comes at a price, but nonetheless things seem to be taking a step in the right direction.

I thought I'd found the holy grail of shops last year, one that championed local produce and sold only organic, Fairtrade, ethically sourced products. Out of This World was one of four organic/ethical supermarkets in the North of England run by a cooperative. It was an eco-shopper's dream and solved all my shopping dilemmas at a stroke. I attended the opening and interviewed the director, Jon Walker, who was very optimistic about the store's prospects, as were the farmers I spoke to who were supplying it. However, within a year it had closed, along with the other three stores, wound up because of financial difficulties. Set up to provide an alternative to 'destructive consumerism', it had fallen foul of just that, being under-cut by the 'Big Four' who, between them, control almost 75 per cent of the UK grocery market. It's sad that, while British consumers are purportedly unhappy with supermarket shopping – most of us would prefer to buy direct from farmers and local retailers, according to research by Oxfam – when it comes down to it, we revert to type. On a positive note, small independent wholefood shops continue to flourish and sustain a loyal customer base. Maybe Out of This World's mistake was to try to emulate the supermarket model. You can't beat them, so don't attempt to join them. The land of local produce doesn't work like that.

Challenge 4:
Does it taste any better? 'Organic vs Ordinary'

I remember when I was in a minority, buying organic produce. It was usually expensive, or at least well over the price of the regular stuff, and my husband used to have a fit when he found out how much I'd spent. That was less than ten years ago and since then there's been a change in attitude. Now, it seems, we can't get enough. In 2007, organic food sales exceeded the £1bn a year mark in the UK for the first time, up 9.3 per cent on the previous year.* The rate of growth is, actually, slowing down – in 2005, sales leapt by almost 30 per cent, a trend driven by *Jamie's School Dinners* according to the Soil Association – but, until recently at least, that was principally only because of a shortage of supply, not because we've lost the taste for organics. And it's not just the chattering classes buying organic stuff: more than half of those earning less than £16,000 a year do too, or did, until the recession hit consumers pockets. Mintel, the research analysts, is predicting that almost half of organic shoppers will reduce or give up buying organics.** So how do we convince people to buy organic, which is not only being squeezed by the credit crunch but also, ironically, by competition from other ethical choice, such as Fairtrade and locally-sourced. Apart from the environmental argument, shoppers also want to know if it tastes better.

We know organic food is supposed to be better for you. It has fewer toxins and other nasties, and claims that it contains more nutrients and vitamins, especially antioxidants, have been bolstered by a University of California study. The study demonstrated that eating organic fruit and veg may be better for your heart and general

---

* Reported in the *Daily Telegraph*, 18 June 2007
** Source: *Daily Telegraph*, 24 November 2008

health (although, having said that, different stories for and against the nutritional benefits of organics seem to be published every week). Whatever the science, proof of the organic pudding is in the eating. Can you tell whether there's a difference in the taste?

To test whether there was a qualitative difference, I decided, as one of my eco-challenges, to hold a tasting session. If I'm honest, it was also a bit of an excuse for a party, but then again, why not? I held it at the St Nicholas Fields Environmental Centre in York, a wonderful building where I know a few people. I invited lots of friends and acquaintances, some of whom were fairly 'green' and some who wouldn't normally come along to a place like that.

It was not, I admit, a very scientific study, as several of the more academically inclined guests pointed out. But for all their ribbing about my methodology, everyone was very, very curious about the results. They took my 'Organic vs Ordinary' taste test very seriously, nibbling and sipping and noting down their preferences on the charts I'd handed out to everyone. There was an organic and a 'non-organic' version of each of the different foods and beverages I'd provided, all of which were bought from supermarkets. Wherever possible, I'd bought the supermarket's own brands (eg Tesco organic carrots and Tesco ordinary carrots) or stuck to the same brands (for crisps I got the organic and the ordinary ready salted Kettle Chips) but it wasn't always possible to compare like with like. All of the foods were removed from their packaging and labelled 'A' or 'B', as were the drinks, which were decanted into jugs or, in the case of the wine bottles, disguised in my husband's old socks. The test was simply to find out which of the two versions of each food or drink the guests liked the most, rather than to test whether they could 'guess the organic', though inevitably people did try to do that, too. Thirty people took part, including a few children, and almost everyone hung back at the end to find out the results. When I told them which was the most popular Somerset Brie there was a sharp intake of breath all round! (Nineteen had sampled it; fifteen had picked the non-organic as their preferred choice.)

Overall, taking into account both food and drinks, there wasn't much in it. The organic versions won out marginally, receiving 55.45 per cent of the votes, against 44.55 per cent in favour of the non-organic varieties. Among the wines, the non-organic Merlot won comfortably by eleven votes against five, though my friend Lucy, who tastes wines as part of her job, pointed out that it wasn't a fair comparison because one was from Chile and one was French. (I'd just gone on the principle that they were both roughly the same price, which is how I've always chosen wine in a supermarket.) People also preferred the non-organic Pinot Grigio (eleven votes against eight), though the organic Soave won the day with nine votes against five. Michael, who runs two restaurants, thought all the wines were pretty bad and he didn't rate the instant coffees either. Neither did the other coffee-drinkers, apparently; the non-organic won again by six votes against two, though organic teabags fared slightly better (seven votes against five). Both were served with organic milk. Organic orange and apple juices (not from concentrate) both had the edge (nine against seven and seven against four votes respectively).

The shock success of the non-organic Somerset Brie (fifteen votes against four) was mirrored by the non-organic mature Cheddar (fourteen against three), though the organic Double Gloucester reversed that (fifteen against five), as did the organic Wensleydale (fifteen against five). The organic ploughman's pickle also won hands down over a well-known brand (sixteen against three).

The crisps, which seem to have higher scores, so I imagine the kids really got into rating them, were again inconsistent: sixteen against ten votes in favour of the non-organic plain crisps, but eighteen against nine in favour of the organic flavoured crisps. Organics won out in the other snacks, too: crispbreads (eighteen against four); rice cakes (thirteen against ten); oatcakes (nineteen against four) and breadsticks (eleven against eight). The non-organic pittas bucked this trend by scoring twelve votes against nine and people also preferred the non-organic houmous with thirteen votes against eleven for the organic.

I also tested biscuits and chocolate, the organic biscuits faring rather better on the whole (digestives, thirteen against seven in favour; ginger biscuits, twelve against five; and shortbread level pegging at six votes each). Interestingly, people liked the non-organic chocolate better: the ordinary dark chocolate got fifteen votes against six votes and the ordinary milk chocolate, thirteen votes against eleven.

I didn't test much veg because this was a party, and no fruit (I'd spent a fortune as it was) but of the two veggies I did test – carrots and red peppers (for the dip) – I've always considered organic carrots to be a kind of standard-bearer. So, apparently, did my guests. The Somerset Brie wasn't the only non-organic to rock the boat, however; the non-organic carrots were rated much higher than anticipated, creating quite a ripple among those who thought they knew their onions – and their carrots – though they still lost out with ten votes against thirteen for the organic ones. The organic red pepper did much better, trouncing the ordinary one by sixteen votes against six.

If there's anything that comes out of this test, apart from the fact that the results are not going to make it into a scientific journal, it is that just because something's organic it doesn't necessarily taste nicer, though there's a slightly better chance that it might. Also, it seems that our perceptions of organic food, when we know that it's organic, tend to colour how we see it – we think it'll taste better because it jolly well ought to, being purer, greener and, let's face it, usually more expensive. We want that satisfaction, that value for money, that confirmation that we're right – witness my 'eco' friends, who were mortified that they'd picked the 'wrong' (ie, non-organic) carrot!

Challenge 5:
Can you grow your own?

Growing your own vegetables makes perfect sense if you're an eco-shopper. To start with, you don't even have to do the shopping bit, or not so much of it, anyway. And as for food miles, it's food footsteps from plot to plate. After all, why buy spring onions from Egypt or herbs flown from Israel when you can grow them yourself? You don't even need acres of space: potatoes can be grown in tubs, cucumbers in bags, strawberries in pots, tomatoes in hanging baskets and lettuces in the flower bed. People are wising up to this; not since Britons were urged to 'Dig for Victory' during the Second World War have we embraced vegetable growing so enthusiastically. According to the Horticultural Trades Association, garden centres have reported a significant increase in the sales of seeds for edible plants and herbs, while the increase has been even greater at supermarkets such as Tesco, particularly for less traditional varieties such as chillies.*

Allotments, on the wane for decades, are now in such demand that some people are on waiting lists for years. The popularity boom has been especially notable in inner cities, where the new breed of allotment owner is more likely to be environmentally conscious female, under 40 and with kids. Even people in flats are transforming their balconies with window boxes, while for those with gardens, raised beds are now hotter than decking.

*Observer, 16 September 2007

It seems the so-called 'Titchmarsh Factor' is at least partly responsible for this, with series such as *How to be a Gardener* taking viewers back to basics in the same way that Delia Smith taught us how to make pastry and boil eggs. And it's not just gorgeous, grinning Alan Titchmarsh: when the BBC2 series *Grow Your Own Veg*, presented by Carol Klein, was broadcast in January 2007 it achieved better ratings than *Celebrity Big Brother*. More recently, celebrity chef Jamie Oliver has got in on the act with his Channel 4 series *Jamie at Home*, a seductive combination of gardening and cooking that encouraged us to 'get down and dirty with nature'.

But the truth is, we're not gardeners in this family. We have a small city garden – that, as I recall, was the reason for buying our property – but we never factored certain considerations into the equation. To start with, neither of us has the time. Second, neither of us has the interest, although in my case it's more that I'm already overloaded with other commitments rather than disliking the idea. In theory, I am very keen and I own five books on organic vegetable gardening as proof, including a 'no-dig' method that I thought was going to be my salvation. In practice, I read the first few chapters, got enthusiastic, went out and bought packets of seeds and then it all fizzled out because other stuff got in the way. The result is that I still have onion sets in the shed that I bought a year ago and packets of seeds for carrots and beets unopened. As for the seed potatoes, I got as far as 'chitting' them (that's spreading them out in a tray and leaving them to sprout little stalky bits, if you're as clueless about gardening as I am) but left them so long they went soft and wrinkled and started to smell funny and I had to chuck them in the compost bin.

Shamed by this lack of progress I have taken things further since then, commissioning a team of enthusiastic young lads from a nearby organic nursery to put in a plum tree for us and create a small raised bed. I left the planting a bit late – for a while next-door's cat thought it had the best loo ever on its doorstep – but despite my undisciplined seed-sowing, lack of weeding and the wet summer, I managed to grow lettuces, radishes, rocket and carrots. I was chuffed. As to the rest of the garden, I decided to work with Nature rather than against my own and am going for a full-on meadow effect. The lawn has been dug over, extended and resown with a grass-and-clover mix, plus half a dozen packets of wildflower seeds. The idea was to create a little urban sanctuary for insects, bees and butterflies, with the additional advantage that it would not need mowing. Unfortunately it produced a plot of what looked like rampant weeds with giant mega-poppies everywhere. In the end I dug them up because the poppies had turned into triffids and I was worried that the neighbours would think I was taking my alternative lifestyle a little *too* far . . .

Heady with the success of my carrots, and refusing to be downcast by the failure to thrive of my courgettes, sweetcorn, broad beans and beetroots, I have since taken a step towards self-sufficiency by signing up for a share in half an allotment plot with a friend of mine. We figured that with two busy people working a half-size plot it ought to be do-able, though we were surprised to be offered one so quickly. Once I saw it – the plot was a hayfield with grasses up to my daughter's shoulder and brambles growing wildly – I realized why. It's February as I write, the ground has been frozen for weeks, and the only thing we've done is dig out couch grass. This is back-breaking work and likely to be never ending. I'm keeping a record of our progress in my blog (www.klockworks.co.uk) but I can tell you now, *The Good Life* it ain't. On the plus side, it makes my little pocket-handkerchief-sized raised bed seem an absolute doddle . . .

AISLE 2

Homemade Challenges:
Dinners, Dairy, Baking, Preserves and Soup

Challenge 6:
Ready meals vs proper dinners

What's wrong with ready meals? In less than five minutes you've got a tasty, calorie-counted, nutritionally calculated dinner on your plate and you're still in time to watch *EastEnders*. Britons are buying more ready meals, or 'meal solutions' as they're now called, than ever before: the UK market is now worth over £2bn annually. People like them because they're quick and easy, and supermarkets like them because they make them mega-profits (40–50 per cent on the premium ranges, according to a Channel 4 *Dispatches* programme, *The Truth About Food*). If life's too short to stuff a mushroom, it's definitely too short to make mashed potato. Handily, you can buy it in a plastic tray, which means no peeling, no boiling and no washing-up, either. There now, I've almost sold it to myself.

Some people I know live almost exclusively on ready meals. Personally, I've never been a huge fan. This is partly because our daughter has food allergies, which makes them impractical for us as a family, but mostly because, however mouth-watering the picture on the box, I tend to find the contents underwhelming. Having said that, I always used to keep a stock of them in the freezer – often bought from the 'reduced' shelf at the back of the supermarket – as back-up for those days when there was no time to cook, or to feed my husband when he got home late. Besides, we liked those Indian dishes that Tesco does and they worked out cheaper than a takeaway. That's all changed since I became an eco-shopper. I still buy pizzas and meatballs occasionally – look, I never said I was an eco-saint – but just about everything else I now make from scratch.

Packaging – all those compartmentalised plastic meal trays – is one of my major bugbears with ready meals. Yes, you can compost the cardboard sleeve, but very few local authorities currently have the facilities to recycle those moulded plastic dishes. The problem is, there are about fifty different groups of plastic with hundreds of different varieties, which means you can't just chuck your chicken tikka masala tray in with the plastic bottles (so stop kidding yourself you're doing the right thing when you sneak in that margarine tub with the plastic milk bottles). I have, in the past, saved plastic pilau rice dishes for mixing poster paints and anything decent with a reusable lid is washed out and kept for food storage or to use in packed lunches. However, there's a limit to how many plastic boxes and containers my cupboard will hold, and I reached it some time ago.

According to Waste Online, an estimated 56 per cent of the 3 million tonnes of plastic waste we produce in the UK annually is used packaging, most of it from households. Only 7 per cent of total plastic waste is currently being recycled; the rest goes to landfill where it takes hundreds of years to break down, and very possibly longer. Plastics haven't been around long enough yet for us to find out when – and if – they finally rot away. Furthermore, the production and manufacture of plastics uses significant amounts of fossil fuels, both as a raw material and as energy (for a detailed look at packaging issues, see Aisle 11).

With ready meals there's a double whammy: it's not just the packaging that's got a high carbon footprint, there's the food, too. When you factor in where all the separate ingredients are sourced from, the food miles involved, the manufacturing process, storage – chilling and freezing are high consumers of carbon – and transport to and from the shop, the price you pay for that three-minute 'ping' doesn't even begin to reflect the cost to the environment.

As for what's actually in those ready meals, described so seductively and depicted looking so mouth-watering on the box or sleeve, that subject could fill another whole book. First of all there's the provenance of the basic raw ingredients. Let's take chicken tikka masala, the nation's favourite dish. How many of us – myself included – have stopped to think about where the chicken in it comes from when we buy our in-store takeout? When I purchase a whole chicken, I'll go for organic or free-range, but the thought rarely crossed my mind when I was buying ready meals. Once again we have celebrity chefs in the shape of all-round-good-(organic)-egg Jamie Oliver and Hugh Fearnley-Whittingstall to thank for exposing what goes on in the British chicken industry. After *Hugh's Chicken Run* and *Jamie's Fowl Dinners* were screened on Channel 4 in January 2008, the entire nation started talking about the conditions in which intensively farmed chickens are produced. I counted three full-page, 'We're-working-on-it'-type supermarket adverts for chicken in one newspaper on one day alone that week, so the programmes clearly hit their target. A month later, sales of battery chicken were down by 10 million and sales of free-range chicken had shot up by 35 per cent – if you were lucky enough to find one, since the supermarket shelves were cleaned out. Sainsbury's has since committed to a target of having 100 per cent of its fresh chickens RSPCA certified and Waitrose and the Co-op have also committed to improving chicken welfare standards across the board, while Tesco has refused to go that far. One can only hope that demand – and welfare standards – will continue to improve and that the surge of public interest isn't just a temporary blip. However, as far as ready meals go, unless it's an organic dish the chicken will almost certainly be the regular intensively stocked variety.

Then there's all the extra stuff that you wouldn't use at home, like modified starch, soya, emulsifiers, stabilisers, hydrolysed vegetable protein (HVP), monosodium glutamate (MSG), artificial sweeteners, sulphites and processed fats such as the ubiquitous palm oil. Palm oil is now present in one in ten supermarket products according to Friends of the Earth. Its expansion as a cash crop for use in food, cosmetics and biofuels has been so rapid that the rainforests of Malaysia and Indonesia are being cleared at a terrifying rate, not only threatening the orang utan with extinction but actively contributing to climate change. All of the major UK supermarkets have joined the Roundtable on Sustainable Palm Oil and Sainsbury's has announced it will only use palm oil from certified sustainable sources, so once again consumer pressure is having an impact. In fact, the supermarkets, aware of a growing concern among consumers, are cleaning up their acts – or rather, their ingredients lists – by cutting back on and even banning traditional ready-meal fodder, namely additives, chemical flavourings, colourings and hydrogenated fats, as well as reducing sugar and salt levels in their own-brand products. It's good, as far as it goes, but even the healthiest 'meal solution' is going to have a bigger carbon footprint than a simple, home-cooked meal, especially if you source the ingredients for the home-cooked version locally. The good news is that the credit crunch has encouraged a return to home cooking.

Did I manage this challenge? Yes I did, but I can tell you now, it is harder work. They're not called convenience foods for nothing. I totally appreciate that when you're juggling a job and a family and the whole kit and caboodle of modern life it can be tricky to find the energy or motivation to start cooking a meal when you get in, and it does take a bit more time. But it's not that onerous, honestly; you can whip up a simple family meal in twenty minutes (ten if you're going for the pasta-and-pesto fallback) but it's never going to be a three-minute ping. Still, is that really so bad? Cooking can help you switch off from the working day and gives you a bit of 'down time'. If the kids grumble, give them an apple, get them to set the table – or, better still, involve them in the cooking. It's a life skill that all too few young (and older!) people have and it will teach them about the provenance of food as well as building up their confidence so that they learn to cook with what's available.

With home cooking, the usual advice is to cook up a storm at the weekend and then freeze stuff, so that you've got your own homemade ready meals. I've tried this, usually when I have a glut of aubergines with brown patches, then I forget to eat them. As a consequence, I have four Mediterranean vegetable bakes in my freezer. The other thing you are supposed to do is plan your week's meals in advance, which I still don't do, partly because I never know what the vegebox is going to bring and partly because I'm just not that organised. Half the time I don't know what I'm going to make until I open the fridge. The other half, when I am a bit more together, I get something out of the freezer the night before – some salmon, say – and look up a recipe before I go to bed. I'm a whiz at homemade fishcakes now and my daughter loves them.

Rather than knock myself out cooking all weekend, I find the easiest way to spread the load is to cook larger quantities when I make something for dinner, so that I can freeze the leftovers for another time. Hey presto, you have tuna pasta or asparagus risotto all ready for pinging, so long as you remember to defrost the night before. I reuse the plastic boxes we get our Indian takeaways in, but I am a bit slack about labelling. The consequence of this is that what I thought was fish pie turns out to be macaroni cheese. You always think you'll remember, don't you? Chicken stew or minestrone soup? The mystery is revealed in the microwaving.

Cooking with seasonal vegetables, especially the unfamiliar ones, has been a bit of a challenge. I decided to keep a notebook in the kitchen and jot down any moderately successful recipes for future use so that next January, when I get a run of butternut squashes and cavolo nero in the vegebox, I'll know what to do with them. I've been cooking long enough to be able to improvise with a degree of confidence but I have a selection of tried-and-tested recipe books that I always return to, including the Women's Institute's *The Big Book of Best Kept Secrets*, which I can thoroughly recommend for its seasonal recipes, *The Food Bible* by Judith Wills, Delia Smith's *How to Cook* (Books One and Two) and Nigella Lawson's *How to Eat*. I've also got an old, much-splodged Cranks cookbook that is excellent for veggie recipes, and I've discovered a website, www.vegbox-recipes.co.uk, which has loads of useful recipes on it as well as a `rogue's gallery,' to identify mystery veg.

One piece of kit that's definitely helped is my Tower Auto Slo-Cooker. Like sales of bread-makers and food-processors, sales of slow-cookers are suddenly booming because of the recession. I got mine second-hand from my friend Janet. I assume Janet, who had never used it, was given it by someone else, because everything about the styling and the accompanying recipe book screams '70s' at me, especially the recipes for beef bourguignon, Black Forest gateau and cheese fondue (also, weirdly out-of-date stuff like tripe and onions, stuffed lambs' hearts and Shropshire pigeon casserole). While I'm not up to bagging bird-life, the Slo-Cooker did turn out a very respectable non-pigeon casserole the other day and it's great for veggie curries and chilli con carne, too. In fact, you can make most things in it. I made a rice pudding, which my daughter loved, and you can use it to make marmalade, porridge, mulled wine, steamed puddings and soup. In terms of energy consumption, it uses no more electricity than a light bulb (which is very good news for the environment). It has the advantage of allowing you to prepare the food in advance and then cooks it very gently at a low heat for a period of hours (anything from four to eleven, depending on the setting) so that you've got a hot supper to come home to. You don't get much readier a meal than that.

One final note on this revival of proper food: it demands that you eat all together, as a family. There's none of this wandering down when people feel like it and consuming a meal for one in front of the telly. When dinner's on the table, especially a dinner that someone's taken a bit of time and trouble with, it requires that people sit down and share it together. Which, given all that's been written about family breakdown, stressful lives and children not being able to concentrate or converse, is no bad thing. And if you serve Bisto once in a while, I'm not going to argue. I can't make gravy to save my life. I heard Janet Street-Porter on telly saying that ready-made gravy was for sluts, so there you go. You've found my weak point. But I do make my own pasta sauce these days.

Challenge 7:
Back to basics: can one woman make her own?

Why would you want to? I mean, isn't making your own yogurt taking the green lifestyle a bit too far? You might very well say that and, in truth, I'm with you on the yogurt. Lovely as it would be to be able to potter around all day making jam, whipping up loaves of bread, trays of cakes and pots of soup, you can only really do that if you don't have a full-time job, or at least have a very flexible job, and preferably not too many small children underfoot either. However, since writing is a flexible job and my child is old enough to entertain herself I felt honour-bound to try these things for the greater good of the planet, if not my sanity, and in an attempt to reduce our carbon footprint. Here's how I got on.

YOGURT: Funnily enough, we used to make our own yogurt years ago when I was a child, using a hay box, as I recall. It all sounds very *Cider with Rosie* to me and when I asked Mother she denied all knowledge of a hay box and said we'd used a yogurt maker. Researching the subject on Google, I first thought that yogurt-making involved an unacceptable degree of faffing about, heating and cooling milk, but you can skip that if you use UHT. Yogurt-making kits that use sachets of dried milk powder are available, though they may not present the eco-smartest alternative because of the industrialisation and distances involved (EasiYo is manufactured in New Zealand). You can buy plug-in yogurt makers that use ordinary milk or you can go back to basics and make it in a flask or an insulated picnic box. Or a haybox, come to that. Allegedly.

You can also, apparently, make yogurt in a slow cooker. 'Great!' I thought. 'I can knock another eco-challenge on the head without having to buy any special equipment.' However, I regret to say this was an abject failure. This may have been down to the quality of the milk I used (an old carton of UHT, originally bought for a camping holiday, that had passed its 'best before' date a month earlier), though possibly it should have been left in the Slo-Cooker for longer than the two hours specified in the recipe booklet. Whether it was the milk or the timing, something went wrong because the end result was a runny, watery gloop that wasn't even yogurty enough to add to soup or make into a dip.

I have succeeded in making more-than-passable yogurt since then, though I did succumb to buying a popular brand yogurt maker, mainly because it was cheaper than purchasing a wide-mouthed flask, which was what I'd been intending to do. Because I wanted to use local produce, I bought semi-skimmed milk from our milkman and did the sterilising-and-cooling thing, which wasn't quite such a deal as I'd thought it would be. Basically, you need to heat a litre of milk, plus a couple of spoons of dried milk powder (if you want a thicker yogurt) in a heavy bottomed pan until it reaches 180F°/82°C – use a jam thermometer – then cool it by standing the pan in a bowl of cold water until the milk temperature drops to 128F°/53°C, at which point you stir in a tablespoon or two of your starter culture of live natural yogurt (use one that's as fresh as possible). Then you put it in your container or flask, depending on what you're using – the system purchased doesn't require electricity, you simply add boiling water to the yogurt maker and put the yogurt jar in – and leave it to stand undisturbed for twelve hours or overnight. Decant if necessary into clean pots or jars and refrigerate, at which point it should thicken up some more. I got a lovely, mild set yogurt doing it this way, a bit like Petit Filous in texture and flavour. I should add that the manufacturer doesn't advise doing it this way, but it's the same principle as the flask/insulated box process, and as long as you use clean equipment and sterilise the milk, I can't see a problem with it.

So, honour satisfied, finally, on the yogurt front. However, buying yogurt from a local dairy seems to me a respectable eco-smart alternative to making your own and this is what I do. The yogurt comes from a farm less than an hour away and, since it's delivered by our milkman, we're supporting two local businesses. The only problem is recycling the pots, which are the wrong sort of plastic – they're actually polystyrene – for most local authority recycling facilities. I now have two tottering towers of empty yogurt pots that I don't know what to do with because I can't bear to send them to landfill. (This is what happens when you start recycling:

you develop Fear Of Throwing Anything Away.) I've emailed a company that makes kitchen units out of yogurt pots and another one that turns them into coasters but they weren't interested in taking them. I'll ask the Scouts and the school if they need them for junk modelling and I use some for our annual worm-charming competition (see Aisle 12). My friend Spit says you can cut yogurt pots into strips to make plant markers for the garden, so I'm going to do that, too. As for the rest, they'll have to be binned. It does go against the grain but until our local authority permits mixed plastics recycling I've come to the conclusion that, for the amount of bought yogurt we consume (one 454ml pot a week at most), it's not worth losing sleep over.

ICE-CREAM: I feel the same way about making ice-cream. We buy ice-cream made on a farm just up the road because I'm keen to support a local enterprise (and do so with some dedication because it's totally scrummy). However, it is expensive so I had a go at making some myself. It wasn't terribly successful, partly because it's difficult to find a recipe for homemade ice-cream that doesn't involve making an egg custard base, which, given my daughter's food allergies, would be positively lethal. You can freeze whipped double cream, which I did, mixing it with a sweetened strawberry puree, but the resulting ice-cream was rock hard and crystalline with ice. Our chef friend suggested making it in the Magimix and then freezing it in the bowl, so that when you take it out you can just plug it in and beat it without any effort. I tried that, making some pineapple and coconut ice-cream (I had a pineapple in the fruit box that needed eating up). However, after half-freezing it and beating it twice I got bored and left it to set. It wasn't as crystalline as the previous lot but it was an hour before it was soft enough to eat and even then it was still pretty crunchy. I'm sure if you used eggs – and, even better, an ice-cream maker

– it would be lovely, but since we can't, I buy a tub of the expensive stuff and we just have it occasionally, as a treat.

SOUP: Now, soup I do make. Love it. I've stopped buying tins of soup completely since we got the vegebox because I make all our soup now and it's much fresher and tastier and better for you. There's no better way to use up the stuff that's beginning to look a bit ropey towards the end of the week, and the possibilities, as they say in the recycling advert, are endless. All you need is a large, strong-bottomed pan, a liquidiser, a supply of onions (tell me a soup recipe that doesn't begin with sautéing a chopped onion) and a tub of Marigold Swiss Vegetable Bouillon (preferably the reduced salt one). I can't make my own stock any more than I can make gravy, though I do boil up chicken carcasses and go through the skimming and reducing lark. It's pretty tedious and the resulting stock still seems weak and watery but I do it for form's sake, freeze it and then generally forget about it. But hey, I didn't waste the chicken.

Because I work from home, I have the luxury of being able to stop and put on a pan of soup for lunch, but you could easily do it the night before and put some in a flask to take to work. The quickest soups – something like minted pea or asparagus – can be ready to eat in less than ten minutes. My standbys, minestrone (everything goes in) and winter vegetable (a versatile home for the kohl rabi) take longer because there's all the scrubbing, peeling and chopping to do, but if you make a large batch it'll keep you going for a week.

My daughter, who is horribly fussy as well as allergic, only ever ate Heinz cream of tomato soup, so she was my ultimate challenge. Thanks largely to my Women's Institute book, she now eats home-made hearty tomato and vegetable soup, tomato and bean soup (secret ingredient: baked beans – sounds yucky but it's a winner), my own chicken soup (adapted from the M&S version) and, if pressed, will deign to sample leek and potato, as long as there are no obviously green bits in it. Neither she nor her father will eat my favourite soup, spinach, parsley and garlic, which I got from *The Food Bible*. It's the quickest soup of all to prepare and brimful of health. You simply fry a chopped onion, celery stalk, white of leek and three cloves of garlic, throw in lots of fresh washed spinach and a small handful of parsley, add 400ml of stock, simmer until the leaves have just wilted then liquidise and serve with a sprinkle of Parmesan cheese or natural yogurt and freshly grated nutmeg. It's gorgeous. Just check your teeth for flecks before you do the school run.

Looking back through my notebook, I've also made: borscht (beetroot soup); Brussels sprout and chestnut soup (using those vacuum packed chestnuts); curried parsnip soup; tomato, carrot and butterbean (a blatant rip-off of my favourite Baxters' soup); chilli-roasted squash and red pepper soup (one I made up; it was a bit oily I recall); celeriac and porcini mushroom soup (inspired by a fresh soup I saw in a chiller cabinet); roasted tomato, garlic and red pepper soup (another *Food Bible* quickie: oven roast the lot on a tray and then liquidise with some stock, half a tin of butter beans for bulk and fresh basil – cinch!); curried butternut squash and apple soup (WI again) and celery and cheese soup (try it with Applewood smoked cheddar, it's divine). I know bread is supposed to be the staff of life, but soup is the stuff of mine.

BREAD: Our bread is also homemade, but by my husband, who has discovered he can do cooking if it involves man and machine, by which I mean a breadmaking machine. It's so quick and easy to make bread this way that I've also begun asking our daughter to do it. And even if you can't get your kids to eat a whole wholemeal, as it were, the 50 or 70 per cent combos, made with strong organic bread flour, are miles healthier than that wishy-washy sliced plastic bread that's marketed to appease mums and please children simultaneously. We originally started making our own bread because of all the other unnecessary stuff that goes into commercial bread, including soya flour, and because of the potential for contamination by allergens such as sesame seeds.

Environmentally, I guess it's the same dilemma as with other plug-in devices, in that you're using electricity to make it (we usually do the rapid bake option). On the other hand, the units are sealed and highly efficient and use much less power than a regular oven, plus you're taking the food miles and manufacturing out of the equation, at least for the finished loaves. Organic flour often has to be imported, which makes it less 'green', though we have managed to source locally grown, artisan-milled, stoneground organic wheat flour, which is so damn wholesome even the white flour is brown. If we don't get round to making any, I try to buy our bread from a tiny independent bakery nearby, because batch-baking is more energy-efficient.

CAKES, on the other hand, are my thing. I come from a long line of cake-bakers (one of my grandmothers carried on baking for the family into her nineties) but even so I probably wouldn't bother that much if it wasn't for the need to find healthy-ish treats for school packed lunches (I sneak grated carrot and apple chunks and dried fruit in whenever I can). In terms of being greener, the same arguments about packaging, food miles, provenance of ingredients and manufacturing processes apply to 'boughten' cakes (as my other granny used to call them), but since cakes aren't exactly essential to one's existence in the way that fruit and vegetables are, I'm not suggesting you have to turn into a one-woman – or man – production line. They do make life a little sweeter, though, and personally, I find making cakes very rewarding. I think it's to do with producing something special for others to enjoy. You know those annoying ingredients lists that state, 'Made with LOVE' when they're actually made on a production line? Well, my homemade cakes really are.

PRESERVES: I was in two minds as to whether to have a go at jams and chutneys. Partly, I guess, I saw them as the preserve (sorry) of WI members and village fetes and all things Ambridge-y, which isn't really my scene, though I realise *The Archers* does feature drug addiction as well as Bert's prize cucumbers and the WI is now as famous for nude calendars as it is for making marmalade. Then there is the special equipment that's needed, namely a special thermometer and Kilner jars and the like. Third, I enjoy buying homemade preserves at farm shops and markets and delicatessens – I bet if you buy nothing else, you'll come home from a farmers' market with a jar of piccalilli – so I didn't especially see the need to make any myself. That was until my husband returned from a car boot sale with a preserving pan, which he'd bought because I'd asked him to keep an eye out for an old saucepan I could use for boiling dishcloths.

It seemed much too good a piece of kit for boil-washing snotty hankies and the like, and since I'd bought a thermometer for my yogurt-making experiment and saved a load of fancy jam jars because they looked so nice I didn't want to put them in the recycling, I thought I'd give it a go. My friend Cath had given me a marrow from her allotment and it had been languishing in the veg basket for several weeks but looked perfectly edible. Ah-ha, marrow and ginger, I thought, recalling my grandmother's standby, and started rifling through recipes in my WI cookbook. In the end, I decided to make apricot and marrow chutney, because it was a twist on the traditional, being flavoured not just with ginger but with pungent cardamom, peppercorns and cloves. I also, in a rush of blood to the head, decided to make strawberry jam, a quick microwave version that I thought my daughter might be encouraged to help me with. I could already envisage our homemade produce at the school harvest festival. I became so enthusiastic about the prospect of stocking our larder with pickles, jams and jellies I was ready to sign up for the WI there and then.

The lure of jam-making did not, however, hold out the same appeal to my daughter as it did to me (she'd much rather play Robo Jam on the PS2). Grumpily, I set to work sterilising the jars, rinsing them with boiling water and air drying them in a warm oven for ten minutes while I washed the strawberries (Belgian, oops; the English season had passed) and peeled a Bramley apple to give the recipe the necessary pectin for setting. It was all going quite well until I stopped tending the microwave and decided to do a little multi-tasking by hanging out the washing while the jam did its thing for ten minutes. On my return, I found the bowl rotating in a lake of strawberry juice and the inside of the microwave bespattered with sticky red goo like the aftermath of a slasher movie. I slopped the juice back in (I advise you not to do this wearing a brand new top, as I did), cleaned out the microwave, covered the bowl with a fresh piece of clingfilm and tried again. Blow me if it didn't happen again, and all I did was turn my back for a couple of seconds this time. What with this and the jam resolutely refusing to reach setting point, I eventually did what I should have done from the start, which was to bung it into the preserving pan, stick the thermometer in it and keep boiling the wretched stuff until it finally reached the magic 220°F. By this time I had two plates covered in daubs of jam (the cold saucer test; when the jam forms a skin that wrinkles when pushed back, it's set) and had spent what seemed to be an eternity staring at the edge of a wooden spoon trying to decide whether the jam was forming drips or flakes, which is the other method of determining whether it's ready. The preserving pan had no lip, so in the process of pouring the jam into the jars I got it all over the work surface and the side of the fridge. I ended up with just two and a half jars of jam, the remaining half being distributed around the entire kitchen. Amazingly, it did taste like proper jam, though it was a bit sweet for me.

Chutney-making did not go without incident, either. The first problem was that I needed muslin to tie the spices in and I didn't have any. Refusing to be stumped by this, I cut up an ancient cotton teacloth that bore the legend 'A Gift From Jersey' on it and used a square of that instead. Then, I realised I didn't have any white malt vinegar in the larder and the recipe called for a pint of it. I raided the cupboard under the sink where the cleaning stuff is kept and found a half-empty bottle with a lid missing. I poured it into a jug. A dead ant floated to the surface. After pondering the implications and ethics of using ant-contaminated vinegar (was it formic acid they produced? Would that help or hinder the preserving process?) I bolted down to Costcutter and bought up their stock of Sarsons. On my return, I noticed the hem of the tea-towel bouquet garni, which was happily simmering away in the chutney, was losing its colour. Fearing a Bridget Jones blue-string-soup scenario I fished it out. The marrow wasn't discoloured; on the other hand, the scenes of St Helier seemed marginally more faded than previously. In the end, I decided it hadn't stewed for all that long and it would probably be OK. I labelled the final product 'tea-towel blend' and made a mental note to sample some myself before I began bestowing pots of it on friends and neighbours. We had it at Christmas and I'm still here, but I've got some muslin in for the next lot. As for joining the WI, I'd be a liability on home produce. On the upside, I'd only need a couple of small buns for the nude photoshoot so the rock cakes are on me.

AISLE 3

Chiller Challenges:
Milk, Meat and Fish

Challenge 8:
The quest to find the mystery milkman

Where do you get your milk? I'll hazard a guess you buy it from a supermarket, either one of the big stores when you do your regular shop or a Tesco Metro or a Sainsbury's Local or something similar. It's a pretty safe bet: back in the early 1990s, the doorstep delivery accounted for almost half of liquid milk sales; by 2005 that figure had dropped to 11 per cent according to a report by the Competition Commission. Today, it's even less and the milkman is set to become an endangered species, though the writing was on the wall way back in the 1980s – I made a radio documentary on the demise of the doorstep delivery as a student. The milkmen I interviewed told me how the supermarkets were taking away their custom by slashing milk prices to customers.

I'm as guilty as the next person of this. Stocking up on a week's milk from Sainsbury's, which I then froze and defrosted as necessary, I initially felt a pang of regret at the passing of Ernie and his fellow milkmen. However, along with 'Two-Bun' Ted who drove the baker's van in Benny Hill's witty ditty, it seemed that the likes of Ernie had had their day. I didn't give it another thought until my eco-shopper's instinct kicked in, at which point it belatedly occurred to me that, from a green point of view, the doorstep delivery is a better option. This is partly because the milk usually comes in glass bottles, which, unlike plastic bottles or cartons, are reused up to sixty times before being recycled. Each time they're reused, it saves the energy that would otherwise be used to make a new one, so reducing CO_2 emissions. Plus, those electric milk floats use far less energy than your own car or a refrigerated home-delivery van, they create virtually no pollution and they deliver to lots of homes. Furthermore, doorstep milk deliveries help to support local employment and diversity and to retain an element of choice.

I knew there was a milkman in our area because I used to write my newspaper column very late at night and often into the early hours of the morning. At around 2am I'd hear the distinctive whine of a milk float going past our house and the faint rattle of milk bottles. Either it was Ernie and his ghostly gold-tops or someone down our road had a milk delivery. Originally, I contemplated running out of the house and waylaying the mystery milkman but I didn't want to frighten the life out of him and, in any case, loitering on the street at two in the morning didn't seem very sensible. Having leant out of the window as the float went past and identified the dairy company, I set to work on Google, only to discover there were apparently no deliveries in our area. The website www.findmeamilkman.net ('Your milkman is only a mouse click away') didn't turn one up; neither did Express Dairies or the Dairy Crest helpline. Yvonne, my neighbour, who can usually be relied upon to know everything, was none the wiser – like many people, she had stopped having her milk delivered because it got nicked from the front step once too often – and a trawl through the Yellow Pages also drew a blank. I was about to resort to my plan of leaping out in front of the poor chap when a casual chat with my friend Cath, who lives just down the road, revealed that she had her milk delivered. She gave me the number for a company that offered 'deliveries and removals', which sounded intriguing (would they take away my old sofa when they dropped off the milk?), and that is how I found Simon Milkman.

Simon Milkman was very helpful and said he delivered down our road three times a week and on Saturdays. He not only did milk in glass bottles, but orange juice, too. He could also deliver yogurt and cream. Other dairies are diversifying like this – I found one in Darlington that delivered eggs, bread, cheese, butter and organic chickens – and it seems like an excellent green alternative. I placed a complicated order for milk, juice and yogurt and we arranged that he would conceal them under the bush by the front door to prevent thefts. Apart from the fact that the bottles get a bit dirty from bits falling off the bush, this has worked well. I have to give them a good rinse anyway before refrigerating them since there are often slugs adhering to the neck, which freaks my daughter out (especially when you're about to pour them on your cornflakes).

Slugs aside, milk in glass bottles was a novelty to our daughter, who had never come across this before and had to be taught the art of depressing the foil cap just enough to be able to flip it off. (I had forgotten that there is always, *always* a milk-bottle top clogging the plughole when you drain the washing-up water.) You do need to bring it in off the step early when it's hot, but at least we haven't had ours stolen yet. The only other quibble I have is that the glass bottles can't be laid on their side like cartons can, so if you've placed a large order – over Christmas, say – they take up a lot of room in the fridge. Our milk delivery service does have organic milk, which I started to get because our daughter drinks a fair amount of it. But since organic dairy herds have lower yields, you need more methane-farting cows to produce the same volume of milk (more on this below), so while it's better for animal welfare and, arguably, for health (organic milk has higher levels of omega-3) there is some debate as to whether it is ultimately a better eco-option so I switched back to the regular stuff.

Now that I get milk, juice and yogurt delivered I make far fewer trips to the Sainsbury's Local on the corner, which makes my little green heart glad. It also saves time and hassle because we rarely run out of milk as we used to. Pint-for-pint, buying milk from a doorstep delivery service does cost more, but to me it's worth it for the sheer convenience of always having milk in the morning for your coffee and cornflakes.

To be unapologetically political for a moment, it's not just the traditional doorstep delivery that has almost disappeared because of cheap supermarket milk. There's always a pay-off for those low prices and it's the UK's dairy farmers that have paid it. Many have already given up because the farm-gate prices paid by supermarkets for milk have fallen so low (to 17p per litre in June 2007, according to a report on BBC News) that dairy farming simply isn't viable. The supermarkets' argument is that this is due to the competitive pressure they're under because we, the customers, demand it. (The corollary to this is the price-fixing scandal of 2002–3, in which some of the major supermarkets and dairy processors were found guilty of anti-competitive practices by an Office of Fair Trading inquiry after they colluded to increase the prices of dairy products.) However, things are looking up very slightly. Dairy companies and supermarkets are now responding to those customers who would rather pay a bit more for their milk and see the extra go to the UK dairy industry than into shareholders' pockets. Tesco has introduced 'localchoice' – milk sourced from around 150 family-owned farms around the UK, to which Tesco pays a premium of an extra 6p per litre over the current rate – and Sainsbury's has raised its premium to all 320 members of the Sainsbury's Dairy Development Group to help farmers improve their businesses. But China is thirsty and EU milk is increasingly being dried and sent east. If we don't support all our dairy producers properly we might ultimately be taking our morning coffee black – whether we like it or not.

To hard-line, deep-green activists, the no-milk alternative is actually the best, because of the greenhouse gases produced by cows. I gave this serious thought, and even experimented with rice milk (too watery) and oat milk (too wince-making) on my muesli. I used to drink a lot of soya milk in the past, before I became wary of the potential effects of the plant oestrogens in it (although it turns out that soya milk has dubious eco-credentials anyway because of the vast areas of rainforest that are being cut down to cultivate soya crops). So what to do? I can drink my coffee black but tea without milk just isn't on and my family certainly wouldn't tolerate a milk ban. I've reached a compromise that probably won't satisfy dairy farmers, milkmen or vegans but it's my best shot as an eco-shopper: lots of porridge (made with water). We still drink milk, but less of it, and I have developed a serious herbal tea habit instead. Nettle tea, anyone?

Challenge 9:
Going veggie: the one-week challenge

York, where I live, is, according to Colmans, the mustard people, the meat-eating capital of Britain. I'm not sure how they worked this out, since we do have a fair number of veggies chowing against the tide of burgers and gristle. My friend Maureen, for instance. I was chatting to her in the street when she was approached by a young couple asking for directions to KFC. Maureen, who was collecting for Compassion in World Farming at the time, gave them directions, then solved her ethical dilemma by giving them a lecture on the unhappy lives of broiler chickens. I hope they gave her a donation.

I'm not vegetarian myself, though I was, for twenty years. Being a reformed vegetarian isn't something I boast about – it feels like a fall from grace – but having a child with allergies to eggs and nuts makes life quite difficult enough. At least the meat we eat is usually organic, which I always assumed meant that it had lived a happy, free-range, cruelty-free life. For proper organic meat this is true – no system of farming has higher levels of animal welfare standards than organic farms working to Soil Association standards. However, there have been revelations in the press about scams being practised by some butchers and farmers, passing off ordinary meat as organic. What with the uncertainties about diseases such as BSE and, latterly, the superbug MRSA infecting intensively farmed animals on the Continent, increased risk of food poisoning (*E. coli*, *Salmonella*), contamination from chemicals and heavy metals (PCBs in farmed salmon, mercury in tuna), and bird flu killing off Christmas turkeys, as well as the hormones and anti-biotics routinely fed to livestock, I can't help thinking vegetarians are going to be the last ones standing.

My reasons for turning veggie all those years ago were influenced heavily by Peter Singer's *Animal Liberation* – our whole sixth form read it and stopped eating meat *en masse* – and a rather emotional connection I'd always felt with the cows lowing and blowing by the gate across the road from our house. As a teen, I used to feel a physical revulsion for meat that I've managed to overcome as a parent (I started eating meat again when I was testing the baby foods I was making for our daughter). This time, though, my reasons for attempting to stop eating meat – at least for a week, which was the eco-challenge I'd set myself – were strictly environmental. Being veggie, or preferably vegan, is much, much better for the planet.

The story about farting cows and sheep contributing to climate change sounds like a joke, but it's true. And it's really serious. Methane is a powerful greenhouse gas – it has twenty-three times the global warming impact of CO_2 – and, according to the Vegetarian Society, farmed animals produce more greenhouse gas emissions (18 per cent) than the world's entire transport network (13.5 per cent). A single cow can produce as much as 500 litres of methane per day. I saw on the news recently that British scientists are experimenting with feeding cows less 'windy' fodder, but even if that were to reduce their flatulence levels, the cost, in terms of resources – land, water, feed, fuel, transportation, processing – of a diet containing meat is three times greater than a vegetarian one, and that's before you factor in the environmental damage to soil, pollution from fertilisers, waste and the sheer inefficiency of the land-use ratio (someone on a vegetarian diet requires less than half the area of land to produce their food than a meat-eater does).

That's the science bit, but on a practical level, how hard was it going to be? Actually, I thought I'd find it easy, having 'been there, done that' before, but I totally failed. I can't blame my family for this. They did it with me – with the proviso that lunches at school and at the office did not count – and although they did it with much grumbling, especially when I served them meals with couscous and aubergines, they gave it a go. My husband didn't mind it too much (he said he wanted to cut back on his meat consumption anyway) but our daughter ended up eating a lot of pasta and baked potatoes and it would have been hard to keep it going for any longer than a few weeks without her becoming deficient in some nutrients. However, it was my own lack of willpower that let me down, and writing as someone who will happily eat tofu and brown rice, that's a rather humiliating admission to make.

In my defence, I only succumbed a couple of times. Or possibly three. The trouble with falling off the wagon is that, once you've done it, you find yourself thinking, 'I might as well be hung for a sheep as a lamb' – a not inappropriate turn of phrase in the circumstances – and eating that cold sausage in the fridge just because it's there. I blame the Murder Mystery party I went to on day two of this experiment, an Austin Powers-style do in which I was cast as an aspiring actress/East End gangster's moll called Babs Crayfish. Having settled on the young Barbara Windsor as my inspiration, I got so into character that by the time the hot buffet appeared I knew she'd have no truck with the stuffed mushrooms and went for the pork and chorizo. It weren't me, it was the Method Acting. Straight up, guv'nor. Anyways, I ate bleedin' bean sprouts practically all week to make up for it. As for that slice of 'am I 'ad on the Thursday, well, if I hadn't have ate it, it would have gorn off.

I did attempt to carry on without meat after the week, and the East-End accent, had passed, but I'm afraid I lapsed again. What's interesting is that, when I had a strong personal motive, as I did in my teens and twenties, being vegetarian, even at a time when your only choice eating out was an omelette or a cheese salad, wasn't a problem. Coming at it from an ethical/philosophical perspective, without the revulsion I used to feel for meat, definitely made it harder for me to summon the same level of commitment. I know this is bad, but the point of a 'Confessions' book is to be honest about what did and didn't work for me and I did struggle with this one. Interestingly, I've felt a renewed personal motivation to go vegetarian since reading about a connection between red meat and cancer, which has definitely been a spur to cut it out of my diet. I've now reduced my red meat consumption to zero, though I do eat a little organic or free-range poultry and sustainable fish. (I work on the basis that fish farts and chicken burps are less gaseous than ruminant animals like cows and sheep, which has been confirmed by Defra: beef and lamb account for 16 tonnes of CO_2 per tonne of meat, whereas it's 4 tonnes for chicken.) Going vegetarian does reduce your carbon footprint, so I compromise with the family by only serving them red meat once or twice a week. Our daughter's become a big fan of what we call 'cheesy beany wraps', which are two flour tortillas sandwiched together with baked beans and cheddar cheese and fried in a little oil. My husband likes baked beans, too, though given their methane-producing potential, I try not to serve them too often. There's quite enough trumping going on from those cows.

Challenge 10:
Fishing for . . . anything that isn't cod

You know the saying, 'There's plenty more fish in the sea'? Well, there isn't. According to the Marine Stewardship Council, there may be no fish left in our oceans in fifty years' time. Even now, more than half the world's fish stocks are being fished to maximum capacity. Apart from a minuscule 3 per cent, the rest are being over-exploited, some to the point of serious depletion. If we don't take action, fish will be off the menu permanently. Then what are we going to eat with our chips?

But hang on a minute. 'Fish is Good For You.' Nutritional experts say we should be eating more of it, especially oily fish which has all that healthy omega 3 which is essential for your brain and your eyes and your heart and your creaky old joints, and it smoothes out your wrinkles if you eat salmon for breakfast, dinner and tea.

Which, by the way, isn't advisable, due to the cancer-causing dioxins and PCBs that can contaminate oily fish (one to two portions a week if you're a girl or a woman of child-bearing age and that's your lot, according to the Food Standards Agency; four if you're male or post-menopausal). Ever since watching the memorable BBC documentary about fish farming, *The Price of Salmon* (2001), I've eaten only organic or wild salmon, but a girl can't live on salmon alone, organic or not. I've also stopped eating fresh tuna (though not tinned: where's the consistency in that?) due to the high levels of mercury and other heavy metals that can accumulate in it. Apparently, swordfish, marlin and shark pose the same risk, but then I've never been a big shark fan.

What I do enjoy is a nice piece of cod, but eating cod is an environmental sin these days due to all the over-fishing. It's a bit confusing, not to say tempting, when you see it in supermarkets and on wet-fish slabs. If it's there, surely it's OK to buy it? (Answer: there is good cod and there is bad cod. It depends where it's fished from.) It's not just cod that we should be forswearing, either; the Marine Conservation Society (MCS) has a long list of fish we shouldn't be eating because they aren't from sustainable stocks. I doubt you're going to lose any sleep over not being able to sample black scabbardfish or Patagonian toothfish, but herring, halibut, plaice, sea bass, skate, snapper and swordfish are all on the list too, along with turbot, tuna (bluefin) and Atlantic wild-caught salmon (oh, no!). Tiger prawns were on the list but aren't now. (Tiger prawns farmed in south-east Asia and Latin America have a whole other saga going on. Next time you consider ordering a king prawn jalfrezi, consider this: their cultivation causes massive and often irreversible environmental degradation, disease, pollution, debt, dispossession, illegal land seizures, abuse of child labour and violence. According to *Not on the Label* by Felicity Lawrence, in at least eleven countries people have been killed in violence linked to prawn farming.)

My challenge was this: could I source a fishy on a little dishy that didn't mean some fisherman hanging up his oilskins permanently when the boat came in? Actually, this challenge is easy. I'm tempted to say just buy it all from Marks & Spencer, which is pretty much what I do, or Waitrose, because they tied equal first in the MCS's 2007 league table and have made a point of selling only fish from responsibly managed fisheries. Tesco, incidentally, came third and Sainsbury's, fourth. The main thing to do is to look for a symbol that shows the fish is from sustainable stocks – either the MCS or the Marine Stewardship Council (MSC), Freedom Food (RSPCA approved), Soil Association, Tartan Quality Mark or the Organic Food Federation. Pole- or line-caught is best because it reduces the likelihood of other sea creatures and seabirds being caught, and dolphin-friendly is essential. If you get white-van man knocking on your door asking (usually a bit shiftily) if you want any 'fresh fish' – which used to happen quite frequently round our way – I'd say 'no thank you'. You don't know where it's come from.

The advice is to diversify your choice of fish and know what you should and shouldn't be eating. There's an excellent website, www.fishonline.org, or you can buy the *MCS Good Fish Guide*, which costs £10. If, like me, you'd rather splash that kind of cash on a new Patricia Cornwell, they also do a pocket guide for free, which you can keep in your wallet and whip out if you're in a quandary by the fish counter. Best choices from the 'fish to eat' list include pollock, Cornish sardines and pilchards, red mullet, Alaskan or organically farmed Atlantic salmon and organically farmed Atlantic cod or, failing that, MSC certified Pacific cod. Some species of tuna (albacore and skipjack) are OK. You can sometimes find organic, sustainable farmed cod from the UK but it's expensive so I make it into a fish pie to make it go further.

Just buying my fish from M&S didn't make this into much of

an eco-challenge, so I set out to source some pollock for myself. My first stop was our local market, where there are two long-established fish stalls. Surveying the piles of cod fillet, haddock, ling and plaice, I asked, 'Do you have any Alaskan pollock?' They looked at me as if I was slightly mad, probably because their fish came from Scarborough and Bridlington, an hour away. No, they said, there was no pollock. Neither, it transpired, was there any hoki. Or Cape hake. They did have farmed salmon, though, and crabsticks. 'Do customers ever inquire about sustainable fish?' I asked. The answer, at both stalls, was 'No'.

'So they don't worry about cod sources being depleted?' I ploughed on doggedly, while customers in the increasingly long queue behind me (it was Friday, fish for tea) sighed pointedly.

'There's plenty of cod!' said one of the fishmongers, insisting that North Sea cod had already made a good recovery.

'So it's not a problem?' I asked, confused. 'It's OK to buy cod?'

'Of course it is.' He waved at the gleaming fillets on ice in front of me. I bought a small piece of cod, not knowing whether to feel like an eco-criminal or a silly middle-class woman talking a load of pollocks. It was pointed out to me later that I was wearing a T-shirt with the words 'Red Herring' in diamanté across my chest, which was entirely coincidental (it's a fashion label; I bought it for two quid down the charity shop).

Continuing my quest, I popped into M&S to see whether they had pollock. Once again I came across the usual suspects, mainly cod (Icelandic), haddock, salmon, plaice and prawns, but nothing out of the ordinary and no pollock. Disheartened – I had counted on them being a bit more adventurous – I returned home via our local chippy. I hadn't seen cod on their menu for some time and the couple that run it told me that fresh cod had become too expensive and hard to get hold of. They buy from four different fisheries on the east coast and sometimes even have trouble getting haddock, which is now their mainstay. I asked if they'd tried pollock but they said people just weren't interested in it. Later, I talked to my restaurateur friend Michael, who confirmed pollock's lack of appeal to customers and suggested it needed rebranding.

That same day, BBC News ran a story about how Birds Eye, which controls 80 per cent of the fish-finger market, was launching 'the world's first sustainable fish finger' made from – you've guessed it – Alaskan pollock. Substituting with pollock across part of their range will reduce their yearly cod catch by 4000 tonnes, said a spokesman, who admitted motivation for the switch was 'enlightened self-interest' (the traditional fish-finger was facing a limited future). As rebranding exercises go, this is pollock's big chance. If kids start eating it, the rest will follow.

As to the cod question, well that really did open up a whole can of fishing worms. To find out whether it really was OK to eat North Sea cod like the fishmonger said, I spoke to the MFA Fisheries office in Scarborough, where my inquiries were treated with some suspicion by a spokesman who thought I was trying to stitch him up. He said that North Sea stocks tended to fluctuate but there was plenty of cod coming in from other sources such as Iceland and the Barents Sea, directing me to CEFAS, the Centre for Environment, Fisheries and Aquaculture Science, for more specific answers ('I'm a haddock man myself'). I also emailed celebrity chef Rick Stein, who is famous for his fish dishes, but his PA emailed me back to say that he was too busy to handle my query personally and they also suggested I contact CEFAS. I did so, and was eventually contacted by Dr Christopher Darby, who told me that, according to the International Council for the Exploration of the Seas' (ICES) May 2007 report, North Sea cod stock was 'at risk of being harvested unsustainably' with the biomass of adults at a very low level. Prospects for the future were looking more optimistic – there had been 'an improved recruitment of young fish to the stock' – but there was still a long way to go and how quickly and to what level recovery would occur was uncertain. As to whether we should be buying it, he said, that was a decision for the consumer to make.

Dr Darby pointed out that North Sea haddock was at full reproductive capacity (ie, plenty of adults) and was classified by ICES as being 'harvested sustainably', so I'm sticking with Mr Haddock Man, even if he was rather bullish with me. Having said that, the situation with haddock isn't clear-cut, either. Haddock is not on the MCS's 'fish to eat' list. Reading the 'advice' box, it appears that while most haddock stocks are at healthy or sustainable levels, haddock occur in mixed fisheries along with cod, which, as we know, is depleted, particularly in the North Sea. Hence, to help reduce the overall impact on stocks we should be choosing line-caught haddock from the Northeast Arctic. This is inevitably more expensive: I sent my mother-in-law, who was in town, into M&S, and she phoned me from the fish aisle to report that two small line-caught smoked haddock fillets cost £7.48. (This in a tone that implied that she, for one, wouldn't be buying it.) Still, it seems that ways of trawling for haddock without catching cod are being explored: M&S has also been working with Scottish fishermen to develop new nets that are raised above the seabed and which have reduced the accidental catch of cod to less than 5 per cent of the total catch.

At least my quest for pollock has finally been satisfied, although it took a while to find any. Loch Fyne, the well-known chain of fish restaurants, had been promoting 'The Alternatives' menu featuring pollock, whiting and red gurnard. The specially created dishes featuring these less-well-known fish from sustainable sources had been designed to help customers familiarise themselves with a broader range of fish and so take pressure off traditional species. Regrettably, the day I visited was a Bank Holiday Monday, not the best day for buying or eating fresh fish, and pollock was off the menu, as were the other two. I described my eco-challenge to the manager, who went to the kitchens and found me a nice piece of Cornish mackerel, even though it wasn't one of the set lunch options. It was very tasty, but it wasn't pollock and by now my curiosity was piqued.

I eventually tracked down fresh British pollock at Tesco's wet fish counter and bought a large fillet. Uncooked, its flesh was firm, white and meaty looking and I had high hopes for it; hopes that were dashed when I served it up to the family and we discovered that it was tasteless, squidgy and grey coloured. 'It's disgusting,' my daughter moaned, poking the rubbery, curled-up mass with her knife. 'It's research,' I retorted, smothering mine with garlic mayonnaise and trying to pretend it was roast cod with aioli. She ate it spoon for spoon with the egg-free mayo, wearing a long-suffering expression. My husband, who was so delighted there were no sneaky little bones that he finished his off, pronounced it 'OK but bland' which, in the circumstances, almost counts as praise. The consensus (confirmed by Rick Stein in my *A Taste of the Sea* recipe book) is that while pollock is not much of a solo performer it would be tolerable in a fish pie. I suppose it is – I had a Young's Mariners Pie made with pollock the other day (more research; the rest of the family abstained this time) and it was acceptable, though to misquote Mr Darcy, it was not flavoursome enough to tempt me. I wish it were otherwise, but I have given up on Mr Pollock in favour of a full-on flirtation with dashing Mr Mackerel. Line-caught and MSC certified, of course.

AISLE 4

Household Challenges:
Cleaning, Washing, Wiping and Wrapping

Challenge 11:
Domestic cleaning without chemicals

Once I started researching the damage that domestic cleaning products can cause, both to ourselves and to the environment, the only thing that brought me any consolation was that, since I am a complete slut where housework is concerned, my toxin load must be at a minimum. I only attack the housework in earnest when my mother-in-law is due to visit, which is not to say I don't keep the kitchen surfaces clean or vacuum up toast crumbs when the floor gets crunchy, but I'm not obsessive about it (unless I have PMS, then I become a mad midnight cleaning woman). That said, the cupboard below the kitchen sink, plus a shelf in the lobby, was, until fairly recently, crammed with the usual cleaning products: bleach, disinfectant, antibacterial wipes, antibacterial spray, spray polish, polishing wipes, brass and silver polish, mould remover, limescale remover, bathroom cleaner, kitchen cleaner, window cleaner, multi-surface cleaner, toilet cleaner, tile cleaner, shower cleaner, oven cleaner, drain cleaner, dry cleaner, etc.

I dusted off the bottles and examined them more closely. At least half of them had a big black cross on the back and instructions not to breathe it in, swallow it or splash it on your person, to the extent that I had bought a ventilated mask for some of the more poisonous preparations. But I never really thought about just how poisonous they were and it wasn't until I started work on this book that I decided to get rid of them. Even then, I hung on to the bleach, the polish and a few other bits and bobs 'just in case'. In case of what, I can't imagine now. Alien attack, possibly.

Cleaning, and the state of one's house, is a fundamental thing to most women. Even if you resist it, it's there, bugging you. I think our preoccupation with it is less to do with keeping things spotless than attempting to exert control over our environment, usually in the face of order-wreckers such as children, pets, partners and mess-making daily routines. The bottles and sprays we employ are our armoury against chaos. Handprints on the windowpane? Ketchup on the carpet? Choose your weapon and it will be magically removed. Moreover, your child will be able to eat their dinner off the floor, if you believe the adverts, because you've blasted every germ into oblivion. And, possibly, exposed your kid to a different raft of problems: according to scientists, asthma, eczema and food allergies may be triggered by our homes being too clean. (Air fresheners and household cleaning sprays have been cited as the cause of the high rates of asthma across Europe, according to a 2007 European Community Respiratory Health Survey, which calculated that use of the sprays on a regular basis increases the risk of developing the condition by 30 to 50 per cent.)

We're used to scanning food labels for ingredients, fat content, etc, but take a closer look at your cleaning products and you'll see that they're not very forthcoming about what chemicals are in them. If there is a warning, for example, 'contains sodium hypochlorite', you may be none the wiser about what that is or does, other than the fact that it's an irritant. Some – 'contains triclosan' – are promoted as selling points. Triclosan is a case in point: an antibacterial agent based on an antibiotic, it's in everything from detergents to toothpaste to plastic chopping boards. It has also been found in human breast milk, where it is not supposed to be. It's toxic to aquatic life, makes chloroform in combination with chlorinated tap water, and sunlight can convert triclosan in sewage effluents to deadly dioxins. Oh yes, and its overuse could be contributing to the rise of resistant superbugs and damaging your immune system.

Many toxic chemicals are extremely hard to get rid of and remain in the environment for many years, accumulating in the food chain and in our bodies. We still don't know all the facts about what these cocktails of ever-accumulating chemicals might do to us but it's clear they are already being passed on from mother to foetus. In 2005, the US Environmental Working Group examined the umbilical cords of ten newborn babies in Washington DC and discovered an average of 200 contaminants, including a chemical used in the production of Teflon. This is from a family of perfluorinated chemicals (PFCs) that remain stable at great heat, can repel water and oil and are extremely resistant to being broken down in the environment. They have been linked with birth defects, immune system deficiencies, disrupted thyroid function, developmental problems and bladder cancer. They are also in everything from non-stick pans to kids' school trousers – tell me if you can find a pair that aren't impregnated with Teflon, because I can't – and stain-repelling treatments for furnishings and carpets.

You used to be able to test your own exposure to toxic chemicals through a World Wide Fund for Nature (WWF) online questionnaire but it has since been removed and WWF-UK toxic programme was handed over to CHEM Trust (www.chemtrust-org.uk). I did the test when it was still up however, with alarming results. Apparently

I have potentially high levels of PFCs and medium exposure to brominated flame retardants, a family of hormone-disrupting chemicals that are now so widespread in the environment that traces have been found in polar bears. And they don't even have soft furnishings. The Arctic acts as a pollution 'sink' for much of the industrialised world, with the result that toxins become concentrated in marine animals. It's not just polar bears that are absorbing the hormone-mimicking pollutants: according to an article in the *Independent**, the Inuits, who eat a great deal of seal meat and blubber, are consuming high levels of flame retardants, too. As a result, twice as many girls are now being born as boys in the Arctic Circle. The imbalance in the sexes is more pronounced in northern Russia, Canada and Greenland, but across much of the northern hemisphere the proportion of boys being born has dropped unexpectedly. Furthermore, infertility is on the rise among young women in their twenties, the very group least likely to experience such problems. It's not *Children of Men* yet, but the futuristic film set in a world where no more babies are being born doesn't seem quite so freakishly implausible.

If the PFCs and the brominated flame retardants don't get me, it seems likely, based on my answers to the questionnaire, that I also have medium exposure to organotins, organochlorine pesticides and PCBs (the family of chemicals that includes banned insecticide DDT), synthetic musks (bioaccumulative, provoke allergies), Bisphenol A (another hormone disruptor) and phthalates (yet another hormone disruptor). The good news is, my exposure to volatile organic compounds (VOCs) is probably low. I wouldn't bet on that; we had our daughter's bedroom painted recently.

After reading all that, I got rid of the 'just in case' chemicals as well and converted to Ecover, a range of ecological detergents

*12 September 2007

and cleansing agents that you can get in supermarkets and elsewhere. I had been using their washing-up liquid for some time,
but had a mental block about how effective their other stuff, such
as dishwasher tablets, might be. It turned out that they performed
just as well, if not better, than my usual brands. What I particularly
like about Ecover is that not only are its products kind to the
environment but you can also refill the bottles at some wholefood
stores, thus saving on the energy required to recycle plastic bottles.
If you like using bottles and sprays and disinfectants and polishes,
Bio D has a satisfying selection, including an excellent loo cleaner
that passed the sniff test when I held a green 'girls' night in' party
(never say I don't know how to get my kicks) and you can refill
some of their bottles too.

Now I realise you don't actually *need* to buy loads of separate
products to do your cleaning but I've always been a bit sceptical
about the lemons-and-vinegar school of housework. As my sister
Claire – a fan of the TV series *How Clean Is Your House?*, which
is big on bicarb, as well as bleach – says, 'It's all very well but
the house ends up smelling like a fish and chip shop.' She had
three plug-in air fresheners that overpowered all pongs, but since
I told her about the chemicals that air fresheners pump out
(formaldehyde and phenol, which have been linked with shortness
of breath and circulatory collapse) she's got rid of them. Back in
the old days people used to clean with vinegar and newspaper
all the time and were perfectly fine with it, though they did spend
a lot of time scrubbing. In these days of squirt-and-go, we have,
as with convenience food, traded our precious time for something
that may ultimately be far more precious: our health.

So, can you be clean and green without being a slave to a
bucket of suds? Well . . . no. Not in my experience. I'd like to
say yes – I was confident, when I started this challenge, that it
would be fairly straightforward – but, after a day of squeezing

lemons, attempting to rinse away very frothy soap flakes, juggling measuring jugs and tubs of bicarb and keeping track of all the different cloths I was using (which I then felt obliged to put in a 60° wash – oh, the guilt – because bleach is bad for the environment), I came to the conclusion that I was giving myself an unnecessarily hard time. Plus, the bath still looked smeary. As with cooking meals from scratch, cleaning the house this way is more work. Having said that, if you do it little and often it's probably more painless. And, despite the smeary bathtub, I did get some good results. I was amazed at the effect a paste of baking soda had on my grotty kitchen sink – it hasn't sparkled like that for years – and a quick scrub with a brush was all it needed. I still do this once every couple of weeks and give the sink a wipe round with a cut squeezed lemon when I'm making a salad dressing the rest of the time. Baking soda, or bicarbonate of soda (it's the same thing), is also said to be a good deodoriser. Claire sprinkles it on the carpet to get rid of damp-dog whiff and I tried leaving some out in a bowl in a musty smelling back bedroom, which helped a bit. The smoked haddock kedgeree was too much for it, though; the whole house stank so I resorted to chef's candles, which have essential oils of basil, patchouli and geranium in them. Unfortunately, candles, unless they're made from beeswax or are vegetable based (like soy), aren't terribly good for the environment either because of petroleum residues, but I was getting desperate. I've also tried using bicarbonate of soda in solution to clean the fridge, chucking a couple of tablespoonfuls into a bowl of hot water. It seems to work, but there's a part of me that prefers washing-up liquid. It feels as if it gets things cleaner, though I suspect the need for bubbles is purely psychological. Baking soda will even unblock drains: you pour half a cupful down neat, followed by half a cup of vinegar and it does that foamy, fizzy reaction that you get in those kids' volcano sets. No more nasty niffs and no fish get killed either – except the stinky old haddock and we'd had him, anyway.

It seems you can't beat hot soapy water for cleaning, and washing-up liquid tackles most jobs, although the environmental formulas can lack welly when it comes to removing stubborn grime. I'm a big fan of them for your actual washing-up, but even my Auntie Maggie, who shuns commercial cleaning products and always has done ('I have an innate suspicion of aisles of squirty stuff. It's all a con'), uses Fairy Liquid to wash out the bath. You can use something like Ecover's cream cleaner instead, but if you want to be completely natural, a solution of soap flakes in hot water with a good squirt of lemon juice added is a recommended multifunctional cleaner. Luckily, I had soap flakes, so I made up some of this in a bucket and used it to do the whole bathroom, adding tea tree oil to the solution to disinfect the loo and the floor. It worked well on the lino but the bath looked less than sparkling and a tidemark was still visible. I scrubbed this with bicarb paste, which was what left the streaky residue even after I'd rinsed it thoroughly, and ended up doing the bath for a third time with an E-cloth and plain water, which finally did the trick.

E-cloths are great and, when you consider that you don't need anything else at all with them, just water, they couldn't be a better investment. When my friend Karen – who recycled all my old domestic cleaning products by taking them off my hands – first saw mine she said, 'It's a flannel', but agreed, on closer inspection, that it was more special than that. They're made from millions of tiny 'clever' fibres that work brilliantly on hard surfaces and can be used damp or dry to clean, dust and polish. Two E-cloths (one general purpose, one glass/polishing) cost me £9.99, which is a fair old whack but then they can be washed and reused up to 300 times. I bought another general purpose one so that I could alternate them but ended up keeping it in my trombone case. It brings up a lovely shine on brass.

Ah, but what of limescale and loos? Coca-cola poured down the toilet will definitely decrust the pan if you leave it overnight, though not completely if recent experience is anything to go by (I got through a two-litre bottle of the stuff). Claire has used Coke in burnt-on pans and says it's great, which makes you wonder what the hell it does to your insides. I've tried baling out the toilet bowl with a yogurt pot, applying a paste of bicarbonate of soda and scrubbing off the limescale with an old toothbrush, which was (a) very time consuming, (b) not very pleasant, and (c) not 100 per cent successful. Life really is too short for these kinds of antics. I also tried a toilet bowl descaler, which is a magnetic ring that you put in your cistern. It's said to polarise the calcium, preventing stains and limescale build-up, but it had no discernible effect on the limescale in our loo at all. Auntie Maggie, who has never entered the Parazone, cleans her loo with vinegar. We stayed at her house and had fish and chips for supper one night but since the only bottle of Sarsons was by the toilet, no one really fancied it. (We had balsamic with our chips instead.) I now use Bio D toilet cleaner, let it stand overnight and give it a good scrub with the loo brush in the morning, which seems to remove the worst.

So what about cost? Well, cleaning like this is also cheaper. Mightily encouraged by Auntie Maggie's compact and very low-tech cleaning kit (E-cloths, vinegar, washing-up liquid, a waxed mini duster, a tin of National Trust furniture polish and some cut-up old vests of Uncle Nick's), I bought the following: five lemons for £1.00; two 250ml bottles of distilled white vinegar (£1.38); a 350g box of bicarbonate of soda (£1.35); a 350g box of borax, which is a natural antibacterial, antifungal cleaning and bleaching agent (£1.35); and a couple of 'proper' dishcloths (the textured kind) that cost 88p and 55p respectively. I also bought a mega

5 litre container of Bio D washing-up liquid, which worked out at £1.50 a litre, on the basis that I'm skipping the soap-flake solution (too scummy and I don't like the smell) and going to use washing-up liquid instead. When you think how long that lot will last, and the fact that they all have multiple uses, I think that's value for money, particularly compared with the bottle-for-every-task approach to cleaning I was using before.

Still, returning to the old ways isn't for everyone. My friend Karen doesn't like the concept of using foodstuffs for cleaning, even though she, like Claire, is a fan of Kim and Aggie's. When I told my neighbour Yvonne about my natural cleaning challenge she said, 'I know all about that; I watch *How Clean is Your House?*,' and then proceeded to tell me she'd just bought a bottle of Mr Muscle. Yvonne likes things to be 'really clean' and my sisters, who favour Domestos and antibacterial wipes, feel the same. They both have young children and are not convinced that 'eco-friendly' products and methods can be truly effective.

I suspect my friends and family represent many (if not most) people who want to be sure they've wiped out germs and who have trust issues with anything that doesn't kill 99 per cent of them stone dead. All I can say is, the 'eco' equivalents seem to me to be equally effective in terms of performance. As for germs, epitomised by those green gurning monsters crawling out of the toilet bowl in commercials, there's no way of knowing how many I'm killing since you can't see them with the naked eye (and even under a microscope they don't scowl and stomp). However, we don't get sick or have tummy bugs and everyone in our house is healthy. Isn't that the main yardstick?

I admit there are times – usually when I emerge shiny faced and damp from scrubbing and sluicing the shower instead of squirting it with something chemical – when I wonder about my own choices. Then I remember that the mould remover I used to have was so toxic that I'd have to apply it in bursts, holding my breath and dashing out of the bathroom every thirty seconds or so to avoid inhaling the fumes. I left it too long once and gasped a lung full, which seared my throat for a couple of hours afterwards. It wasn't very pleasant, but I don't think there were any lasting effects. The trouble is, you don't know. My child was born with eczema and allergies. Did I pass toxic chemicals on to her? Or was I perhaps too handy with the antibacterial spray on her high-chair? Are my hormones being disrupted? I'll say: it's gone midnight, I've got mega PMS and there are bathroom tiles to wash.

Challenge 12:
Green washing: laundry the eco way

It was my dance teacher, Joel, who first told me that I should be washing my clothes at 30 degrees. We have little chats while we catch our breath when he's teaching me the quickstep and it was during one of these breaks that he proudly announced that he was doing 30-degree washes, as recommended on *Good Morning*. I was shocked to hear I was already behind the times – I'd dropped from 60 to 40 degrees, thinking that was the realistic lower limit for normal cleaning – and couldn't quite believe that such a low temperature could get the job done. When I got home I stuck a load on at 30°C and it washed absolutely fine, and in no time at all. Not long after that, in April 2007, Marks & Spencer announced that it would be encouraging customers to reduce their impact on the environment by lowering their washing temperature to 30°C. This simple move, designed to help combat climate change, saves a remarkable 40 per cent energy per wash. According to M&S boss Stuart Rose, if every load of laundry was washed at 30°C, the saved electricity could power every street light in the UK for ten months. Now, the 30-degree recommended wash temperature is even printed on boxes of detergent.

The 30-degree initiative was developed as part of the 'We're in This Together' campaign, led by The Climate Group. It brings together businesses, government and non-government organisations with the aim of helping households reduce their emissions by 1 tonne over three years. They calculate that, if every British household made this simple change, up to 25 million tonnes of CO_2 could be saved, which is more than the combined emissions of Scotland and Wales (annually, one assumes).

Talking to friends, it seems that this message is one that has definitely hit home and lots of us have lowered our washing temperatures to 30°C – or even lower, which makes huge energy savings. But when it comes to grimy whites (especially T-shirts), grotty handkerchiefs, underwear, sheets and towels I never really feel that a 30-degree wash is sufficient and they can still look stained or soiled. I've started boil-washing things like dishcloths in a saucepan for ten minutes with some soap flakes, throwing in my husband's manky hankies for good measure. (Only use a few, though, and keep an eye on the pan or it'll foam up like a giant cappuccino and put out the gas.) As for sheets, towels, pillowcases and knickers, I used to vacillate between putting them in at 40 or – shock horror – 60 degrees, depending on the state of them, until our washing machine of ten years finally gave up the ghost and we bought an all-singing, all-dancing, A-rated-everything digital washing machine that has a 40°C 'eco wash' (and much more besides), which takes the angst out of the whole thing. I've looked for a definitive answer to the environmentally friendly laundering of bed linen and the like and have been unable to find anything, though Marks & Spencer's advice states, 'Sheets, towels, nappies and heavily soiled clothes will still benefit from a hotter wash.' Hopefully that means I'm doing it right. If you're an allergy sufferer, you will definitely need to wash bedding at 60°C as anything lower won't kill dust mites (dust mites in bedding can trigger asthma and rhinitis attacks).

So what to do about whites? The dancing line of spotless shirts, clean white socks and pristine T-shirts beloved of TV washing powder ads has become iconic. A woman, they imply, is judged by the brightness of her whites. It is a standard few of us are happy to let slip, though it's a harder act to pull off at 30 degrees, if you don't use regular detergents (more of this below). My friend Cath, who uses Ecoballs, summed it up when she told me, 'I know the kids' clothes are clean. They're just not very white.' However, dazzling whiteness comes at a high environmental price. Modern washing powders perform well at low temperatures but they contain optical brighteners which attach themselves to fabric to reflect white light, making clothes appear cleaner. Optical brighteners are extremely difficult to biodegrade, cause mutations in micro-organisms and can cause severe skin irritation. Chlorine bleaches, which break down to form carcinogenic substances, are another ingredient used to make washing look whiter, while phosphates, used to soften water and boost a product's cleaning power, stimulate algal bloom and kill plant and fish life.

Fortunately, there are ecological alternatives. I use Ecover's Laundry Bleach after my friend Lucy recommended it. Lucy was trialling Ecoballs for me and, like Cath, found they needed a bit of help in the whites wash. Laundry bleach is an oxygen-based bleaching agent that claims to be 'the most ecological bleach except for sunshine'. As well as keeping whites white, it helps to combat soiling and stains on colourfast laundry. Another option is to add half a cup of borax to the dispenser drawer. I've done this and a splodged tablecloth (decorated with half of breakfast after a sleepover party) came out looking just like its old, pre-Marmite-coated self.

Laundry liquids and washing powders that are free of environmental nasties are widely available in supermarkets now. However, a word of warning if you regularly use laundry liquids on a low-temperature wash: the combination can make your washing machine go mouldy. Apparently, using biological washing powder helps but you'll also need to do a once-a-month empty 95°C maintenance wash using soda crystals to dissolve the grease.

One laundry product you're unlikely to find on supermarket shelves is Ecoballs. This is because once you've bought a pack you won't need to make a return visit for another 1000 washes. They contain special pellets and work by ionising the water, allowing it to get deep into your clothes and lift the dirt away. If the initial outlay seems expensive (a pack of three costs around £30 and includes stain remover and refill pellets) bear in mind that this works out at about 3p a load. They have soft rings around them, which make them look like mini models of Saturn, and they are quite large. You use all three in the wash and I immediately found the space they took up in the drum rather off-putting. I didn't really get on with them, largely for that reason, but Lucy borrowed them and loved them so much that she bought them from me. She says they pass the male-sweaty-armpit-T-shirt test (you know, when a shirt's clean and dry but it still whiffs?) but warns that you mustn't leave them in a load of wet laundry because they need to dry out between washes.

The other reason for me rejecting the Ecoballs was that I had, by then, become a soap nuts fan. Soap nuts are entirely natural biodegradable washing shells grown from the Chinese soapberry tree (confusingly, in Nepal) and have been used for centuries in India. They work out at roughly a third of the cost of conventional washing tablets and, when the shells are done with, you simply put them on the compost heap. Soap nuts contain saponin, a natural soap, and when they're wet they go shiny and tacky, a bit like a horse chestnut bud before it's opened. You put between six and eight half shells in a cotton bag or knotted sock (not one of those little nets for washing tablets; I tried that and got sticky bits in my knickers) and bung them in the washing. One lot of shells does four to six washes, depending on the hardness of your water and the temperature you wash at. The first use will be the most powerful, so use fresh ones for really dirty stuff and pre-treat marked or soiled spots with stain remover. They don't lather much – I've sat and watched the drum going round wondering if they were actually doing anything because I couldn't see suds – but they do clean efficiently.

I don't use fabric conditioner (I find the perfume overpowering) but you definitely don't need it with soap nuts because they make your washing beautifully soft. My daughter put on a freshly laundered dressing gown this morning and remarked on how snuggly it was. All that was used to produce this effect was soap nuts and fresh air. Soap nuts don't fade colours, either – amazingly, they seem to enhance them. They can also be boiled up in a saucepan to make a liquid soap, which you can use for doing the hand-washing or for cleaning surfaces, windows or even your hair (though, after trying it, I don't recommend the latter; my hair went like string). The brown colour is a little unappealing and the lather goes quickly but I used it for hand washing my stockings and they came out lovely and only needed one rinse instead of two. I think soap nuts are fab but you may find them hard to locate in shops, in which case you can buy them online. (Just a note to nut-allergy sufferers: they aren't recommended if you're extremely allergic but my daughter hasn't had a problem with them. I guess you have to err on the side of caution.)

So much for washing clothes, but what about drying them? The cheapest, simplest and possibly most energy saving thing I've done is to get a washing line rigged up in the garden. I very rarely use the tumble dryer these days, because it's the most carbon-hungry appliance in the house. Besides, on a nice day I can get things drier more quickly (and with minimal creasing) on the line. OK, your towels will dry a bit stiff and scratchy – giving them a good shake before pegging them out helps – but when my husband complains that ours are like something out of a Russian bathhouse I tell him they're good for the circulation. You do have to cope with the occasional beetle in your bra and pollen on the pillowcases, but that's more than compensated for by the lovely 'outdoorsy' smell. Unless, that is, you've had to drag it all in and out three times that day because it's been raining, in which case it can develop a rather less pleasant 'damp washingy' smell.

Rain's a pain and during the soggy summer of 2007 I had to dry a lot of my washing inside. We don't have a utility room or anywhere to hang one of those old-fashioned laundry dollies (the kitchen's no good; everything ends up smelling of sausages or stir fry), with the result that the house has sheets over the banisters, socks on the radiators (even when they're turned off) and clothes horses in the living room, where our daughter and her friends are wont to set up camp beneath them. In the winter, with the heating on, things dry much more quickly but during that summer I did occasionally resort to finishing some things off in the tumble dryer if they'd been hanging up for two or three days and still weren't fully dry. I used dryerballs, which are spiky plastic balls you pop in with the load. They're said to reduce drying time by 25 per cent, as well as softening fabrics and reducing wrinkles. Dryerballs do fluff up towels well, which removes the scratchiness problem, but I can't honestly say whether they cut the drying time or not because I keep it to a maximum of twenty minutes anyway. They are very noisy, though – the first time I used them I was worried the racket would disturb the neighbours – because they bang around in the drum. I guess a fuller load would deaden the volume, but then it would also take longer to dry.

Ironing is another consumer of domestic energy that we are being told to keep to a minimum. I am gratified that this is one carbon reduction measure that actually requires me to do less, though speaking as someone who only gets round to it when the ironing basket is overflowing, that doesn't represent a huge lifestyle change. It does mean I have ceased to iron the aforementioned hankies into neat little triangles and I don't bother with pressing T-shirts these days, either. I find that if you hang clothes up straight away, the creases fall out of most things, though I do iron my husband's shirts if I'm feeling generous. The advice is to switch off the iron before the last item as it will retain enough heat to finish it. I tried this and it basically only works for something small and easy; it certainly doesn't get through an entire shirt. I tested it twice on my husband's and each time was left with crumpled sleeves and wrinkles and crinkles because the iron had run out of steam. Literally. Also, mine started to puddle and descale. It didn't even do a man's T-shirt particularly well, and I only tried this as a test. In fact, the only item I managed to press successfully without power was . . . a handkerchief. Not into triangles, of course.

Challenge 13:
Does recycled toilet roll pass the test?

As far as I'm concerned, buying recycled loo roll is a no-brainer. You recycle your newspapers and magazines (I hope). So why on earth would you support the clearing of virgin forest just to wipe your bum? Each year, 25 million trees go into the production of new toilet paper, paper towels, napkins, facial tissues and handkerchiefs for EU consumers, while boreal forests in Canada are being logged at an alarming rate by paper giant Kimberly-Clark, which makes Andrex and Kleenex. These trees, by the way, are taking in the CO_2 that we are pumping into the atmosphere in ever-increasing quantities, which is what is bringing about climate change. And we're throwing them down the toilet.

It astounds me, when I get to the toilet-roll aisle in a supermarket and see the piled up multipacks of cushiony, quilted, printed, aloe-impregnated, puppy-gambolling, bear-decorated, cutesy-kitten toilet paper brands, that the recycled stuff is such a small proportion of it. You really have to hunt for it and there's comparatively little choice. There's Nouvelle, Naturelle and some supermarket own-brands, and if you go to small independent shops you'll find Suma's Ecosoft and Cotton Soft, which is unbleached and made from organic cotton as opposed to paper. The latter is gorgeously soft and, because it's unbleached, produces none of the dangerous toxins associated with traditional chlorine bleaches in the manufacturing process. Furthermore, it's made from discarded cotton waste, and it takes much less processing to make paper out of this than from wood. So I've switched to Cotton Soft now, though I always used to buy Nouvelle, partly because it is better quality than most (it's quilted, natch) and partly because it supports the Woodland Trust, so I was surprised to find that *Ethical Consumer* was calling for a boycott of the brand. The magazine named Nouvelle number three on its Climate Criminals 2007 list because of the activities of Koch Industries, which owns Nouvelle's parent company, Georgia-Pacific. Georgia-Pacific also came bottom of a WWF sustainability rating of the top five so-called 'tissue giants', scoring only 27 per cent (SCA, which owns Naturelle, came top with 69 per cent). All the more surprising, then, that the Nouvelle website was claiming that it is the only recycled UK tissue brand recommended by the WWF. I contacted WWF about this and they told me that, while 100 per cent recycled or recycled with an FSC logo was best, WWF did not endorse a particular brand. The matter was taken up with Nouvelle, who subsequently withdrew the claim from their website.

Ultimately, it's important to 'close the loop', that is, not just to recycle, but also to buy recycled goods. According to Nouvelle, if every household in the UK purchased a four-pack of recycled toilet tissue, the waste paper used would replace the equivalent of 170,000 trees' worth of virgin pulp. And if those trees were planted, they would cover an area the equivalent size of 265 football pitches. Don't you just love those wacky stats? Recycled loo paper has, in the past, had a reputation for being a bit thin and not tearing off cleanly, but overall the quality has improved. As for whether recycled loo rolls pass the 'love your bum' test, I have this to say. We are truly spoiled these days. I remember visiting my granny's house when I was small and I used to dread a visit to her outside lavatory, and not just because it was cold and draughty and hung with a framed copy of Rudyard Kipling's 'If'. We had to use that shiny, hard, crinkly, single-sheet stuff, which not only didn't absorb but was positively painful on little bots. So let's not get too anal, so to speak, about recycled loo paper's properties. The stuff works. Save the trees, my son.

I wish I could say the same of recycled kitchen roll, but I can't. I bought some kitchen roll made from 100 per cent recycled paper from my health-food shop and when I tried to mop up a spill with it the paper practically dissolved in my hands. However, there are some supermarket own brands available and they're not too bad – in fact, Tesco's own brand 100 per cent recycled kitchen towel is really good. Use recycled kitchen towels for draining the fat from sausages and the emergency staunching of cut fingers (I'm forever slicing my thumb when I'm cooking) but for mopping and wiping my advice is to use dishcloths and change them daily. It makes for less waste, too.

For all that I've been ever-so-slightly hectoring about recycled rolls, it hadn't occurred to me that I was still quite happily buying boxes of snowy white Kleenex and so contributing to the razing-of-the-forests problem myself. I dashed down to Tesco to check out whether they offer any recycled alternatives, which they didn't at the time, though I'm delighted to report that they do now and other supermarkets have got in on the act too. Also, some of this paper) is made from FSC (Forest Stewardship Council) mixed sources – that is, produced from well-managed forests and other controlled stocks. It is considered to be the best standard according to WWF but although it supports forests and the people who live and work in them, it doesn't significantly reduce the impact of climatic change. So I try and use more sustainable alternatives where I can. For that reason I've stopped buying those little packets of tissues to keep in my handbag and have taken to pinching a few of my husband's nicer cotton hankies instead. Clean, they double as scarves, headbands, receptacles for apple cores and lost teeth (my daughter's, not mine) and bandages. If that isn't a good example of the three 'R's' (reduce, reuse, reycle) I don't know what is.

Challenge 14:
Can a girl live without clingfilm!?

Clingfilm is one of those household products one always has in a drawer (or on a natty dispenser, if you're that way inclined), along with aluminium foil, greaseproof paper, food wrap and freezer bags. I used to be a bit obsessive with clingfilm, covering every last leftover with it, and I always used it in the microwave, too. It's a habit I've been determined to break, since clingfilm doesn't biodegrade. Not only that, but it's made from plasticised PVC, which contains DEHA, a potential endocrine disruptor that can leach out of the wrap and into food. The plastics industry claims that DEHA migration levels are safe and disputes the health concerns, but my hormones are quite disrupted enough already, thank you, and I haven't even hit the menopause yet. You can buy non-PVC food wrap, and I have done, but you're still left with the fact that it doesn't degrade. So what to do?

To get round the microwave problem, I've invested in a tempered glass container with a plastic clip-on lid. I also use a microwavable steamer, which is brilliant for cooking fish (unfortunately, I can't use it for anything else now; the salmon odour seems to have stuck). I've also bought some food covers made of food-grade silicone that adapt to fit all types of containers. They create an airtight, waterproof seal, can be used for reheating food in the microwave as well as in the oven and are said to last indefinitely. They are remarkably stretchy, though I've found they don't 'cling' if there's any moisture on the surface of the bowl. Also, you need to leave a small gap when you're microwaving, which means they can slip off.

As for storing stuff in the fridge, I wash out houmous pots and anything else with a lid and use them to save halved lemons or cut onions or uneaten baked beans. My fridge is, I admit, rather crammed with pots and tubs, some of which tend to migrate to the back and founder there, but if they're clear plastic they stand a fighting chance of being noticed and their contents consumed before they go off. Larger dishes of leftovers I cover with a plate or with foil, which I wash and reuse as many times as possible before recycling. It is a bit of a pain cleaning foil if it's got really dirty but you can put it in the dishwasher if you're careful, which is what I do with foil trays. The foil ultimately gets recycled and to 'close the loop' I've started buying recycled aluminium foil from our local wholefood shop, which uses only 5 per cent of the energy required to make regular foil. It feels thinner to me, but it serves its purpose and covers a roast chicken without tearing. It's more expensive, though, so I use it sparingly.

Making packed lunches for school is a bit of a challenge without clingfilm, so I'm using foil to wrap sandwiches now. I did use grease-proof paper for a while, assuming that it would compost, but on checking with the nice people at www.recyclenow.com it seems the consensus is that it may take a long time to break down. Since greaseproof paper isn't recyclable their advice was to add it to the compost bin sparingly and shred it into tiny pieces first, making sure it was free of any food residues that might otherwise attract rats. I also recycle lots of the aforementioned little pots for fruit and snacks. If your child prefers a customised container, you can get some that hold precisely two biscuits, though I've had a year's worth of use out of an old mozzarella tub with no objections from my daughter.

For storing loose vegetables I now use paper bags, saved from trips to the greengrocers, whereas previously I bunged everything into separate plastic food bags. I've also bought some Onya Weigh bags, which are tulle bags with a drawstring neck that you can put fresh produce into for weighing, washing and refrigerating; they also stop your veg or fruit sweating and bruising (go to www.onyabags.co.uk). Bread goes into a cotton bread bag to keep it fresh. I do still keep a roll of medium-sized all-purpose plastic bags in the drawer but they're those resealable ones that stand up to being washed out with hot soapy water and reused several times (I peg them out to dry above the bath). Even so, I hardly ever need to use a plastic food bag these days. I'd say that's a wrap.

AISLE 5

Healthy Challenges 1:
Beauty Products

Challenge 15:
Staying lovely without chemicals

I love beauty products. Always have done, since my mother introduced me to Quickies Cleansing Pads at 13. I've cleansed, toned and moisturised ever since, though it has come at a massive cost financially. I hate to think how much I've spent on beauty products since I began my twice-daily regime, but it would run into thousands. Suffice to say they know me by name at the Clarins counter.

I'm not alone. A 2006 survey commissioned by *New Woman* magazine revealed that British women spend £3000 a year on beauty products and treatments, with 81 per cent of women wearing make-up every day. According to analysts Mintel, British women are the largest users of make-up throughout Europe, capping even the French (and Clarins is cheaper there, *n'est-ce pas?*). All well and good, but there's a lie in these ointments and it is this: the very products that are promoted as making us look younger, sexier, healthier and more attractive may ultimately be doing the opposite.

'Getting Lippy', a groundbreaking report by the Women's Environmental Network, published in 2003, claimed that cosmetics and beauty products may contain ingredients that impair fertility, increase the effects of ageing(!) and are linked to cancer, allergies and other health problems. 'There is increasing evidence that we are all victims of a great big con.' I'll say. You expect the food you buy to be safe, and there are huge public outcries when it isn't, yet the same stringent standards are not universally applied to cosmetics companies. This is especially true in the US, which is less regulated. However, since the implementation of the EU Cosmetics Directive REACH (Registration, Evaluation and Authorisation of Chemicals) in 2006, consumers in the UK have been better protected from chemicals that are considered mutagenic, carcinogenic or reproductive toxins. All UK cosmetics and their ingredients must be safety tested and there is a list of chemicals that are not permitted for use in cosmetics and maximum concentration restrictions on some others.

That's still not enough for campaign groups, which are continuing to put pressure on Brussels to tighten up their approach to chemical regulation by asking for legislative proposals to recognise, among other things, that endocrine disruptors such as parabens and phthalates cannot be 'adequately controlled' and should be substituted by safer alternatives. Even though three phthalates (DBP, BBP and DEHP) are now banned from cosmetics in the EU, the phthalate DEP (di-ethyl phthalate) is still widely used in deodorants, hair care, aftershave lotions, skincare, make-up and perfumes. A Greenpeace study* of thirty-six perfumes revealed that at its highest concentration, DEP formed 2.23 per cent by volume. The EU's Scientific Committee on Consumer Products (SCCP) considers its use safe** despite epidemiological

*An Investigation of Chemicals in Perfumes, February 2005
**Opinion on Phthalates in Cosmetic Products, 21 March 2007

evidence (although it is claimed to be inconsistent) that DEP can impair reproductive function, according to WEN. In individual products phthalates may represent a trace amount but the cumulative effect – women can use more than twenty different products as part of their daily routine – can amount to a substantial internal dose.

Women aged 20–40 have been found to have the highest levels of phthalates in their bodies from their use of hairsprays, gels and nail polishes, which may have implications not just for their own fertility, but the reproductive ability of their offspring. And it's not just women: teenage (and, increasingly, pre-teen) boys lashing out on antiperspirants, body sprays and grooming products are also putting themselves at risk.

Another cause for concern is the widespread use of parabens in cosmetics. Parabens are synthetic chemicals that are used as preservatives to inhibit the growth of bacteria, moulds and yeasts. You'll find them in one incarnation or another (methylparaben, ethylparaben, butylparaben, propylparaben, isobutylparaben, benzylparaben) in many beauty and personal care products from deodorants and moisturisers to sunscreens and shampoos and they are also used extensively as a preservative in food. Parabens are known to disrupt hormone function and more than twelve research studies have shown them to mimic the effect of oestrogen in animals and in tissue culture (this activity occurs only when parabens are applied to the skin, not ingested). The link between oestrogen and breast cancer is already well proven but what had not been shown until more recently* was that intact parabens have been found in human breast tumours, with methylparaben accounting for 62 per cent of the total paraben recovered. It was a small study but a significant one in the eyes of many researchers,

Journal of Applied Toxicology, February 2004

who point to our daily application of parabens-containing products and their potential cumulative effect.

Cancer Research UK's website (www.cancerresearchuk.org) gives a possible parabens link with breast cancer short shrift. Under 'Cancer Controversies' it states that 'finding parabens in tumours is a far cry from saying that it causes breast cancer. In fact, breast tumours have large blood supplies and are likely to have traces of everything in our bloodstream'. Interestingly, some other cancer charities are more open to exploring the issue. A UK charity called The Genesis Appeal (www.genesisuk.org/), which is entirely dedicated to preventing breast cancer, is funding research into parabens and aluminium levels in breast tissue. 'We do share the concern that many commonly used chemicals in the cosmetic and plastics and household products industries could have adverse effects on health, given prolonged exposure,' Lester Barr, the chairman of the appeal and a breast cancer physician himself, said in an email to me. 'At present, we are taking the pragmatic view that there is insufficient evidence to permit us to make definite recommendations about specific products. This may change as more evidence is gathered.' The US-based Breast Cancer Fund (www.breastcancerfund.org) also takes the parabens research seriously, arguing that 'although not a conclusive link between exposure to parabens and breast cancer, this . . . signals the need for a precautionary approach to the manufacture and use of these compounds'.

There's clearly a need for more research. A Channel 4 programme called *Beauty Addicts: How Toxic Are You?* (11 October 2007) followed two sisters who between them used over seventy beauty products per day – and showed that they both had high levels of parabens in their urine. After a complete detox from chemical-laden beauty products, including antiperspirants and deodorants, one of the sisters had no parabens at all (the other still had some, probably due to something she'd eaten). What effect were all those parabens having? Women need answers. The oestrogen/breast cancer connection is indisputable and the wide-spread use of parabens (which act like oestrogens in the body) seems to me to be a dangerous prescription for our health. One in nine women in the UK will develop breast cancer in their lifetime according to statistics from Cancer Research UK; and rates of breast cancer are increasing world-wide. Millions of pounds are spent on research to treat it and a massive amount of publicity goes into promoting awareness, yet only 2 per cent of all cancer research funding is spent on prevention. I find this extraordinary. Around 5 per cent of breast cancers occur in women with a strong family history of the disease. That means 95 per cent of breast cancers are caused by other factors, including age, repro-ductive history, hormones, lifestyle (being overweight is a signif-icant risk factor) and the environment. So why isn't our intake of chemicals such as parabens investigated more fully?

Multiple exposure to potentially harmful chemicals in everything from perfumes and aftershaves to deodorants and body lotions is enveloping us in a toxic cloud that's further concentrated by the chemicals in the washing powders, fabric conditioners and house-hold cleaning products most of us use daily. In some individuals, the onslaught of so many chemicals has an immediate and debil-itating effect such that they become chronically ill with a range of symptoms from nausea, dizziness and headaches to arthritis, memory problems and fatigue, a condition known as Multiple Chemical Sensitivity or MCS. It's more likely to affect people with a genetic predisposition to allergies or with compromised immune systems. I once ran a support group for people with candida, a systemic yeast overgrowth, and many of those who came to meet-ings, including a number of ME sufferers, felt very ill in the presence of such chemicals. My system is strong enough to cope but those who are affected badly can end up being unable to work, and becoming prisoners in their own homes. As it is, I'm still affected if I get close to someone wearing perfume. My eyes water, or, worse, I start sneezing, which can be embarrassing if you're at the theatre.

Having cut as many man-made chemicals out of my life as I can, I've become super-aware of synthetic fragrances and, if anything, they seem to be affecting me more. 'Perhaps you should start using perfume again,' my friend Pauline said when her Issey Miyake set me off streaming. My friend Sandi's Christian Dior Poison also made my eyes water and as for my sister's Aldi fragrance, by the end of a car journey with her the combination of the perfume and the car's dangly air-freshener tree made me want to throw up. My daughter is equally sensitive: I took her into the Body Shop with me to check some ingredients labels (her eyes are better than mine) and in the time it took her to decipher 'parfum' on a body lotion her nose was running and her eyes were itching. I suspect it was triggered by the overwhelming scent of strawberries that permeated the shop.

If you're appalled, as I am, by the potentially harmful effects of the chemical cocktails we happily use on our bodies in the quest for youth and beauty, go to the Campaign for Safe Cosmetics' product guide, 'Skin Deep' (www.safecosmetics.org). It allows you to check out ingredients and products, though bear in mind that formulations differ as EU restrictions are tighter. I went through a selection of mine, cross-referencing with *Ethical Consumer* magazine resources, and this is what I found in just one shampoo (pay attention now, here comes the science bit): ammonium laureth sulfate (irritant); dimethicone (a silicone emollient that is occlusive, ie it coats the skin, trapping anything beneath it); methylchloroisothiazolinone (concerns include allergies/immunotoxicity, organ system toxicity); paraffinum liquidum (mineral oil, clogs pores), sodium benzoate (organ system toxicity); parfum (also known as fragrance; associated with allergies and immunotoxicity) and disodium EDTA (EDTAs are 'penetration enhancers' that may carry themselves and others into the bloodstream; there's still a big data gap on their effects but disodium EDTA is in a 'moderate hazard' category because of concerns about carcinogenic effects).

Guess what? I stopped using the shampoo. Along with pretty much all my other products. Once you start reading cosmetics labels like food labels, it opens up a whole new and, frankly, terrifying world. Even 'natural' products are not exempt – and, indeed, some such products aren't very natural at all; only 1 per cent of a commercial product has to have the natural ingredient to earn the claim. I was surprised, on reading the ingredients of a very expensive stick deodorant with organic plant extracts, to see that the first ingredient listed was propylene glycol (PG). While PG is considered safe by the cosmetics industry, its ability to penetrate the skin quickly, carrying other chemicals with it into the bloodstream, and the impurities that can be generated by its manufacture (including 1,4-dioxane, a probable carcinogen) give it a less wholesome pedigree.

From a green point of view, beauty products generate a massive amount of completely unnecessary packaging of the jar-in-the-card-supported-by-more-card-and-encased-in-a-plastic-carton kind, most of which is currently difficult or impossible to recycle. As a veteran consumer of quality products, I admit that I'm seduced by 'luxury' packaging; the first thing I did when I brought a new purchase home was to sit and read (and often re-read) all the comforting claims about the product's effectiveness. The fact that the small bottle of whatever it was came encased in layers of packaging and sealed in nice crinkly cellophane made me feel confident that the contents must be special. Psychologically, it was reassuring to think that something I'd spent that amount of money on (and almost certainly felt guilty about) was well presented; the packaging reiterated the promise that the hit on my credit card would be well worth it. We're such suckers, aren't we? Modern marketing recognises our emotional neediness; the quest for a product that will, we hope, transform not just our skin but our lives. Plush packaging, with its 'eye candy' appeal and suggestion of added value, invites this kind of aspirational buying, but it's a con: research shows that packaging for health and beauty products can cost three times as much to make as the contents. Where does it go? In the bin. Now that I'm more aware of how I'm being manipulated I look for ethical products with minimal packaging. The more consumers do this – and ethical products are the latest buzz in the cosmetics industry because, as manufacturers see it, there is even more cash in consciences – the better off the environment will be. Though not necessarily our wallets, unfortunately.

Then there's the whole issue of animal testing which, I have to admit, I thought was over and done with since 'not tested on animals' seems to be a ubiquitous claim these days. That was before I spent the weekend reading research papers and toxicity reports for this chapter, which described how many rats, mice, guinea pigs and rabbits had had various chemicals put in their eyes, dabbed onto their skin or fed to them in such high concentrations that it caused them physical pain, not to mention giving them tumours or stimulating them to give birth to babies with abnormalities (which were then 'sacrificed' so that their organs could be tested and measured). Clearly, I was wrong. The product itself may not have been tested on fluffy bunnies but the individual constituents may well have. What this tells us about how the stuff may affect humans is debatable; much as I love our own guinea pigs I don't feel they're the target audience.

One of the reasons I really like the Lush range of products is because they not only operate a supplier-specific boycott policy (which means they don't engage with any suppliers who test on animals) but they also use human testers for their products, which seems to me to make much more sense. I gather no cruelty is inflicted on the volunteers, either, because a nice young man in one of their stores told me all about the process. He turned out to be a chemistry undergraduate, which was useful because the challenge I'd set myself was to buy a moisturiser that didn't contain any potentially harmful chemicals and was effective and not too expensive. It was proving harder to source than I'd realised because methylparaben and propylparaben seem to be included in just about all moisturisers, even the Body Shop ones and those hand-made by Lush. I left the shop empty-handed, deciding to do a little more research, and emailed Lush a few days later on the parabens issue, having discovered that Tesco made one – it's called bnatural Skin Quenching Body Milk and they also do an Enriching Body Butter in the same range – which contains no parabens, mineral oils or synthetic fragrance, which was just what I wanted. If Tesco could do it – and a big well done to them – why couldn't Lush? Lush sent me some information on the two parabens they use (methylparaben and propylparaben), saying they were the oldest, safest and mildest cosmetic preservatives they could find and that 'everything is known about them'. Furthermore, the parabens were only used at half the maximum permitted level in products that required them and 65 per cent of Lush products did not contain any. I emailed them back and was subsequently rung by Mark Constantine himself, who founded Lush. He called the two parabens Lush uses 'the best of a poor bunch' adding, 'You don't want them really', but said that they were necessary to preserve products containing water. He also felt that they were being highlighted above other, potentially more dangerous stuff, notably hair dyes: 'They're mutagenic and carcinogenic . . . The frightening thing about hair dyes is that they pass through every organ in your body.'

Scary as that thought is to a woman who tints, I continued my quest for a parabens-free moisturiser. Next stop was Boots the Chemist, where I regularly buy my health and beauty products. Boots, I realised, had a lot of activity going on around the No 7 stand, where its Protect & Perfect Anti-Wrinkle Serum was on conspicuous display. The serum, which was highlighted as the most effective anti-ageing product on the BBC's *Horizon* programme in March 2007, originally had shoppers queuing up at 5am to get their hands on a bottle (which was limited to one per customer when demand took off). Curious, I went over to check it out, along with its companion serum, Refine & Rewind. The first thing I noticed was that the latter had five parabens listed two-thirds of the way down the ingredients panel (methylparaben, butylparaben, ethylparaben, propylparaben and isobutylparaben), which meant it didn't fit my eco-challenge requirements. On the other hand, I reasoned, if millions of people are fighting over it, ought I not to test it for efficacy purposes? As I was mulling this over, highly tempted by a special offer that gave me a free bag of No 7 goodies if I spent £18 or more, I bumped into Margaret, a friend-of-a-friend, who was out shopping with her mother. Margaret's mum, who was in her 60s, was having a dilemma over which serum to go for, which was settled when the No 7 assistant told her Refine & Rewind was for the over-40s. 'Aren't you going to buy one?' I asked Margaret. 'No way,' she replied. 'I think they're all a load of rubbish. I use udder cream myself.'

While I recovered from this shock cosmetic revelation – at 41, Margaret has clear, baby-smooth unwrinkled skin, so she was obviously sitting on a successful secret – Margaret went on to explain that udder cream is not just used on cows' teats but by quilters because it's non-greasy and keeps their hands really soft.

It's also favoured by country singer Shania Twain, who has called it 'better than Botox'.

'What's in it?' I asked, curiously.

'I don't know,' Margaret replied, 'but it works.'

I looked up the product on the Internet – it's called Udderly SMOOth (no sexy names here) – and found that it contains minimal ingredients: allantoin, dimethicone, lanolin and propylene glycol in an emollient base (which does, I've since discovered, contain parabens unfortunately). Allantoin, which is found in comfrey (and the urine of some mammals – I do hope the source is the herb, though I suspect not), is a very safe natural substance that is healing, soothing, exfoliating, encourages new cells to form and is ultra moisturising, increasing the water content of skin cells. Lanolin is basically sheep's wool grease, another moisturiser. Like allantoin, it's widely used in the cosmetics industry, especially in handcreams, though it can be a skin irritant. The other two ingredients are common to many beauty products, as already noted (though not without reservations). It sounded as if I could have accidentally stumbled upon the holy grail of cheap effective moisturisers. Margaret promised to drop a sample of udder cream round to me so that I could try it. I bought the No 7 serum, too, for research purposes. Fair's fair. The third moisturiser I got was Green People's Fruitful Nights, a skin repair 'magic' night cream made from pure, natural organic ingredients, free from parabens, petrochemicals, artificial perfumes and other unnecessary synthetic ingredients.

Over the next few weeks, I trialled each of the three skin treatments for fourteen days, leaving a seven-day gap between each, during which I went back to my regular products. I'm not claiming it's a scientific test and I didn't measure the depth of my wrinkles or anything as objective as that. I simply tested them as normal women test beauty products, putting them on and noting how I thought I looked after using them. I chose fourteen days because that was how long my Boots serum lasted, using it morning and night, so it seemed logical to give the other two the same testing period. Ideally, one would probably test for a month each, but I couldn't afford the time or the expenditure on products.

No 7's Refine & Rewind claims to improve the appearance of lines and wrinkles, especially around the eyes, by 29 per cent after the very first application. How this is measured I have no idea, but having put it on and gone to bed I awoke the next morning and met a markedly more youthful, perky me in the mirror. This was astonishing and, to tell the truth, a little perturbing. Skin can't change overnight. Not that drastically, anyway. I asked my husband, who said I looked nice because I was smiling instead of frowning (I had been rather stressed and grumpy) but didn't see a difference in my skin. Still, I was happy, because I thought I looked better, which made him happy, so job done, eh? Well . . . seven days later, the lines around my eyes seemed to have lessened and by fourteen days the upward trend had continued, though the improvement was less striking in comparison with first use and the effect seemed to have plateaued out. It has been scientifically proven to improve sun-damaged skin and lessen fine lines and, from my brief experience, I'd concur with that. Even so, I was glad to stop using it. Call me paranoid or a worrier if you like, but I kept thinking about those parabens and my age and breast cancer and decided I'd rather find another way to rout the wrinkles.

The Udderly SMOOth Udder Cream came in a 340g tub splodged with black patches like a Friesian dairy cow. There were no contraindications for humans, but there was a warning about washing teats and udder before each milking and instructions not to use on parts affected by cow pox. I can't believe I'm writing this, let alone that I used the stuff on my face for a fortnight, but

I did, and you know what? It wasn't half bad. My first impression, once I'd got over the udder ridiculousness of this particular trial, was that it didn't smell very nice. However, when I analysed this reaction I realised that it wasn't that it smelt unpleasant, it was just that it wasn't perfumed in any way. I guess perfume might taint the milk or give them itchy teats but then cows aren't fussed about smelling like roses anyway. It's interesting that smell is such an important consideration for me, though, especially since the synthetic perfumes and fragrances routinely added to beauty products are potentially harmful to our health. Its texture was light, midway between a cream and a lotion (Margaret says it starts out thicker when you first open a pot) and it sinks in immediately without any greasy residue. I can see why quilters like it; I can use it as a hand cream and get straight back onto my laptop, and there are no greasy fingerprints or palm prints at all. It has a reputation for being good for chapped and chafed skin, and is apparently recommended by the Eczema Society, round-the-world yachtsmen and Tour de France cyclists, as well as being beneficial for psoriasis sufferers and soothing skin conditions caused by chemotherapy. However, it's not promoted as a face cream but rather as a general emollient. I found that it did slightly sting, irritating my skin one night when I applied it more liberally than usual to my face, neck and décolletage – my skin tingled a bit, but it was only the once and I did slather it on. Also, my skin is very sensitive and reacts that way to lots of things. On the whole, Udder Cream made my skin feel really comfortable and gave my complexion a soft matt finish. There were no dramatic next-day improvements but what I did find over the two-week period was that it seemed to give my skin what I can only describe as an amazing clarity. My skin looked brighter, smoother and the complexion evened out, while scarring from blemishes seemed reduced. It also appeared to have a tightening effect, which is perhaps why it earned the 'better than Botox' tag. I can't honestly say it's got any claims to being 'natural' but in the sense that it's effective, cheap, (340g costs £7.99), multi-tasking and has minimal packaging, it works out a reasonably economical choice in these cash-strapped times (www.udderlysmooth.co.uk)

What all this brought home to me was the phenomenal power that advertising plays in our choice of skincare products. So often what we're buying into – often at very great expense – is a marketing concept, the suggestion that if you use such a cream, serum or lotion you will have the gorgeous, dewy skin of the (heavily airbrushed, cleverly lit and flatteringly photographed) model. In fact, many models, I've since learned, swear by unglamorous Udder Cream! Dove is the exception to this with its Campaign for Real Beauty, which uses real women of different ages, shapes, sizes and ethnicity in its adverts. They tell us you can be beautiful in your own skin and are big on promoting self-esteem. Great. Now you're empowered, you can say, 'Bugger that, I'm fine without the cocamidopropyl betaine and the butylphenyl methylpropional, thank you very much'.

The third and final facial moisturiser I tested was Green People's Fruitful Nights, which was voted 'Best Night Cream' by *Natural Health & Beauty* magazine 2006. It contains organic apricot, hibiscus and rosehip and claims to lift dead skin cells away using pineapple and wild berry extracts to reveal younger skin beneath. Natural fruit acids and firming plant ingredients – which are all listed along with a translation explaining what the ingredient is so you can clearly see and check the preservative system – are said to minimise fine lines and give skin a soft, even texture; the product even boasts of making blemishes and imperfections become less apparent. It sounded magic indeed, and wonderfully ethical – none of Green People's products and formulations are tested on animals, they give 10 per cent of the net annual profit to environmental and 'green' charities and only use recyclable and non-air-freighted packaging. But does the stuff work? Fruitful Nights did have a lovely fruity smell and a lovely texture, but I was initially put off by the rather greyish colour of the cream (but then there are no artificial colourants so what you see is what you get). It sank in well, wasn't at all greasy and, although it's not recommended for very sensitive skin (presumably due to the fruit acids), it didn't make mine react. My skin looked fresh and relaxed in the morning, not as dramatically as after the first use of the Boots serum but, considering the lifestyle factors working against it (coffee, stress, late nights) I thought it did a commendable job. I can't say it's made me look dramatically younger but while it does make claims to magic it says nothing about miracles.

Challenge 16:
Can you make your own skin-care stuff at home?

A couple of months ago I calculated our family's carbon footprint using the WWF's carbon calculator (http://footprint.wwf.org.uk/). Alarmingly, it revealed that, despite all my eco-challenges, as a family we were still emitting 8 tonnes of carbon a year (the national average is nearer 11 tonnes; that flight to my parents', who swanned off to live in France, is what blew it). The calculator has a list of recommendations to further reduce your footprint and high up on mine was the blunt instruction to 'cut down on beauty products'. I considered using Nivea Creme for everything, but the prospect of making my own products appealed more. Having studied the lists of chemicals that are in many beauty products I thought it was high time to simplify what I put on my skin. Also, I was curious to know whether it was possible to make your own stuff and for it to be any good, or whether it would just turn out to be, well, a load of yuk.

I thought I should seek some expert advice before diving straight in, so I went to the Lake District to meet Jane Holroyd, who started the Mother Earth organic skincare range by cooking up night creams in her own kitchen and selling them on market stalls. Jane, a holistic healer and aromatherapist with a background in massage and counselling, has since developed an extensive range of products and has opened three shops in the last two years. Mother Earth products are also stocked by Harvey Nichols and her Raindrops and Roses Body Butter was voted one of the top six body moisturisers in the UK by the *Sunday Express*. I've used several of the products, including the Avocado Organic Night Cream with rose and frankincense, which has a truly amazing de-creasing effect on the face overnight so that you wake up with skin like a petal.

Jane attributes the rapid growth of the business to feedback from customers, many of whom have testified to the efficacy of the products not just for general skincare but, incidentally, for conditions such as psoriasis, rosacea and eczema. The attractiveness of her holistic skincare range lies in the simplicity and purity of the products. At a time when ever-more scientific solutions are being sold to us, the fact that Mother Earth's wholesome, hand-stirred preparations are not made of dubious and unpronounceable man-made chemicals but from organic oils, plant and flower extracts and basic natural ingredients like witch hazel, olive oil and cocoa butter is deeply reassuring. 'People said I would need to include chemicals to give them a shelf life but I've got no plans to include preservatives because they're so stable,' says Jane. She attributes the keeping qualities of the products – unopened, they last three years, or twelve months once opened – to the natural preservative power of the essential oils. She hasn't used chemicals on her own skin for twenty years. 'If I've done one thing, it's to show that you don't need those products.'

The transparency of Jane's formulations is something that visitors to Mother Earth's Skincare Kitchen beside Coniston Water can see for themselves. The business has expanded from Jane's cottage into a small industrial unit where two full-time employees make the products in front of you, stirring them up in Pyrex mixing bowls or blending them in bubbling *bain maries* on a stove top. When we visited, my daughter was soon involved in making a bath soak with lots of dried flowers and salts and essential oils, and we watched as the two employees, Amy and Heather, made up a batch of New Baby Balm, melting beeswax with cocoa butter, coconut oil, sunflower oil and carrot oil and decanting it into glass jars.

Inspired by this, I went home and decided to source my own ingredients. They weren't as difficult to find as I'd thought. Essential oils are easy enough to locate, but you have to make sure they're pure and not diluted (with the exception of the very expensive ones such as rose absolute, which you normally buy in dilution). Carrier oils, like almond and jojoba, are also easy enough to find. I ended up getting some of the raw ingredients from Culpeper, since they have a line of base products to create your own cosmetics, including cocoa butter. I bought solid bars of beeswax, a pot of coconut oil, some Jan de Vries flower essences, dried herbs and flowers from our wholefood shop, and witch hazel and Epsom salts from the local pharmacy. The rest of the ingredients I already had at home: oatmeal, cider vinegar, lemons, rosewater, ground almonds, sea salt, cornflour, bicarbonate of soda and aloe vera gel (I keep it in the fridge and use it for soothing sunburn and sore skin). I spent around £60 in total, which is a lot of money but, to put it in perspective, that's roughly equivalent to two Clarins products and it makes a great deal more than that.

The easiest homemade products to concoct are scrubs and masks, so I started with these. Mashing half an overripe and slightly brown avocado with yogurt, honey and a squirt of lemon juice took me back to those try-it-at-home masks from my *Jackie* magazine days. The end result was a sweetish and rather lumpy guacamole which, when plastered on my face, made me look as if I was covered with troll bogies but once I'd washed it off, my skin felt tighter and looked much brighter. I also put it on my daughter's nose, which was all she would permit, and it vanished a little spot. Plus, there was enough of the original mixture left over for my pudding (or a dip, had we any nachos). Top tip: use Greek bio yogurt. It stays on better.

I also experimented with a kaolin mask, which you make by blending kaolin powder with a carrier oil (I used jojoba, then wished I hadn't because it used up a quarter of a bottle and it's quite expensive) and a few drops of essential oil (lavender). It made a fine, silky smooth paste that smelt and felt like that Guinot's Essential Radiance masque, which is the one that make-up artists swear by to perk up models' complexions after a night on the razz. It didn't set, but it stayed on without slippage and my skin looked ace afterwards. (By the way, I checked the Guinot masque; it has lavender and jojoba too, which makes the oil worth the money.)

As to scrubs, I tried a sugar mixture from *10-Minute Facelift* by Tessa Thomas, a blend of raw brown sugar (I used unrefined molasses cane sugar), cornflour, almond oil and lemon juice. It made a thick, sticky sludge that smelt like Christmas pudding when you mix it and make a wish. It massaged on and washed off cooperatively, leaving my skin nice and soft but rather too pink. I think I overdid the scrubbing; raw sugar is quite abrasive so if you've got sensitive skin try mixing fine oatmeal with ground almonds and a little cream. If you make too much you can cook the rest and hey presto! Porridge!

Since I had my pinny on and was enjoying all this cosmetic cooking, I next tried a cleansing paste from a recipe in *The Fragrant Pharmacy* by Valerie Ann Worwood. This involved blending ground almonds with almond oil, cider vinegar, spring water (I used Evian) and essential oils (I added orange and grapefruit). The end result was like tahini, only slightly thinner. It smelt heavenly when I made it but the next day the whiff of vinegar was a little over-powering so I added a few more drops of the sweet orange oil. I can't say it looks pretty and it is a bit messy to use – I got ground almonds in my hair – but it does cleanse well, plus it exfoliates. My friend Karen has been trialling it for me and she says it's 'absolutely gorgeous' so I'm quite chuffed.

As to toners, they're simple to make – you just need flower water (orange or rose), some essential oils, cider vinegar and witch hazel. Moisturisers, though, are harder to get right. You can buy ready-made emollient bases, but that seemed like cheating as I wanted to do it all from scratch. In the end, I succeeded in making a super-rich cream by grating the beeswax bars (I recruited child labour for this: my daughter had a friend round) and melting them in a measuring jug placed in a pan of gently boiling water. To this I added cocoa butter (and yes, that is the stuff they put in chocolate), which comes as a solid, coconut oil, which is also solid at room temperature, sweet almond oil and essential oils of rose absolute, frankincense and geranium. I ended up with a yellowish oil that set quickly once I'd decanted it. I used an old glass jar that I'd washed and kept after a previous moisturiser had run out but you can buy lidded pots easily online (we got some from eBay). The moisturiser smelled divine but in truth it was more waxy than creamy and it was rather too oily to use on the face. It turned out to be excellent for rough, dry skin; the beeswax gives it a slightly granular texture which is exfoliating and it makes a great treatment for knees and elbows and hands, especially if you put it on last thing at night and wear those white cotton gloves to bed. It's also brilliant on cracked heels; after using it on mine for just two days the splits closed completely.

I have perfected my nightcreams now, with help from Josephine Fairley's *Ultimate Natural Beauty Book*, which has some great recipes, but I still haven't managed to make a day cream (solidified oils are too greasy for daytime use). However, I met a lovely lady called Sally who gave up graphic design to make beauty products and she told me that you need to go on a course and learn how to emulsify. Sally runs Shea Alchemy (www.sheaalchemy.co.uk) and has a range of fantastic moisturisers based on wild shea butter with no 'nasties' that sink in beautifully and smell divine. I use their daycream, which is made locally and delivered by bike – very eco-smart!

Finally, I threw caution to the winds and made a foot powder, inspired by Lush's T for Toes that I use regularly after swimming and had just run out of. I threw kaolin into my Magimix, along with bicarbonate of soda and cornflour, which gives a lovely slippery texture, then added a small handful of chopped dried horsetail (the herb!), some lavender heads, tea tree oil and a few drops of Jan de Vries' Vitality Essence, to invigorate. It needed a lot of whizzing to get a smooth powder and a little adjusting of the cornflour content to stop it going oily, but once the bits of herb and lavender buds had been sieved out, the powder looked the real deal and smelt as if it could out-pong the smelliest of feet, in the nicest, if slightly medicinal, kind of way. I gave a trial pot to a friend, whose son is prone to 'trainer feet'. He loves the smell of it and the deodorising effect seems to work; she got close enough to his tootsies for a sniff test – and on a non-bath-night – and could barely detect a trace.

I did, as you can probably tell, get a kick out of making these products. It had the same kind of appeal as cooking, which I enjoy, or potion-making, which I also enjoy (albeit on Halloween and only to make up gunk for the kids). I make most of my own products these days and am forever foisting sample pots of hand-cream or moisturiser on my friends to test, who have all been very enthusiastic about the results and have (though I say it myself) all got fresh glowing skin. This challenge has proved to me that skincare products are simple to make if you're prepared to invest a little time and effort, and that one can have a lovely complexion without chemicals. I don't feel the cost was prohibitive, partly because the raw ingredients made so many products (and half of them have culinary use, too), but mostly, as they say in the ad, 'Because I'm worth it'. We all are.

AISLE 6

Healthy Challenges 2:
Personal Care Products

Challenge 17:
Do natural deodorants really work?

Being eco-friendly does tend to invite comparisons with hairy hippiedom at times, and I'm not just talking about flowing locks on people's heads. However, 'Doing a Julia' (as in Roberts, who flashed her fluffy pits *on the red carpet*) isn't for me. Neither am I a fan of 'the natural smell'. So what's a girl to do? There's a plethora of health and environmental concerns about what we do to our underarms: plastic disposable razors and roll-ons clogging up landfill; foams and gels containing toxic chemicals; aluminium in antiperspirants and deodorants causing breast cancer, not to mention those nasty parabens. Can we really stay fresh 'n' dry without harming ourselves or the planet? Or – I always see this as the test of an effective deodorant – putting off partners at a salsa class?

Shaving's a personal thing. I still do it, but I use pure aloe vera gel instead of shaving foam to avoid the chemicals and I buy replacement blades so I'm not throwing a whole razor away. But if, like me, you shave your underarms, be aware of this: using an antiperspirant straight afterwards could put you at increased risk of developing breast cancer. A possible link between breast cancer and antiperspirants, based on the theory that nicks caused by shaving allow harmful substances in these products to enter the body, is relatively old news and has been the subject of several contradictory studies. However, at the time of writing – indeed, the very day I took my antiperspirant-free pits to salsa – the story made headlines again, with statements such as, 'I'm a breast cancer expert and I won't let my family use antiperspirants' splashed all over the *Daily Mail*.* The writer, Professor Robert Thomas, who was named UK Oncologist of the Year 2006, stated that 'Giving up using deodorant could be as effective in reducing cancer risk as a diet rich in disease-preventing antioxidants.' Professor Thomas was responding to new research at Keele University that had found that the aluminium content of breast tissue was significantly higher in the outer regions of the breast in close proximity to the area where there would be the highest density of antiperspirant. This is also the area of the breast known to be most prone to developing tumours (although that could simply be because it contains a greater proportion of breast tissue, according to another researcher). Furthermore, the researchers claimed that evidence existed that skin is permeable to aluminium (which is used to block pores and prevent sweating) when applied as an antiperspirant.

I contacted one of the report's authors, Dr Chris Exley, about the shaving issue and he confirmed that 'any activity which might lead to abrasion of the skin is very likely to increase the uptake of aluminium across that surface'. This is a concern because aluminium is capable of mimicking the actions of oestrogens in the body and has been shown to be carcinogenic. 'My own view

*4 September 2007

is that we should all do as much as we are personally prepared to do to reduce our exposure to aluminium,' he said. While scientists and the cosmetic industry continue to argue the toss over whether clear proof exists between the application of anti-perspirants and breast cancer, Professor Thomas's view is that 'it seems sensible to be cautious and not take unnecessary risks'. This is important for women, but particularly so for women who have already had breast cancer, especially if there is a family history of this cancer.

Robert Thomas recommends thorough daily washing and just using a deodorant (which masks the smell rather than preventing you sweating) on occasions when you really need it. In the article, he said that his wife used a natural crystal 'and she smells just fine', which was reassuring, since the thought of going without any kind of protection against whiffiness brings me out in a cold sweat straight off. It made me feel braver about getting up close and personal with a lot of strange men with only a crystal deodorant stone for protection, though I had used one before and found it surprisingly effective at preventing perspiration pong, even after a bike ride. Still, an hour of hot latino rhythms and cross-body leads and all those arms-above-your-head-and-twisty-turny-movements has got to be the ultimate challenge.

I used PitRok, a natural, smooth, shaped crystal that you dampen or apply to wet skin. It dries quickly and leaves an invisible layer of natural mineral salts (no aluminium) that prevent bacteria from multiplying. It doesn't stop you sweating, but unlike other deodorants, which cover up body odour, it works by eliminating the bacteria – the source of the smell – in the first place. In my experience, one application lasts twenty-four hours and the crystal itself is extremely long-lasting. It also has minimal (recyclable) packaging, which gives it great green cred, though you can buy a push-up one in a plastic tube (to make it more like a roll-on, presumably) and a spray version, should you feel the need for something less basic.

I've tried a variety of aluminium-free deodorants in the past: roll-ons with lavender or ylang-ylang, stick deodorants with active enzymes, clay and baking soda, propylene-glycol-free ones, Japanese spa mineral ones and unscented ones and I had been tortured with doubt about the effectiveness of every single one under salsa conditions. Indeed, I had become so concerned about my armpits 'humming' that I had taken to using Sure on salsa nights, feeling that an application of aluminium was worth it for the extra confidence it gave me. I confess I popped it in my bag when I used the crystal stone, just in case I needed to dash to the Ladies to put some on, but it wasn't needed. At least, I hope it wasn't. I'm pretty sure I know when I whiff – I didn't feel I could wave an armpit in some poor bloke's face and go, 'Smell this, can you?' – but just in case my ultra-sensitivity to odours had let me down I got my daughter to test on my return home. 'You smell of clean clothes,' she pronounced, after inhaling deeply. I'd call that a result. I've had a jive lesson since and, let me tell you, I can do an entire routine to 'Hit the Road, Jack' and still smell fresh as a daisy.

Challenge 18:
Sunscreens: what's the safety factor?

I never tan and I burn within minutes of being in the sun so I'm fanatical about slapping on sunscreen when I'm out and about. My equally pale-faced daughter gets an application of factor 40 on all exposed bits before she sets off for school and my husband is given a lecture about wearing his hat. We do these things because we want to protect ourselves and our loved ones, but increasingly I'm frustrated by the feeling that you can't do right for doing wrong. Never mind the parabens or the PABAs (para-aminobenzoic acid, a skin irritant); depending on who you believe, there is yet another cause for concern prevalent in our sun creams: nanoparticles.

Without getting too technical about it, nanoparticles are minute structures that exist at the scale of atoms and molecules. They are a product of the emerging field of nanotechnology, an as-yet insufficiently regulated or tested brave new world of scientific innovation that has been enthusiastically embraced by the personal care and cosmetics industries, particularly manufacturers of sun cream. They are present in sun cream as micronized particles of zinc oxide and titanium dioxide, ingredients widely used to protect against UVA. In their regular form, these materials have an opaque white appearance and can make the wearer look pallid. At nano-scale, because the particles are so tiny, this effect is broken up and the product 'disappears' into the skin without leaving a white residue. While zinc oxide and titanium dioxide are non-toxic, the concern is that in their micronized or nanoparticle form they may be able to penetrate the skin, especially if it is broken or inflamed by acne, eczema or shaving nicks, for example. Once in the bloodstream, they could potentially accumulate in areas of the body that larger particles cannot reach, with serious consequences (it's already known that they can react with other materials in the lungs). There appears to be a great deal of speculation about what nanoparticles might or might not do and the consequences for us as consumers. There is also the question of the exposure suffered by workers manufacturing the products and the knock-on effect of releasing nanoparticles into the environment, things we'll only know about further down the line (by which time it may be too late, of course). The confusion is not helped by the fact that even environmental

NGOs themselves have come to different conclusions about it. In the US, Friends of the Earth has called for a moratorium on the release of any more personal care products containing nanoparticles and the withdrawal of any such products already on the market (this is likely to go down like a lead balloon since it covers everything from anti-ageing creams to toothpaste). The Environmental Working Group, however, after extensively reviewing the studies, has come around to recommending some sunscreens containing nano-sized ingredients on the basis that, given the dangers of skin cancer, such products offer the safest and most effective protection.

Tellingly, the Soil Association has announced a total ban on manmade nanomaterials in all its certified organic products, from health and beauty products to food and textiles. A Soil Association press release on 17 January 2008 stated: 'We are the first organisation in the world to take action against this hazardous, potentially toxic technology that poses a serious new threat to human health.' Gundula Azeez, Soil Association policy manager, said: 'There should be no place for nanoparticles in health and beauty products or food. We are deeply concerned at the Government's failure to follow scientific advice and regulate products. There should be an immediate freeze on the commercial release of nanomaterials until there is a sound body of scientific research into all the health impacts. As we saw with GM, the Government is ignoring the initial indications of risk and giving the benefit of the doubt to commercial interest rather than the protection of human health.' I'd say that sets the benchmark, and it certainly throws down the challenge to companies such as Unilever, Boots, L'Oréal and Lancôme – not to mention the British Government, which, according to the Soil Association's press release, was warned by scientists three years ago that nanoparticles should be avoided 'as far as possible'.

It's hard to know whether sun cream contains nanoparticles or not, partly because the ingredients on bottles are often in such minuscule print (nano writing?) that, even with my 'granny glasses', I find it impossible to decipher them, but mostly because nanoparticles aren't listed as such, cosmetics manufacturers are steering shy of the subject. Still, it seemed wise to ask, and since my regular product, L'Oréal's Solar Expertise Active Anti-Wrinkle & Brown Spot Sun Cream, had a number for consumer advice on the box, I gave them a call. A very nice girl noted my query and went off to speak with L'Oréal's scientists. She rang me back the following day to confirm that yes, it did contain nanoparticles. Am I still using it? No, I'm not – even though I've got a couple of unopened new tubes in my bathroom cabinet as the result of a 'buy one, get one free' offer from Boots.

I might have gone with the nanos, my vanity being what it is – I've spent a fortune testing other, more 'natural' sun creams, including some that settled in embarrassing white rings in the creases round my neck – had it not been for yet *another* ingredient scare. Aargh! Just when I thought it was safe to go back in the water (reapplying sun cream liberally afterwards, etc, etc), a report from Keele University popped up questioning the safety of aluminium in sunscreens.* I came across this when I was Googling – strangely, although the aluminium-in-antiperspirants was well reported, the sunscreen research didn't get the same publicity – and the implications are breathtaking. It suggests that aluminium salts might be a factor in the increased incidence of skin cancer. In three of the products tested, Simple Sun Protection Cream SPF35 Garnier Ambre Solaire SPF30 and Piz Buin Mountain SPF50, aluminium salts were at levels higher than the researchers were able to measure. They estimated that, for those three products, an average day on the beach would result in up to 1g of aluminium being applied to the skin, a significant amount over a summer, let alone a lifetime.

*Free Radical Biology and Medicine, 43 (2007) 1216–17

More immediately concerning is the combination of aluminium, a pro-oxidant (that is, potentially cancer-causing), with the action of UV filters in sunscreens, which have also been shown to have a pro-oxidant effect on the skin. Together, says Dr Exley, they could 'very likely exacerbate oxidative damage in the skin and they may be involved in the increasing incidence of melanoma'. He adds, 'I do not use these products'. Neither do I now, having binned my sun cream since it cites aluminium hydroxide halfway down the ingredients list (when I asked the L'Oréal customer advisor how much aluminium it contained, I was told they were unable to give percentages of ingredients for legal reasons). The four other products tested were Boots Soltan Kids SPF30 and SPF50, Nivea Sun Moisturising Sun Lotion SPF15 and Hawaiian Tropic Sun Lotion SPF15, all of which contained aluminium, though in smaller amounts (it wasn't listed as an ingredient on the latter two).

Can sunscreens actually cause skin cancer? It's a controversial question. Aluminium hydroxide is in sun cream for babies, for heaven's sake (I found it in Johnson's Skincare Baby 40). Can it really be that bad? I corresponded with Cancer Research UK over Dr Exley's conclusions, which they called 'speculative and premature', adding, 'There is no strong evidence that aluminium compounds could increase the risk of cancer in animals and humans' and denying a link between sunscreen ingredients and skin cancer: 'Studies have shown that people tend to use sunscreens as an excuse to spend more time in the sun and this cancels out some of their benefit.' Dr Exley questioned whether this explanation was based on scientific merit and also asked why Cancer Research UK is against the possibility that sunscreens might actually be exacerbating the problems of skin cancer. 'Surely they want to find out what causes cancer and do all that they can to prevent it?'

Surely we can trust manufacturers to provide safe products – and our governments to ban those that aren't safe? At the heart of all of the research I've done on toxic chemicals in personal care products, this issue of trust is paramount. The industry is well aware of how crucial, and fragile, consumer trust can be. Noting that the ethical products sector is 'making real waves', an article in *European Cosmetic Markets* states, 'Trust is a big factor when buying into a brand.'* It cites Charles Laroche, Vice President of External Affairs, Unilever Europe, pointing out that 'the upside of this is that the industry has the ability to gain the confidence of the consumer if it is seen to be doing the right thing. The downside when it gets it wrong . . . is a huge fall from grace.' And, possibly, ruined lives. Not that the article adds that, of course. The marketing feature goes on to talk about Body Shop pioneer Anita Roddick, a vigorous and outspoken campaigner for ethical values, who herself came under fire for selling up (many said selling out) to L'Oréal. Whatever you think of her argument that she was able to bring greater influence to bear on cosmetics companies from within, her untimely death in September 2007 is a massive loss. Catherine Bennett wrote in the *Guardian*, 'It is hard to think of anyone, least of all anyone in the beauty business, who will alert women to the lab-coated frauds who continue to exploit their horror of looking old.' I'm no Anita Roddick, but I will say this: keep asking questions. Demand answers, seek explanations. If you're not happy, don't buy their stuff. It's simple.

Simple, yes. Easy, no. Do you know how much trouble I've had finding sun creams that fit my increasingly long list of criteria now? Fortunately, I discovered Green People's Sun Lotion 22 SPF, with edelweiss, green tea and avocado. It sinks in well, doesn't

*February 2007

leave a white residue, has good UVA and UVB protection and no aluminium. There are other sun creams on the market without parabens – Eco Cosmetics SPF30 with sea buckthorn and olive for example. However, there was no information about what level of UVA/UVB protection the latter afforded.

Then, waddya know? I came across a warning that we shouldn't be slathering ourselves in sunscreens all the time anyway because in doing so we're preventing our bodies from absorbing vitamin D. Vitamin D, which we get from the sun on our skin, plays a crucial role in protecting against heart disease, diabetes and, yes, cancer. Not getting enough of it has been linked with high blood pressure, schizophrenia, multiple sclerosis and bone health. See what I mean? You just can't win.

Here's what I do during the summer. I take a short walk without sun cream before 11am when the sun's not too high or too hot. I lurk indoors from midday to 3pm, after which, before I go out, I apply my sunscreen. I never sunbathe. Moreover, I have tried to reintroduce the parasol but people just look at me oddly because I'm walking round town with an umbrella up and *it's not raining*. (I took it to the races on a blisteringly hot day, too, but someone behind complained they couldn't see.) If you think that's mad, here's the latest: mice given the human equivalent of one to four cups of coffee a day – not as a latte, they had caffeine drops in their water – and free use of a running wheel were found to have the highest resistance to skin cancer. I can do that; it means I just drop by Pret a Manger on my walk. Though I like the irony of the running wheel whizzing round and going nowhere; it describes how I feel exactly.

Challenge 19:
Girl talk: the gory details on sanitary protection

Modern sanitary protection being what it is – discreet, disposable and highly absorbent – makes you wonder how on earth women managed before the invention of Lil-lets and Always Ultra. It wasn't until 1896 that the first disposable sanitary towels came into being and tampons didn't become popular until the late 1920s. Prior to that, women had to make do with whatever they had available, fashioning a variety of ingenious solutions for capturing the blood from their menses with strips of sheepskin, wads of cotton, knitted pads, wood-pulp bandages, menstrual aprons or towelling rags (hence the term 'on the rag', apparently), which were washed and reused. Bothersome, messy and I'd question their effectiveness, but they were, at least, environmentally friendly. We may be able to whizz around on roller skates wearing a pair of white hot pants (those old Tampax adverts have a lot to answer for) but there's a high environmental price for this liberation.

According to who you read – and I'm not even going to attempt to calculate my score – a woman uses between 10,000 and 12,000 towels and tampons during her lifetime. And where do they go when we've finished with them? Either down the loo, which is VERY BAD INDEED because they block drains and get washed up onto beaches, even if the manufacturers insist that they're flushable and/or biodegradable (10.4 per cent of the total litter recorded in the 2006 Beachwatch survey was sanitary products – euww) or, if you're bagging and binning as recommended, into land-fill. There's a huge emphasis on disposable nappies and the space they take up in landfill sites but very little about sanitary products, even though the same principle applies. I assume this is partly because periods and the mess they create is still a taboo subject (which is why sanpro manufacturers demonstrate the absorbency with blue dye) and partly because the alternatives, if women know about them at all, seem at best Mother Mung Bean-ish and, at worst, a return to the pre-Kotex days of rag-washing. Moreover, you are highly unlikely to find them in Asda or Sainsbury's or any of the other supermarkets because we women are a captive market, committed by our cycles to spending a fortune on packets and boxes of tampons and towels – and let's not forget panty liners for the rest of the month – and the more variations there are (night-time, deodorising, cotton-fresh, silk-feeling, aloe-impregnated, tanga-fit, etc, etc), the more money we'll spend.

So what are the alternatives? Well, there are two main reusable options: washable towels and pads that you fasten into your knick-ers with poppers, or menstrual cups such as Mooncups or Keepers, which sit inside the vagina and collect the blood. Mooncups are shaped like a kind of mini wine goblet, complete with a stem that you trim according to your size. They're made of soft silicone (the Keeper is similar but made of natural rubber) and come in a little cotton bag tied with ribbon. Mooncups come in two different sizes, depending on whether you've had a vaginal birth or not, and do not require special fitting. Once they're in, they only need emptying every four to eight hours and can be used overnight.

Ivana, a girl I know who has used a Mooncup for two years, is full of praise for it. 'To start with it was a bit tricky,' she admits, 'but when you get the knack it's quite easy. Once it's in you just forget about it.' She says it's saved her a fortune, and although she does still use sanitary pads on a heavy day 'to be on the safe side' she points out that overall she's still cutting down on waste. Ivana was surprised to learn that her GP and nurse hadn't heard about menstrual cups; she was less surprised at the reactions of her friends and housemates. 'I do tell them about it and their first reactions are always, "Oh my God, why would you do that?" But they're getting more curious now because I keep going on about it.'

Keely, a friend of mine who volunteers with Ivana, had the same initial reaction. 'I thought it was the most outlandish thing I'd ever heard of. But I came round to the idea and now I've made a pledge to try it out.' I asked her if she had, in fact, fulfilled this pledge and she admitted she hadn't, so she went online there and then and ordered one. She rang me a few days later to thank me for giving her the push. 'It's been so much better than I thought,' she said. 'It's really no more trouble than a tampon, plus you don't have to change it so often.' Keely admitted that some people might find the idea of emptying and rinsing a Mooncup 'a bit of a no-no' but found it coped with a very heavy period extremely well. She was delighted with the freedom it gave her and the drier nights; the only downside was that, since she had omitted to read the instructions first, she hadn't realised you have to release the internal seal (it adheres to the wall of the vagina by suction) before removing it. As a result, it came out with a noise that would have been hard to explain in a public convenience ('I prefer a silent operation'). She admits it might not suit a young girl – 'You have to know your way around your body' – but says she found the trial 'rather jolly'. She's now a total convert. 'I can't believe I left it so long,' she enthused.

Encouraged by all this, I bought one myself. At first, I couldn't see how it would ever go in (you fold it), but I managed it relatively easily. Removal was trickier – 'Try not to panic if you can't find the stem,' the booklet advises – but if you follow the instructions you'll be fine. By day three of my period I was quite laid back about the operation and confident enough to go to a party wearing my Mooncup and a white dress. I had a brief moment of terror when I thought 'Why have I done this?' and dashed off to the Ladies to check (all was well) and then forgot about it for the rest of the evening. It's the nearest I'll get to roller-blading in hot pants but I'd say boogieing to Shakira gave it just as good a workout.

My Mooncup cost me £18.49, which I reckon I'd recoup in savings on sanitary protection in about four months (Keely bought hers online for £15 with free delivery, so shop around). Looked after and used correctly, they can, apparently, last years. Mine has already been tested to the extreme – I was sterilising it in the multi-steamer (without veg, before you ask) and forgot all about it. It wasn't until an unpleasant smell of singeing wafted into the room that I realised I'd left the pan on the gas and had melted my Mooncup. Actually, the Mooncup was OK – though it smelt rather off-putting for a while – but the steamer's had it.

If you're not up to trying menstrual caps, the washable reusable pads are worth considering. They come in all sorts of funky colours, including brocade backed, and you can buy washable panty liners too. If you're good with a sewing machine, you can even run up your own. I commissioned a friend, Anastasia, to do this for me since I'm hopeless at needlework. The Women's Environmental Network has templates and also lists of stockists; go to www.wen.org.uk and search on sanpro. Anastasia managed to whip me up a really rather lovely one that could be (and was) mistaken for a sunglasses case. It looked as if it had been made from one of her husband's ties, which made me feel slightly uncomfortable about using it 'down there' since I know him quite well, but she insists it's a Liberty offcut. We are rather tickled by the thought of recycling our partners' ties in such a femme-friendly fashion, but I don't know what our husbands will make of it.

In the meantime, she brought round some Lunapads that she'd ordered from www.twinkleontheweb.co.uk. These are as soft and lovely as a slipper and have a thin layer of breathable nylon concealed in the layers of flannelette to prevent leakage. The great thing about them is that they have removable liners, of which you can use as many as you need, but they're held in place by a couple of pieces of ribbing and we can envisage the ribbing rubbing, if you get what I mean. Also, they come from Canada, which is a long way to fly your sanitary protection from. I didn't try them myself, since I was going strong with the Mooncup by then, though I could see the appeal of having half-a-dozen washable panty liners as back-up. Anastasia gamely trialled the Luna-pads and reported that, while they looked nice and felt soft, they were a bit bulky to wear ('OK for jeans but not for skin-tight leggings'). Furthermore, a normal wash with Ecover at 40 degrees didn't combat stains, despite pre-soaking in cold water. 'At the sort of price we're talking (£10.99 for just one regular maxi pad and liner), we want them to look good as new for several months, if not years.' She had no problem with the soaking and washing regime but wondered how it would appeal to teens or students. 'You'd have to be pretty up-front to conduct it in shared accommodation.' I imagine that travelling or working away from home would also be tricky, not to say icky.

I've since become a convert to washable pads and panty liners myself as a back-up to the Mooncup, which is pretty good but not infallible when it comes to leakage. This was after another friend dropped by for a coffee and we got onto matters eco. I showed her my Bokashi bin (see Aisle 12) and she nipped home and returned with her Moonrabbits. Desperate Housewives, eat your heart out. Moonrabbits (www.moonrabbits.co.uk) are a range of simple poppered cotton pads that you can get with or without a waterproof lining. They are handmade in Aberdeenshire and my friend absolutely swears by them, particularly if you get itchiness or dermatitis. They come with a useful little drawstring bag for your handbag, too. I found they washed well at 40°C and air-dried quickly but I was a little too self-conscious to hang them out on the line. I also put a warning on the lid of the ice-cream tub in the bathroom that I use to soak them in. You really don't want children or house guests idly investigating its contents . . .

I guess how far you want to go with alternative sanpro depends on how intimate you are prepared to get with it. Squeamishness is a matter of degree once you get round to washing your own but when Anastasia polled a group of friends about the pads she received a universal 'yeuch' at the idea. Still, she's planning to use the Lunapads again. 'I'm rather thrilled and felt pretty smug not to be chucking away more stuff, so I'll persevere even if it only allows me to cut down,' she concluded. Atta girl. As for me, I'm a 100 per cent Moon Mama now. I'm thinking of starting up a sect.

There is a middle way, which is to opt for biodegradable natural pads and organic cotton tampons, which are not only better for your health but better for the environment, too. Earlier this year our local pharmacy started displaying the Natracare range up front in the shop window, which can only be a good sign. I've been trying out Natracare for a while and they're great, even if the night-time pads are bulky. The panty liners are really soft and do the job well, though you may need to change them slightly more often, and in my opinion the curved panty liners are much better than the regular ones. You can also buy those super-thin jobbies with wings, which I really like. In fact, they make everything you can get from the big-name manufacturers. What you don't get is perfume (an irritant), non-biodegradable plastic (from backing strips and applicators; these form a significant proportion of sewage-related debris on beaches), pesticides or GM material (organic cotton tampons apparently reduce the risk of developing toxic shock syndrome, which can be fatal) and synthetic materials such as rayon or polyacrylic absorbents, which can cause vulval itching, soreness and other thrush-like symptoms. Crucially, they are not bleached with chlorine, which contaminates the food chain with dioxin. I remember watching the 1989 *World in Action* documentary that exposed the extent of dioxin pollution in the

UK and being appalled by it. Dioxins don't just poison the countryside, they're hormone disruptors, potentially carcinogenic and have been linked with endometriosis. The original chlorine bleaching process has since been largely phased out but most of the replacements, including elemental chlorine, still produce dioxins.

If I hadn't had this down as an eco-challenge I doubt if I'd even have considered giving such 'hands-on' approaches to sanitary products the time of day, which just goes to show how important it is to step out of one's comfort zone occasionally. Give it a whirl, girls.

AISLE 7

Liquid Challenges 1:
Hot Drinks

Challenge 20:
Does Fairtrade tea make the best brew?

Every time I buy tea I have the same dilemma. I go for a general purpose, fairly robust kind of tea, something with a bit of welly that will get me out of bed in the morning and will pep me up when I'm flagging at four o'clock. I have, in the past, experimented with different kinds of leaf tea, but I tend to forget about them and find them in the back of the cupboard three years later. So, like 96 per cent of the British population, I buy teabags. The problem I always have is deciding which ones to get. I want to support farmers by buying Fairtrade. I want to protect the environment by buying organic. And I want a tea that will, metaphorically speaking, slap me round the chops, without causing suffering to anyone else. Basically, an ethical, organic tea that tastes nice and packs a punch. Is that too much to ask?

Morally, I feel I ought to buy Fairtrade, and I often do. There's much more choice now than when I first started buying Fairtrade products a few years ago: back in 2002, UK sales of Fairtrade goods amounted to £63m; by 2006 this had jumped to a staggering £293m. Over 270 UK towns now have Fairtrade status and more than half the UK adult population recognises the distinctive logo of the Fairtrade mark. (This is not the same as something that is marketed as 'fairly traded'; the Fairtrade mark is an independent stamp of approval guaranteeing that the product has met with the standards required by the Fairtrade Labelling Organizations International or FLO. This doesn't mean that a 'fairly traded' product isn't authentic, but nonetheless it's an important distinction.) Awareness was given another huge boost after Marks & Spencer's announcement in April 2006 that they would sell nothing but Fairtrade tea and coffee and other retailers have since followed suit. It's all good, though it begs a socking great question about precisely how *unfair* regular trade is, not to mention our own compliance with it.

So how does Fairtrade work? First, by paying a fair price to farmers and producers in developing countries, a price that covers the cost of sustainable production and living. Not only does it give them a better deal, it's also dependable and can sustain them through market fluctuations. Globalisation, the monopolistic practices of powerful multinationals, government intervention and extreme weather events such as droughts and hurricanes all affect prices, which are sometimes so low that farmers cannot even cover their production costs. As a result, they have no money for basics like healthcare, electricity or schooling for their children and frequently live in conditions of desperate poverty. This has been particularly true for small-scale coffee producers, who have been badly hit by plummeting world coffee prices, but depressed prices on the world tea market have also caused terrible hardship (in some more remote parts of India, hundreds of workers have died from starvation and disease).

To show the effect Fairtrade can have, in Uganda, when tea prices fell to $1.52 per kg in 2007, which is below the growers' production costs, Fairtrade brand Cafédirect was paying $2.33 per kg. The same year, Cafédirect announced it was increasing the amount it paid for tea by 8 per cent, meaning that 88 per cent more was going back to those who traded with them compared to what they would receive from non-Fairtrade companies. For workers on tea plantations, Fairtrade certification ensures that they receive decent wages, have the right to join a trade union and are provided with good housing; also that health and safety and environmental standards are met and that no forced child labour is used.

Beyond that, Fairtrade pays a premium that is set aside for farmers and workers to spend on social and environmental projects. Whether it's drilling bore holes to collect clean water, establishing a healthcare center or setting up their own processing plant, the initiatives (which are democratically chosen by committees of elected workers and farmers) don't jnust raise the quality of life for communities, they also give long-term viability and security and help to develop businesses. For example, the Stockholm Tea Estate in Sri Lanka, which supplies Clipper Fairtrade tea in the UK, has used the premium from Fairtrade sales to enable workers to install elecricity in their homes, build recreation halls, buy a new ambulance and set up a loan fund to finance small-scale income generating schemes. As a result, the workforce is coop-erative and happy and prepared to put in the overtime, when necessary, to pluck flushes of new growth, producing high-quality teas that command better prices at auction.

This is the kind of stuff I want to know if I'm going to pay extra for my tea, though the cost differential is certainly not exorbitant. Given Cafédirect's policy of paying a higher premium you would expect Teadirect Fairtrade tea to cost more and it does, but it still holds its own against other premium brands and works out cheaper than some, especially speciality teas such as Sainsbury's Taste the

Difference blends. What makes the whole tea-buying process more confusing is that many well-known brands, including almost all of the non-Fairtrade ones, state on the packet that they are 'working in an ethical partnership' or some such wording. This, you might be forgiven for thinking, amounts to much the same thing as Fairtrade, and I admit I always assumed this was the case, in the I'll-spend-ten-seconds-considering-this-oh-it-must-be-OK kind of way that you do when you're dashing round the supermarket. However, having looked into the subject more closely, I can tell you that it's not.

The Ethical Tea Partnership (ETP) is an alliance of tea-packing companies that have come together to ensure that the tea they buy is responsibly produced. They pay for rolling monitoring programmes in twelve of the main tea-growing countries that, between them, produce 70 per cent of the world's tea. The monitors themselves are independent, though I note that Norman Kelly, executive director of the ETP, was formerly Operations and Development Director for Unilever Tea, Kenya. Unilever owns PG and Liptons, which are members of the ETP along with the Tetley Group, Betty's, Taylors of Harrogate (makers of Yorkshire Tea), Tazo and Twinings. Typhoo, incidentally, is one of the few major players that is not a member; it has its own Quality Assurance Programme, an in-house supplier-monitoring scheme conducted by its buyers, and is a member of the wider Ethical Trading Initiative (see Aisle 10).

So what does the Ethical Tea Partnership actually do, and how does it differ from Fairtrade? Essentially, its focus is on working conditions – employment, education, maternity, health and safety, housing and some basic rights – and ensuring that estates comply with local laws, trade union agreements and some international standards. The monitors grade estates, and producers are given support to make improvements, though what this 'support' amounts to and whether it is financial or not I've been unable to discover, as they haven't replied to my emails. Ultimately, if suppliers do not comply, they are de-listed. The Ethical Tea Partnership is laudable, but it's not an official certification mark and, unlike Fairtrade, the ETP does not guarantee a fair and stable price for workers, nor does it pay a premium for development and investment. Because of this, some have accused the big brands of exploiting the burgeoning ethical market and attempting to con the consumer, though the ETP denies this. In its information leaflet it states that the two schemes are complementary and 'provide for consumer choice'. So I guess you have to make up your own mind on that one.

But what about organic teas? After all, I don't want to imbibe pesticide traces in my cuppa and I'll always buy organic when I can. Aren't organic teas 'Fairtrade' by their very nature? I'd always assumed this was a kind of default position, but it turns out I was wrong. True, certification with the Soil Association necessitates compliance with the UN Convention for Human Rights and the core standards of the International Labour Organisation. Specifically, this means employees must have the freedom to associate, the right to organise and the right to bargain collectively. Employers may not use forced labour or child labour that interferes with children's education. Failure to uphold any of these requirements can result in organic certification being withdrawn. However, that falls a long way short of the proactive stance taken by the Fairtrade Foundation. At the time of writing, progress has been made along this path, prompted by prices for many organic products being driven down to levels at or below the cost of production. Following a four-year pilot scheme, the Soil Association has now launched a voluntary Ethical Trading Standards (ETS) certification in addition to its Organic Standards. Its range is small as yet, though the ETS document states that, 'In the future we may introduce these standards as an integral and mandatory element of the Soil

Association Organic Standards.' The first step towards that seems to have been taken already, with the announcement on 25 October 2007 that air-freighted organic food must, with effect from January 2009, meet the Soil Association's Ethical Trading Standards or the Fairtrade Foundation's standards. Reading the Ethical Trading Standards certification requirements, it makes stipulations about paying a 'fair wage' but says nothing about a social premium; however, the employer must be able to demonstrate that they have made 'a positive social and cultural contribution' over and above their legal requirement to the community.

So, the organic movement is moving towards Fairtrade. But is the Fairtrade Foundation moving towards becoming more organic? I ran into Mark Dawson, who chairs the York Fairtrade Forum, and told him about my organic vs Fairtrade dilemma. He told me it was something that concerned the Fairtrade movement as a whole: 'Ideally, the aim is for the Fairtrade producers to all have greater environmental standards. We're working towards that, though there's still some work to be done.' I went on to tell him about my quest for the perfect ethical cup of tea and he agreed that, in the early days of the Fairtrade movement, the quality wasn't so good. 'In the 1980s, we were buying it out of charity, whereas now that definitely isn't the case. Some of the best tea and coffee is Fairtrade.' Which is where my challenge for this section originally came in.

Over the years I've experimented with many different brands of tea – Fairtrade, organic and bog-standard types – and the taste issue is one I keep returning to. I've had some pretty unimpressive Fairtrade teas, to put it kindly, with the notable exception of Teadirect, which always seems to deliver. And that delivery, that lip-smacking sigh of pleasure, is critical: ultimately, no matter how worthy my tea is, if it tastes like floor sweepings – and, while I'm not impugning Fairtrade teas in this, some tea bags, particularly cheap supermarket own-brands, have been identified as being little more than that – then I'm certainly not going to buy it again. Being an eco-shopper doesn't mean you stop being discerning about quality, after all. So, leaving organic tea out of this (I trialled them in the 'Organic vs Ordinary' taste test in Aisle 1), I set out to discover whether Fairtrade tea made the best of the brews.

Once again, I'm not claiming any scientific basis for this test. It was simply to try and discover my preferences and dislikes when I didn't actually know which brand of tea I was drinking. To do this, I enlisted the help of my daughter, recently granted tea-maker status now that she's 10, since the appearance of the teabags would have been a give-away had I been making it. I bought five brands originally – PG Tips (not Fairtrade), Typhoo (not Fairtrade), Clipper Fairtrade Tea, Equal Exchange Breakfast Blend Tea (Fairtrade) and Nilgiri Tea from the Just Change Network (not Fairtrade as such, but it's picked by a network of disadvantaged tribal groups in South India for 'mutual social and economic benefit'). My daughter decanted them into clean, numbered yogurt pots and kept her master list stashed away so that I couldn't peek. Every day after school, when I hit my four o'clock low, she made me a different cup of tea, using the same kind of mug and with strict instructions to mash each teabag fifteen times before removing it, which is the kind of technical detail that only lovers of fairly strong tea can appreciate. I gave each tea a rating, based on colour, pick-me-up power and taste. The clear winner turned out to be PG Tips, which had a good body, great taste and plenty of pep and scored 5/5, with the Just Change tea nipping into second place with 4/5. Clipper and Equal Exchange both got 3/5 and Typhoo an underwhelming 2/5. It was a bit lukewarm and milky though, so I got my husband to repeat that one. However, even made stronger (my daughter had forgotten the mashing instructions) it still only earned 3/5.

I decided to repeat the experiment the following week, since there had been a few technical difficulties – principally, the tea-maker getting distracted by *Tracy Beaker* – adding another non-Fairtrade brand (Yorkshire Tea) to even the numbers out. This time, the mashing instructions were adhered to carefully, the milk was measured into a medicine cup so I always got the same amount (15ml) and the tea was brought to me promptly, which is the kind of child labour that should, I believe, be encouraged. The results were as follows: Yorkshire Tea got a rating of 5/5, which doesn't surprise me as I love it and drink it quite often, and Clipper Fairtrade also earned a 5/5 this time. PG Tips and Equal Exchange got 4/5 and the Just Change Network tea a 3/5. The only consistent result was the Typhoo did not give me much of an 'oo' at all, rating just 2/5.

After two weeks of tea-testing I've come to the conclusion that, while one can have favourites, only two of the teas were really distinctive (the Nilgiri tea had a slightly twiggy, almost liquorice note and Typhoo was harsh and made the insides of my cheeks ache). The rest were fairly interchangeable, given the variation in the way I rated them, though I reckon Yorkshire Tea has a very slight edge.

Is that bias? Possibly. I enjoyed the Clipper tea equally as much second time around, and it's Fairtrade. It was a dilemma: head said Clipper, heart said Yorkshire, tastebuds said both. In the end, I decided to email Taylors of Harrogate, who make Yorkshire Tea, to find out how ethical it was. On the box they claim to pay 'fair prices' to their growers. Did that mean they went above and beyond the remit of the Ethical Tea Partnership, I asked? I was contacted by Cristina Talens, Ethical Trading Manager, who told me that the 'fair prices' claim was entirely on behalf of Taylors of Harrogate, which was a family firm that believed in building good, long-term relationships with suppliers. They often offered a price over and above the market rate to ensure that quality was maintained, she said, which meant revenues for tea growers were dependable and helped them to pay good wages and guarantee decent working conditions. The majority of their tea was purchased direct from estates rather than from auctions (which is where most of the big tea companies buy – they are notorious for driving prices down). Taylors of Harrogate had also, she said, won a Queen's Award for Enterprise for Sustainable Development. Not only that, but they were Fairtrade licensees and have their own Fairtrade Breakfast Tea (sold in Morrisons). You can't say fairer than that, can you? Well, you probably could, but only by interviewing individual tea plantation workers personally. Other than that, there comes a point when you have to decide whether to trust. In this case, I do, mainly because this is a small UK company and it is putting its reputation on the line.

So, what am I buying? Well . . . both. Mostly the Clipper Fairtrade but I do buy Yorkshire Tea from time to time. Fair compromise or a cop-out? Look, give me a break, I'm supporting a local business. And yes, I know they don't grow the tea in the dales.

Challenge 21:
Does ethical coffee hit the spot?

Instant may not be the 'greenest' way to take your coffee (there's far more industrialisation involved; to be a true eco-shopper you should buy your organic, Fairtrade coffee beans and hand-grind them yourself) but since that's the way most people in the UK drink it, that is what I'm focusing on in this Aisle. Besides, the ethical issues are the same whether you use whole beans, ground or instant coffee.

Apart from Fairtrade, there is Rainforest Alliance certified coffee in the Kraft, Lavazza and Lyons ranges, though confusingly Kraft also has Kenco Sustainable Development coffee, which you might think is a different scheme but is also certified by the Rainforest Alliance. (This is the brand that fast-food chain McDonald's now uses in the UK and Ireland.) The Rainforest Alliance is a New-York-based environmental group that works in countries around the world to conserve biodiversity and ensure sustainable livelihoods. As well as coffee, it covers cocoa, bananas, citrus, flowers and ferns, tea and timber.

For coffee growers to be certified they must adhere to a list of principles laid down by the Sustainable Agriculture Network, including conserving wildlife and water resources, minimising soil erosion, treating workers fairly and protecting the forest, replanting where possible and retaining some shade cover. Being awarded the Rainforest Alliance seal of approval means that a farm is managed according to the highest social and environmental standards and gives small producers a competitive edge. Financially, this distinction promotes greater long-term security, allowing farmers to enter premium markets and command higher prices. However, unlike the Fairtrade mark, the Rainforest Alliance seal of approval does not guarantee a minimum price; neither does it pay a social/environmental premium for reinvestment. Moreover, the seal only guarantees that 30 per cent of the beans in a jar of coffee have been sustainably produced.

Manufacturers argue that this mixing of sustainable crops with the mainstream improves the reach of such farming methods. Fairtrade campaigners, while welcoming the scheme's environmental credentials, have accused the big companies of using it as ethical window-dressing. 'Kenco may have got the seal for its Sustainable Development Coffee [which is 100 per cent Rainforest Alliance certified] but it's important to realise it's not across the board,' says Mark Dawson. Of course the same criticism could be – and has been – levied at the Fairtrade Foundation, notably in respect of Nescafé's Partners Blend, which carries the Fairtrade mark. Despite that, some shops have refused to stock it because of the Nestlé baby milk boycott (Nescafé is owned by Nestlé).

Ethical appeals for brands of coffee are being given a more human face these days, literally in the case of Fair Instant coffee, which carries pictures of weatherbeaten farmers on the jars. Fair Instant coffee is manufactured by European company Fine Foods International and is Fairtrade certified, but it gets added eco-cred for its partnership with Save the Children, which benefits from 20p for every 100g jar sold. Fair Instant's target for 2007 was to raise £200,000 to go into Save the Children projects in coffee-growing communities. A laudable initiative – I will gloss over the fact that the amount would barely buy you a house in many parts of the UK.

There is another brand of ethical coffee called Good African Coffee. It doesn't carry the Fairtrade mark but in some respects it goes beyond the Fairtrade concept by taking the approach that Africans need to lift themselves out of poverty through trade, not aid. The coffee is supplied by a network of 14,000 farmers in the Rwenzori Mountain area of Western Uganda who are organised in cooperatives with up to fifty farmers in each group with an elected leadership. Fifty per cent of Good African Coffee's after-tax profits are invested in the growers and their communities and there is specific support for initiatives that protect vulnerable and disadvantaged groups, such as orphans and people living with HIV/AIDS, as well as for community health and education projects. Good African Coffee (which started as the Rwenzori Coffee Company in 2003) is owned, and the coffee produced, by Africans under dynamic director Andrew Rugasira, whose answer to the Live Aid lot is that if Africa were to increase its world trade by 2 per cent it would generate $150bn of wealth. Mr Rugasira's robust championing of African producers – he is reported to have said that Bob Geldof would be better off lobbying Tesco for 2 per cent of its shelf space for quality goods from Africa rather than asking governments to increase their aid budgets – makes a welcome change from the patronage (usually for a tiny proportion of their overall coffee output) of the multinationals. And he's been successful, getting shelf space in Waitrose, Tesco and Sainsbury's for his coffee.

When it comes to buying coffee – well, instant coffee, anyway – I have much less of a dilemma than I do over tea because I've always bought the same brand, Clipper Organic Freeze-Dried Arabica Coffee, which is also Fairtrade. Not only does it tick both of those boxes but it's also, in my opinion, the closest to ground coffee in taste. When my parents paid us a visit once, I made Dad a cup of Clipper Organic and he said, 'Hmmn, it really tastes of coffee, doesn't it?', in a surprised voice, as if this was above and beyond what he expected of an instant coffee (and to some extent, compared to 'proper' coffee, it is). They drink Nescafé Colombie themselves and have stuck with it for donkey's years. Brand loyalty is a comfort zone that we have to be challenged, persuaded or enticed to desert and I guess I too am unadventurous when it comes to coffee. For that reason, it was enlightening to take up this challenge and see what else is out there, though since I'm no connoisseur I called in some help for this one.

Teachers, I reasoned, are probably more in need of a good cup of coffee than most, so I approached the head teacher at my daughter's school to ask if they would mind being guinea pigs in a coffee taste test. The staff agreed, with the proviso that I supplied biscuits (I bought them Fairtrade chocolate chip cookies). I made thermos flasks of six different brands of instant coffee – Clipper Organic Arabica (Fairtrade), Percol Perfect Coffee Original (Fairtrade), Nescafé Gold Blend (not Fairtrade), Kenco Rich and Smooth Roast (not Fairtrade), Good African Coffee (not Fairtrade but see previous page) and Cafédirect (Fairtrade) – loaded them all into the panniers on my bike and wobbled off to my daughter's school.

The teachers, who were in the staff room, sipped and rated the various coffees, which I'd made up using three teaspoons of each instant coffee to one-and-a-half litres of boiled (but not boiling) water. The coffees were simply numbered one to six and the teachers didn't know which brands they were. Everyone was very interested in the results, six of them being occasional Fairtrade coffee buyers and two of them regular Fairtrade coffee buyers, while one never bought Fairtrade coffee because 'I don't usually like the taste'. I asked them to rate the coffee they liked the best, which turned out to be a tie between Nescafé Gold Blend, Kenco Rich and Smooth Roast and Clipper Organic Arabica. The coffee they liked the least – it was unanimous, everyone hated it and some poured it down the sink – was the Percol Perfect Coffee, although a couple of people said they didn't like the Cafédirect coffee either.

I've just repeated the taste test on myself at home, making up six cups of coffee with the numbers on the bottom so that I didn't know which brand was which, and then switching the cups around like you do with that 'find the lady' trick, to make sure I couldn't memorise them. My results mirrored the teachers' exactly. There wasn't much to choose between Kenco Rich and Smooth, Nescafé Gold Blend and Clipper Organic Arabica, which were all really nice, though I thought Kenco had the edge. Percol Perfect Coffee had an off-putting smell and tasted pretty nasty and the Cafédirect wasn't that great either, plus it left a scummy tidemark around the cup. The Good African Coffee was better, though I thought it left an ever-so-slightly bitter taste on the tongue. Having drunk six black coffees in a row, I was left with the jitters and palpitations but I'm prepared to go that extra mile in the name of eco-shopper research, even if does mean running up and down the stairs to the loo for two hours.

What to conclude from all this? I'm pleased they (and I) liked the Clipper, though I wasn't surprised that Gold Blend did well since Nescafé is the market leader and Gold Blend is a premium brand. Kenco, in particular, smelt like fresh roasted coffee, which is what swung it for me. Apart from the Clipper, Fairtrade brands didn't fare very well in this tasting and while, like my other trials, it's not supposed to be scientific but more of a straw poll, I think it is revealing. I had, a couple of weeks earlier, trialled all but the Good African Coffee at a Fairtrade coffee morning in our local church and even someone who is a passionate advocate of Fairtrade and speaks for the movement chose Nescafé Gold Blend as 'suitable for breakfast' in a blind tasting, although he did say that all the coffees were OK. (I haven't included the results of that particular trial because it chucked it down with rain and hardly anyone came.)

On the basis of the teacher survey and my own observations I'd say that Fairtrade coffee can't rest on its laurels just because it's ethical. That may sound faintly heretical but, while there are some people who shop ethically because that's their main motiva-tion, most consumers want nice-tasting coffee as well. I am happy to pay the extra, but only if I like the coffee. If you want to get people to switch brands, you've got to give them a reason to in terms of the product, otherwise they might as well give the money to a suitable charity and stick to what they like.

Conversely, and perhaps more importantly, it highlights the power the big brands have that could be used as a force for good. After all, we wouldn't need to have Fairtrade coffee if the rest of the system wasn't so unfair to begin with. While the individuals and their families who grow the beans that make our coffee struggle (and frequently fail) to even scrape a living wage, the coffee companies are making profits of hundreds of millions of dollars by controlling global prices. I'm delighted that Sainsbury's is switching its own-brand coffee to Fairtrade by 2010 (it's already made Red Label tea Fairtrade effectively tripling the amount of Fairtrade tea sold in the UK) because that's not only great news for producers but it puts the other big companies on the spot. Personally, I feel the likes of Kraft (which owns Kenco) and Nestlé (Nescafé) should be hanging their heads in shame. Their coffee may taste good but ethically they leave the bitterest of aftertastes. Until they pay fairly across the board and not just for one niche brand to improve their corporate image, I won't be buying them. Thank goodness that Clipper, once again, sets a benchmark for quality, ethics and taste. I know what I like and I'm sticking with it. And I'm sending my parents a jar.

AISLE 8

Liquid Challenges 2:
Cold Drinks

Challenge 22:
Does organic booze beat the hangover?

It's often claimed that drinking organic wine gives you less of a hangover than non-organic wine because it doesn't contain additives or preservatives or any other nasties, specifically sulphites. Sulphites can produce allergic reactions and asthma-type symptoms in susceptible individuals but they're also blamed for the thumping headache that wine can give you, which is something that most of us have experienced at some point in our lives. This seemed as good a reason as any for examining the health benefits of choosing to drink organic, although of course there are compelling environmental reasons too.

Non-organic viticulture (grapevine cultivation) relies heavily on industrialised farming, chemical fertilisers and pesticides. Quite apart from the loss of biodiversity, water pollution and soil erosion this can cause, the news that conventional grapes are the most heavily sprayed of all agricultural crops is not encouraging. Pesticide residues do get into wines – up to 240 chemical compounds from spray residues* have been detected using gas chromatography. And if that doesn't make you put your glass down sharpish, the fact that the grape industry occupies 8 per cent of the area invested in agriculture in the EU and yet requires as much as 46 per cent of the 1 million tonnes of pesticides used each year in Europe definitely leaves an unpleasant taste. Interviewed on www.wineanorak.com, organic wine expert Monty Waldin cites Bordeaux, Burgundy, Champagne and Australia as the worst offenders and claims chemical abuses in Chile are so bad that children of vineyard workers have been born with deformities.

Wine made out of grapes that were grown organically will not have been produced using any of the pesticides, herbicides and fungicides (up to eighteen per crop cycle) that grapevines are routinely sprayed with. Some sprays are permitted, principally copper sulphate (called Bordeaux Mixture), which is allowed for use on a restricted basis to counter vine fungal diseases. Furthermore, organic wines are not, as is commonly thought, sulphite-free. Sulphites, in the form of potassium metabisulphite, are added to wines to 'disinfect' them from bacteria and to act as a preservative, particularly important for wines that are made for export and may have to travel long distances and undergo temperature fluctuations before sitting on supermarket shelves. Organic regulations stipulate that only two-thirds of the normal permitted amount of sulphur dioxide (SO_2) may be added, though most organic growers strive for the absolute minimum and some do not add any at all. However, even if sulphites aren't added by the wine-maker they occur naturally as part of the fermentation process, which is why no wine is sulphite free. Wine labels now have to carry a 'contains sulphites' warning, which, since SO_2 is ubiquitous, would be more helpful to people with a lower threshold to sulphites if they stated the sulphite levels.

*Friends of the Earth

Consumers seem to have embraced organic wines enthusiastically. Sales of Sainsbury's SO organic wine range increased by 492 per cent in 2006, and it now has a no added sulphites Cabernet Sauvignon too. It's not just organic wines that are making inroads in the market; biodynamic wines, grown in harmony with seasonal and lunar cycles (sometimes called 'super organic' to avoid baffling consumers), are also available from independent organic wine merchants, and Fairtrade wines are increasing in range and availability, too. In the cause of research, I went to a Fairtrade wine tasting – some of the wines were also organic – taking my mate Adrian with me because I can't drink alcohol (it would seem I lack the enzyme that metabolises it).

It is a bizarre thing to go to a wine tasting and be the only person not drinking. We were seated at a table with the Sheriff and his Lady, both resplendent in gold chains, who took their tasting duties very seriously, sniffing, swirling, glugging and spitting while I sipped apple juice and tried to appear inconspicuous. I did, actually, do the swirling and sniffing bit for form's sake, but halfway through the evening I developed a blinding headache, the result, I assume, of sticking my nose into all those glasses and inhaling deeply (kind of like aromatherapy, only bad). Ade was happy to drink for two and nobly finished my wine off, writing copious and at times questionable notes on his tasting sheet (I doubt that anyone else got turbot in the Cabernet Sauvignon/Merlot 2005; you can take the boy out of Bridlington but you can't take Bridlington out of the boy).

During the interval, I spoke to the sommelier, Dr Gareth Morgan of Oinoudidasko Wine Education, about sulphites and whether organic wine gives you less of a hangover. His comment was that this was 'a bit of a myth', because all wines make use of sulphur dioxide, added or naturally occurring. He pointed out that there are 'huge differences' in production methods that are more to do with the calibre of the winery than whether it is certified organic or not. 'Good winemakers will get their wines squeaky clean, so the better quality wines have less sulphur dioxide in them.' His recommendation, which surprised me, is to go for red wine rather than white wine if sulphites affect you: 'They use less in reds because of the tannins, so if you're sensitive to them, drink cheap red wine rather than cheap white wine.' You may still feel groggy the next day – 'Young red wines with intense tannins can do your head in a bit' – but you're less likely to have the asthma. I did briefly consider using myself as a guinea pig, but decided against it. It's my liver on the line, after all.

Although levels of sulphites aren't printed on the bottle, they are available in some cases on technical data sheets. However, that kind of information isn't easy to come by, as I discovered when I set up a trial to test whether organic wines really did give you less of a hangover. It soon became apparent that sulphite levels could only be found out by contacting the winemakers themselves, which I didn't have the time or the means to do. Also, I was going to need to test non-organic wines, too, which meant there was a lot of sourcing to be done in a very short space of time. However, I got there in the end thanks to Jem Gardener and the team at Vinceremos (www.vinceremos.co.uk), the Leeds-based organic wine specialist, who kindly provided me with four free bottles of organic wine and information on their respective sulphite levels. That left just the non-organic wines to source and a quick call to my friend Lucy, who is in the restaurant business, led me to Peter Fawcett of local wine merchant and delicatessen Field & Fawcett, based at Grimston Bar, York. Peter generously donated four bottles of wine and tracked down their sulphite levels at very short notice. I'm grateful to him and to Jem for their help with this trial.

Finding participants for the trial was also a bit of a poser. It wasn't that I had a shortage of volunteers willing to down free wine; rather that I wanted to conduct it properly and to have some means of quantifying the results. I didn't have the scope to undertake a formal scientific experiment, but it struck me that by enlisting a group of academics I could at least be confident that they'd take a methodological approach. I contacted Gary Haq, who is part of a team at the Stockholm Environment Institute at York University, who agreed to rustle up some researchers for me. We had worked together once before – Gary had asked me to chair a public debate on climate change – so it was good to have a scientist to call on who was working in the same field (the Stockholm Environment Institute formulated WWF's online carbon footprint calculator). I told him I wasn't asking participants to drink to excess but to stay within limits they were comfortable with and fill out a questionnaire the following morning. The trial was conducted blind with each participant drinking from a numbered bottle that had had the label obscured. No one knew whether they were drinking organic or non-organic wine. Ideally, one would have conducted the same experiment with the same people twice, once with an organic wine and once with a comparable non-organic wine, giving them the same number of glasses each time, but I just didn't have the resources to run a more complicated trial. Despite a suggestion that I write it up as a paper and present it formally, I doubt that my questions would pass academic muster ('How did you feel the next morning? (a) Fresh as a daisy (b) Fair-to-middlin' (c) Awful (d) Zombified'), let alone my methods. It was basically a bit of fun, but with a serious purpose nonetheless.

The trial took place in a meeting room at the Stockholm Environment Institute and very jolly it was, too. I felt a bit out of it, sitting there with my Dandelion and Burdock (the first two sips are nice but after that it's just like drinking medicine) and, once the first couple of glasses of wine had been drunk and everyone had started to kick back, tell jokes and generally become more lively,

I left them to it, reminding them to count the number of glasses they'd had and note it on the form while they could still remember. The following day I returned to the unit to pick up the forms (some of them emailed them to me) and to attempt to analyse the results.

Predictably, perhaps, the results were not clear-cut, principally because there were still too many variables. Individuals' capacity to tolerate alcohol can vary a great deal, as I know only too well, besides which some people only had two or three glasses while others drank an entire bottle. Still, having said that, none of the four who had organic wine suffered a headache the following morning, while two of those who drank the non-organic wine did record 'slight' headaches (one drank red, one white, but since they both drank the most – six glasses – I'm not sure we can blame their headaches on the sulphites). For the record, the following are the wines and their sulphite levels. The total level of sulphites is the more significant figure in terms of 'next day impact' according to Dr Gareth Morgan, with whom I corresponded about the trial; 'free' sulphites are those remaining that have not bound with other substances in the wine. The latter can be more easily smelled and tasted and are the ones that can cause an allergic reaction in sensitised individuals.

The two red organic wines were a Côtes du Rhone Villages Valreas 2001 and Rioja Usoa de Bagordi 2005. Both had total SO_2 of 48 mg/l and free SO_2 of 25 mg/l. Incidentally, both testers suspected their wine was organic and neither of them liked them very much. The two non-organic red wines were The Lizard Merlot Vin de Pays d'Oc 2006 (total SO_2: 64; free SO_2: 28) and a Louis Soft Red Vin de Pays de Vaucluse 2006 (total SO_2: 64; free SO_2: 25). The Louis Soft Red rendered the tester 'drunk but happy' – an 8/10 he reckoned – and resulted in a slight headache. He enjoyed the wine very much and noted 'not organic – it's too nice!'. The other tester rated his wine as 'OK' and guessed correctly that it was not organic. What's equally interesting is that, although the non-organic reds have higher total sulphites than the organic wines, the free sulphite levels are almost identical.

As to the organic white wines, these were a Bordeaux Blanc Sec Chateau Vieux Georget 2005 (total SO_2: 80; free SO_2: 16) – the tester had four glasses, felt 'drunk but happy' yet still awoke 'fresh as a daisy' with no headache, which I'd say was quite good going – and a Vouvray Sec Les Troglodytes 2005 (total SO_2: 162; free SO_2: 16), which the tester only drank one glass of, with no side effects at all apart from feeling 'a tiny bit sozzled'. The non-organic wines were The Lizard Sauvignon Blanc 2006 (total SO_2: 157; free SO_2: 32), of which the tester had three glasses and felt 'fair-to-middlin'' the next day and a Louis Soft White Vin de Pays de Gascogne 2006 (total SO_2: 153; free SO_2: 37), of which the tester drank six glasses, scoring herself 7/10 on a 'most pissed' score (that's scientists for you; why didn't I think of numbers?). She did have a headache, though not a 'raging' one and felt 'a bit spaced out and dizzy' the next day. Comparing sulphite levels, the whites all had much higher total amounts but the organic whites had half the level of free SO_2 compared with the non-organic, so one can see that, for those sensitive to sulphites, organic wine might be a better option.

Challenge 23:
Juicy fruit: squashing your own

People assume fruit juices are healthy but they aren't necessarily. Indeed, some experts say they're as bad as sugar-laden, carbonated drinks and load children with far too many calories. Fruit juice consumption has also been linked with childhood obesity and shortness of stature, although it depends which of the numerous studies conducted on the subject you read. I've seen kids knocking it back like there's no tomorrow and the sugar-rush effect is striking. I've also observed that those children tend to be the ones who eat more sweet stuff and less (or no) veg. Can you get kids to down healthier, homemade versions including (dread word) vegetables? That was my objective with this challenge, not just from an eco-shopper's perspective but because my own daughter is still pretty rubbish at eating her greens (and other fruit and vegetables, regardless of colour).

It seems common sense to me not to pour too much juice down children's throats, especially if you don't want them bouncing off the walls. But pure juice has undoubted health benefits if you have trouble persuading children to eat fruit and vegetables, since one glass – and only one glass, no matter if it's of a different fruit or vegetable – counts towards your 5-a-day. The 5-a-day campaign, along with increased awareness of healthy eating, has been one of the driving forces behind the continuing rates of growth in the juices and smoothies market, which, in 2006, saw them become star performers in the UK Top Products Survey by ACNielsen/The Grocer, up 19 per cent from the previous year. Within the category, premium brand Innocent grew by a staggering 168 per cent, taking an even more staggering £96m.

It's not just sophisticated smoothies that have grown in popularity: 'not from concentrate' (NFC) juices, which have diversified into all sorts of fortified (eg with omega3) and vitamin-enriched formulas, are also doing well. These are made from pure squeezed juice, as opposed to the cheaper 'made from concentrates' juices that have been heated and the water evaporated off leaving a thick syrup, which is reconstituted with added water at the bottling stage. Juice made from concentrates may not have the same nutritional value as a 100 per cent pure fruit juice, but on a descending scale it's better than juice drinks, which have added sugars and can contain rubbish like high-fructose corn syrup (HFCS), which is thought to be the number one cause of the childhood obesity epidemic.

Health issues aside, is there anything intrinsically wrong with drinking orange juice, concentrated, adulterated, smoothified or otherwise, from an ethical standpoint? I won't labour the point about Fairtrade, globalisation and multinationals again (Tropicana, the market leader, is owned by PepsiCo); suffice to say that orange plantations require a massive quantity of water to produce a dispro-portionately small amount of juice and that they are very highly sprayed with pesticides, which has a knock-on effect on biodiversity and human health. According to the UK charity Sustain, half the world's supply of orange juice comes from the Brazilian state of Sao Paulo and oranges in Brazil are frequently picked by children who work long hours for little pay.

Since most of the world's OJ starts life in Brazil or in Florida, it is also high in food miles. As noted in Aisle 1, that doesn't necessarily make it a carbon 'baddie': it's important to factor in the volume of the product – which affects the space it takes up in transit – and also whether refrigeration is required to transport and store the juice. In April 2008, Tesco joined forces with The Carbon Trust to introduce a 'carbon reduction label' across four different categories, including orange juice. From a consumer's point of view, this makes assessing the carbon impact of a product much easier. The story was reported on the BBC News and, as a result of learning that Tesco's ambient OJ has less of a carbon footprint (240g CO_2 per 250ml serving) I have switched to ordering UHT juice from the milkman, rather than buying the not-from-concentrate juice I was getting before (Tesco's pure squeezed version works out at 360g CO_2 per 250mls).

I have to admit that, up until now, my main issue has always been a practical one, namely that orange juice (and most of the other juices we drink at home) comes in cartons that can't easily be recycled. However, Tetra Pak recycling has come on apace recently and a programme is now being rolled out across the country in partnership with ACE UK (go to www.tetrapakrecycling.co.uk to find out about your area). There are now banks for recycling beverage cartons where I live, but until then the only option I had was to send off my old cartons to a depot in Somerset – and pay the postage. I didn't do this, and I suspect most other people wouldn't either.

There is a simpler way to get round the packaging, health, environment and ethical issues with juices and smoothies and that is to make your own. A few years ago I developed an enthusiasm for home juicing and bought an expensive juicer and a juice recipe book (*Juices: Nature's Cure-all for Health and Vitality* by Jan Castorina and Dimitra Stais, published by Time Life). As with many of these gadgets, I used it for a while and then the novelty wore off and it was left to gather dust. However, since I've been getting the organic vegetable and fruit boxes I've been deploying the juicer again – it's an excellent way to use up less-than-perfect produce – though it's been mainly for me. Could I find some homemade juices that were (a) not too sweet, (b) contained vegetables and (c) were acceptable to my daughter and her mates? (Ideally, of course, they should be eating whole, unprocessed fresh fruit and vegetables to get maximum nutritional benefit, but fresh, homemade juices whizzed up and served immediately are still better than pasteurised, shop-bought ones.)

The first one we concocted, banana, mango and orange, was, to be honest, more of a shake than a smoothie because I made it in a liquidiser and added a banana yogurt (for the gut-friendly bacteria) along with the fresh mango, bananas and fresh squeezed orange juice (you can add a couple of teaspoons of wheatgerm, a few sunflower seeds, and some honey and thin it out with milk if you're having it for breakfast and it's all you need). It had a thick, slurpy consistency, so much so that I ended up doling out teaspoons to them, but the kids loved it and voted it 34.25 out of 40 (each being allowed to award it up to ten points). Obviously there were no pesky vegetables in it, plus the yogurt had some sugar in it, so it wasn't the healthiest smoothie in the world but it did supply lots of vitamins.

I went for a more adventurous combo for the next one, apple, pear, beetroot and ginger, made in the juicer using fresh, washed but unpeeled apples and pears (two of each), half a raw beetroot and a chunk of fresh root ginger. Beetroot increases liver activity and ginger stimulates the circulation so it's got real health benefits, but it's quite a strong juice and they are distinctive flavours (beet is earthy, ginger is hot) and I wasn't sure what the children would make of it. Grace, my 14-year-old assistant, thought it needed a squirt of lemon juice to lift it, which we added afterwards, giving it a good whisk. The juice went down quite well (Niall, who is 11, gulped it down enthusiastically and got a pink moustache) and they awarded it 28.25 out of 40 (my daughter giving it a grudging 5/10). We made lemon, carrot and orange juice next (four carrots, two peeled oranges and half a lemon, which I should have peeled and chopped but didn't), which is a recipe from my juice book. This scored a very satisfactory 32.75 (Niall drained his glass again and got an orange moustache this time) and even my daughter deigned to drink it, though she complained that the lemon made her right nostril tingle. Coral, who is 11 and a bit fussy about her veggies, gave it a personal best of 8.5 out of 10, writing, 'I don't like carrot or lemon but I like this a lot! You can't taste any carrot!' The grown-ups, who had come to collect the kids, liked the apple, pear, beet and ginger the best, and it's my personal favourite, too.

There were still more recipes incorporating veggies that I wanted to try, so the following week I repeated the experiment with yet more of my daughter's friends and a couple of their mums. My helper, Jack, and I devised the ultimate veggie challenge, which we named Super Seven, though maybe it should be called Secret Seven because of the undercover ingredients. This was made in my juicer and combined two apples, two pears, two carrots, a stick of celery, half a beetroot, a few florets of raw broccoli and a small handful of baby spinach leaves. Despite the greens, it still came out pink because of the beetroot, and the others didn't know what was in it when they tried it. My nine testers (seven kids, two adults) scored it an amazing 74 out of 90, two of the children rating it top marks and only my daughter, once again, turning her nose up ('3/10 – horrible'). As Jack commented, it was a bit of a Willy Wonka combination (remember the chewing gum?). 'You get first course, main course and pudding coming through one after the other.' Martha, also 10, liked it so much that her mum came up to me the next day and asked for the recipe. Success! We also made a Red Pepper Booster from half a red pepper, half a beetroot and a peeled orange, which got the thumbs up and scored 33 out of 40 with the four remaining testers (the rest had run off to play hide and seek by now).

We had great fun with all of this and it was interesting to see how well the children (and adults) accepted raw vegetables in juices if they were combined with a little fruit. I still haven't cracked our daughter though. She likes the Innocent Strawberry and Banana, but if I make the same thing at home . . . take a guess. However, since Innocent is an eco-smart company – all their bottles are made from 100 per cent post-consumer recycled plastic and they carry carbon footprint information on some labels (they also compost their fruit waste; I emailed them to check) – I can't complain. You win some, you lose some. I suspect it's the special Mum ingredient that's the problem. Seasonal smoothies are fine in a bottle, but when you're related it's hard to be Flavour of the Month all the time.

Challenge 24:
Water: what's the best?

Why bother to do an eco-challenge with water? Because, according to Sustain, drinking tap water can help you save the planet – but only if you stop consuming bottled water. Plastic water bottles create an unimaginable volume of waste. Britons already drink more than 2 billion litres of bottled water a year and only about 10 per cent of the bottles are recycled,* the rest go to landfill or litter the countryside and coastline. Even if you do your good citizen bit and recycle your bottles, think on this: it takes vast quantities of oil and energy to manufacture the plastic in the first place, and that's before you add in all the carbon created by extracting the water, processing it, transport and shipping.

All this for a product whose health benefits, compared to what comes out of your tap, are unproven. The World Health Organization (WHO) states that it is 'unaware of any convincing evidence to support the beneficial effects of consuming such mineral waters'. Yet the craziness continues and consumers are swallowing it. You can buy water to relax you, harmonise you, 'funk' you (I dread to think), lower your blood pressure and give you fibre. As for adding colourings, flavourings, preservatives and sweeteners to it, as is the trend judging by the lurid displays in the chiller cabinets,

*Independent, 29 June 2006

if you drink that rubbish, you're daft. That's not from WHO, by the way, it's from me.

Our obsession with bottled water is, say green campaigners, environmental madness. And it's not just lobby groups: commenting on the findings of a 2005 report from the Chartered Institution of Water and Environmental Management, its director, Nick Reeves, said: 'Branding and bottling of water where there already exists a wholesome and safe supply of mains drinking water cannot be seen as a sustainable use of natural resources and adds to the overall levels of waste and pollution to be managed in modern society.' This heightening of awareness has started to produce a backlash against the bottled stuff, notably in San Francisco – where conversations round the water cooler are set to become a thing of the past since water dispensers are themselves being dispensed with – and in New York, where city officials launched an advertising campaign in July 2007 to promote drinking tap water.

Here in the UK, some restaurants have begun to serve tap water (top London restaurant Claridge's has unashamedly gone the other way: it has an extensive 'water list' offering water from Hawaiian lakes, extinct New Zealand volcanoes and Patagonian peaks). A few government departments and agencies have switched to tap, too – though not enough, according to Sustain, which points out that not only is buying in bottled water bad for the environment, it is also being bought with taxpayers' money.

One possible solution to the problem created by plastic bottles is the bio-bottle, a compostable bottle made from cornstarch, which is being trialled by Innocent and is also being used by innovative UK company Belu. Belu sources its mineral water in the Shropshire hills and its net profits go to water aid charities so that, for every bottle you buy, one person gets clean water for a month. The company, which is carbon neutral, is also funding water projects in the UK including a 'rubbish muncher', a machine that will be used to remove litter and junk from the Thames. If it's a little gimmicky – Belu says its water is 'penguin approved' because it doesn't contribute to global warming and the melting of the ice caps – maybe that's not such a bad thing. The little animation on its website is slightly reminiscent of Internet phenomenon, Club Penguin, which kids love, so there's plenty of potential for pester power.

I do, however, have reservations about the bio-bottle's compostability, which, Belu admits, isn't a straightforward operation. The bottles need to be shredded and composted at 60 degrees or higher, which means a hot heap system and dedicated management. Since many people don't do composting, and most of those who do have a cold heap system, I wonder how much this will actually happen. Municipal composting facilities are still relatively rare and although the bottles can be recycled along with ordinary PET bottles, people might assume they will biodegrade in landfill, which they won't unless the specific conditions of heat, humidity, etc are met.

I, like many women, carry a plastic bottle of water around in my bag, particularly during summer. Every so often I buy a new one but I always reuse them, often time and time again, washing them out with hot soapy water, letting them air dry and then refilling them from the tap. This is partly to cut down on the amount of plastic we consume and recycle but mostly because I think paying all that money (a 50cl bottle of Buxton has just cost me £1.20) for stuff you can get for pence is plain stupid. Then I started to hear there had been a warning about refilling plastic water bottles and that they were only designed to be used once, which sounded to me like a ploy to get people to buy more bottled water. In fact, the warning that was circulating, which was about carcinogenic chemicals leaching from the plastic into the water, seems to have been an Internet hoax, based on an unpublished student masters thesis. However, there had been enough written about the dangers of phthalates, particularly DEHA, getting into food and drink from PET (polyethylene terephthalate) plastics, which is what your average water bottles are made from, to make me want to investigate this allegation further.

Trying to track down the truth on the Internet is problematic, since much of the information is out of date, biased or unreliable. Because of this, I decided to find out the official government position here in the UK, which proved harder than I'd thought. The Department of Health referred me to the Department for Business, Enterprise and Regulatory Reform (BERR), and BERR told me to speak to Defra. Defra, in turn, advised me to contact the Food Standards Agency. I was eventually emailed by Bradley Smythe, a senior press officer for the Food Standards Agency, who sent me a detailed reply. It seems that the confusion has arisen because there is more than one chemical abbreviated to DEHA: di-ethylhydroxylamine, a potentially carcinogenic one, and di (2-ethylhexyl) adipate, a plasticiser, which is what goes into PET. While the latter has been shown to induce liver tumours in rodents, the Scientific Committee on Food concluded that the very small intakes of DEHA from its uses in food contact materials (such as film and bottles) would not pose any carcinogenic hazard for humans. Also, there are regulations to control the amount of a substance that may be present in a finished product or that may migrate from it into food: these are set at 18mg per kg of food for DEHA. The Tolerable Daily Intake for DEHA in humans established by the SCF is 0.3mg/kg bodyweight. So now you know. As to whether it's safe to continuously reuse plastic bottles, the official position is that, providing the condition of the bottle has not deteriorated and it can be effectively cleaned, it would be safe to use. This is further qualified by the general advice that 'products should be used for the purpose the manufacturer declares they are intended'. However, the Food Standards Agency also says that 'it is not possible to give a guarantee of safety/or an approval' regarding the reuse of plastic bottles. After all that?

There is a reason, beyond fads and convenience, why people assume (wrongly) that bottled water is of a better quality, and possibly safer, than tap water, and that is the sporadic incidences of contamination of drinking water, usually by micro-organisms such as *Cryptosporidium*. Water can also be contaminated by pesticides, nitrates (from fertilisers) and metals such as lead and iron. The 2006 report of the Drinking Water Inspectorate, which is responsible for checking the safety of our drinking water, reported that 99.96 per cent of all tests met national and European drinking water standards. This is reassuring, though heavy metals from domestic plumbing (old pipes are notorious) can still contaminate your water.

If you're in any doubt, a water filtration jug might be worth considering. These also remove chlorine, which is added to disinfect water and has a distinctive smell and taste, though personally I think the best reason for using a filtration system is that it removes temporary hardness from water, which is what gives you scummy, filmy tea and furs up your appliances. Being eco-smart means that, if you go down this route, you need to recycle your old filters, which there is no excuse for not doing now that Brita has finally (and about time, too) introduced in-store recycling bins for its filter cartridges. However, that's only for Brita systems; if you use another kind you'll need to contact the manufacturers to find out whether they'll take old filters back (and if they don't, make a fuss and ask why).

If you're so inclined, you can get home filtration systems installed under your sink, which means you have filtered water

153

on tap (the dual system allows you to have normal or filtered water, depending on which direction you turn the tap). My friend Janet has one – she got it put in along with her new fitted kitchen (their joiner swore by them, apparently). Janet's husband Dave has his doubts about it: apparently the water isn't as cold as regular tap water and the flow is too slow for his liking. Also, she's since discovered that the filters (which should be replaced every six months) start at about £30. She poured me a glass of filtered and a glass of normal water, making me turn my back so that I didn't see which was which, and I detected the filtered water straight off because it looked clearer and had less of a chlorine-y smell. It tasted more pure, too.

Still, that was very subjective, which is why I needed volunteers for a taste test to see if it was possible to detect a difference between tap water, mineral water and filtered water. I decided to ask the members of the brass band I play in, since it's thirsty work doing all that blowing. I took home a litre of Janet's home-filtered water, poured out another litre of jug-filtered water into a second bottle, filled a third with my own tap water and picked up a litre of Sainsbury's Caledonian Mineral Water. They were all chilled in the fridge for an hour and a half and then transported to band practice in a cool box, where I simply told the band members they were tasting numbers 1, 2, 3 and 4 and asked them to give me their preference. The results were split identically, with each type of water receiving two votes. Geoff, my mate on solo trombone, refused to vote on the basis he couldn't tell any of them apart. Given that the band was equally divided about the merits of the four waters, I have to conclude that there really isn't much in it.

As for me, I've stopped using my jug filter and simply pour tap water into some sturdy old glass lemonade bottles that I bought for pennies at an antiques shop. I keep the bottles in the fridge so that we always have cool water to drink and it's fine. I also bought my daughter a special drinking bottle with a protective lining (from a hiking shop) which she takes to school. If you like funky bottles, Tap (www.wewanttap.com) makes a 400ml reusable tap-water bottle and is conducting a vigorous campaign against the bottled-water industry on its website. Tap's bottles are free of Bisphenol A (BPA), a chemical used to manufacture hard plastic water bottles (and baby bottles) that seems to have a complex and insidious effect on the human endocrine system (see Aisle 4). It has been implicated in breast cancer, miscarriage and male reproductive system defects and more recent research has linked it with diabetes and obesity.* Incidentally, Canada has now banned BPA from baby bottles and, in the USA, the FDA has been forced to re-evaluate BPA by its own scientific sub-committee.**

I give plastic bottles a miss these days. Not that I'm paranoid (much). It's my stand against those 2 billion plastic bottles sitting on the wall . . . and in the gutter . . . and in dustbins . . . and in the park . . . and in landfill . . . and in the sea . . . Now there's a twenty-first-century 'nursery crime' to sing to the kids.

*The Toxic Consumer by Karen Ashton and Elizabeth Salter-Green (Impact Publishing)
** Environmental Working Group (www.ewg.org)

AISLE 9

Baby Challenges:
Nappies, Milk and Toys

Challenge 25:
Do real nappies do the business?

At just two weeks old, Arlo is already a master of timing. I had come to visit Arlo and his mum, Lara, to talk about reusable nappies. And, since it's been eight years or so since I last had to deal with a baby's bum, to change one. As I walked through the door I was greeted by an all-too-familiar pong. 'Right on cue,' said Lara, pouncing on the towel where the semi-naked Arlo was relieving himself. 'I'd stand back a bit if I were you,' she added when I leant over him to coo (I am unfamiliar with the peeing range of baby boys). She swabbed his bottom and handed me a soft, pre-shaped cotton nappy, the same sort of size and shape as the disposable ones I was familiar with, placing a strip of fleece inside it. 'There you go,' she said. I slid the nappy under Arlo's bum, made a minor adjustment to the liner, pulled the nappy up in front and pressed the Velcro strips together at either side to secure it. This without any training at all (that's how easy it was).

Lara poppered the waterproof outer cover on, which looked a bit like a swim nappy, and Arlo was good to go.

As she made me a cup of tea, Lara told me about her history with reusable or 'real' nappies. Arlo is her third baby and all three of them have been in cloth nappies. The ones she had dug out of her baby box for Arlo had already been used on baby number two, Felix, and a couple of friends' babies in between, and were still going strong. They included quite a selection of shaped nappies and wraps, including a couple of really funky designs, one in leopard print and one with spacemen on it. I was amazed at how real nappy technology had moved on: the last time I had anything to do with them was when my youngest sister was a baby. That was in the days of terry towelling squares, large and potentially lethal safety pins – which my mother, wearing a look of grim determination, used to grip between her teeth as she tried to stop Claire from wriggling free – and waterproof over-knickers with tight frilled elastic at the leg-holes that my mother referred to as 'mack pants'. You can still buy flat terry nappies, though the shaped ones are much more popular these days. Nappy pins, it seems, have been phased out in favour of 'nappy nippas', which are plastic clips or grippers that hook into the fabric and fasten the nappy securely. As to 'mack pants', I had assumed they would be a 1960s curio by now, but it seems you can buy something similar in Boots.

Lara uses fleece liners that she made herself from a fleece blanket, bought for the purpose and cut into strips. ('Fleece is brilliant. It's lovely and soft and it repels the poo.') The poo gets flushed down the loo and the soiled liners and nappies are soaked in a lidded bucket with water and tea tree oil, a natural antiseptic. The dirty nappies are washed every other day at 60 degrees with a very occasional 95-degree wash to remove any stains. They are then air dried on the line or next to radiators. Lara believes in letting her babies lie nappy-less on a clean towel every day. 'Babies get used to having the air on their bits and do their business then. It was my mother's best gift to me – that, and twenty old towels!'

Lara runs a group for parents and young children that meets in our local park, and I joined them at a lively picnic to canvass other mums for their views on real nappies. Some of them used eco-disposable brands such as Nature Baby and Moltex, which are partly biodegradable, unbleached and chlorine-free, but apart from Lara none of the women I spoke to used cloth nappies. Objections ranged from the laundering and tumble drying involved ('It defeats the object') – the alternative, having every radiator in the house festooned with nappies, didn't go down too well, either – to confusion about all the different types and styles of cloth nappies, as well as sheer lack of time. The principal objection, though, was to the cost. A birth-to-potty pack can cost £250 or more, while individual shaped nappies cost from about £7.50 to £9.00 depending on the material. This works out much cheaper overall, compared with buying disposables (a saving of £500, on average, for a first child and much more thereafter), but it's a sizeable chunk of money to find up front. One mum suggested that, instead of putting money into an account for the child, grandparents could invest in a full set of nappies, which sounds like an excellent idea. Plus, they get to appreciate their investment firsthand when they come round for a spot of babysitting.

I have to confess, when my daughter was a baby we used Pampers. Every time I put them in the bin I felt a twinge of guilt, but my husband made it clear from the outset that he would have nothing to do with real nappies and so (not without a little relief, if I'm honest) I gave up on the idea. Now, knowing that almost 700,000 tonnes of waste in the form of disposable nappies goes into landfill annually, I wish I'd been a bit more sussed about it. According to a report in *Ethical Consumer* magazine,* landfill conditions do not enable the breakdown of even the biodegradable parts of nappies (and the same is true of eco-disposables, by the way). As a result, the methane emissions for nappies in the UK are equivalent to 98,600 cars, each driven an average of 12,000 miles every year. Moreover (this from my local authority's website), every disposable nappy that has ever been buried in a landfill site still exists and could take several hundred years to decompose. So those nappies of my daughter's are going to be there, making methane, and choking her grandchildren. Now I really do feel bad.

Life is confusing and draining enough with a first baby, particularly if you don't have family around to support you, and I completely sympathise with anyone who feels that washing real nappies is one load of hassle they don't need. But is it really the hassle that people think it will be? The purpose of this eco-challenge is not just to assuage my own guilt, but to try and find out whether real nappies are practical and easy to use and whether someone who might not have considered them as an option can be persuaded to give them a try (and perhaps even switch to them).

First, though, I wanted to do some research for my nappy trial, so that I could get together an information pack to pass on to my team. It was then that my preconceptions about the environmental benefits of real nappies were challenged. Perhaps it was because my daughter was older and I was no longer focused on baby issues, but a lifecycle study on nappies published in 2005 had completely passed me by. The report, which evaluated the environmental impacts arising from every stage of the lifecycle of

*November/December 2007

disposable and reusable nappies, had concluded that there was little or nothing to choose between the two. Commissioned by the Environment Agency, it claimed to be 'the most comprehensive and thorough independent study of its kind ever undertaken in the UK' and based its conclusion on the calculation that the energy consumed by laundering reusable nappies was equivalent to the energy produced by manufacturing disposable ones (including raw material production and waste management). Commercial nappy laundering services were also compared and found to have an equal environmental impact when fuels and electricity consumed were taken into account. Oh dear.

Naturally, the sceptics and green-bashers had a good old laugh at what they saw as this backfiring of political correctness. The Women's Environmental Network (WEN), which had been repre-sented on the project board for the study, was deeply unhappy with the conclusion and hit back, on the grounds that the nappy report was 'seriously flawed', saying that the conclusions were based on 'poor quality data' and that it missed the point of its own findings. Concerted lobbying, spearheaded by WEN, even-tually prompted the Environment Agency to acknowledge that 'things had changed' and to commission a follow-up report.

Sadly, the damage had already been done. Many parents did hear about the original report and decided that real nappies weren't worth it. That, at least, is one reason posited for the failure of the government-funded Real Nappy Campaign, which had aimed to divert 35,000 tonnes of nappy waste from going to landfill annually and had actually achieved a measured diversion of 25,000 tonnes across England and Scotland over the three years. And, as critics pointed out, at considerable cost to the public purse. The poor figures didn't take into account the work done at grass-roots level, or the knock-on effect of the broader campaign, and, while manufacturers of real nappies reported increased sales, the

Government remained unconvinced. Funding for the Real Nappy Campaign, which had been running for three years under WRAP, the Waste Resources Action Programme, was quietly withdrawn. This only came out in an answer to a Commons question by then Environment Minister Ben Bradshaw during Gordon Brown's cabinet reshuffle and it was given very little attention by the over-excited media.

I went to the Real Nappy Campaign's website (www.realnappy campaign.com) which still seemed to be active and was advertising its helpline. Confused as to whether the campaign was over or not, I emailed WRAP and was rung back by Phillip Ward, the director with responsibility for support to local authorities. He said that the campaign would continue but not under WRAP, which was in the process of handing it over to another group of stakeholders (members include the Nappy Alliance, WEN and the Local Authorities Recycling Advisory Committee) and a new operator, Rezolve Kernow, based in Cornwall. While retaining an interest as a stakeholder, WRAP would be redirecting its resources into reducing food waste, which forms a much higher percentage of landfill than nappies do (nappies form 2–3 per cent of household waste annually). 'It's obviously been quite difficult,' Phillip Ward admitted of the Real Nappy Campaign's failure to meet its targets. 'We had some successes but we were a little bit blown out of the water by the Environment Agency report.' He described the report's comments about equivalents as 'pointless and stupid': 'The main problem they had was they couldn't find a representative sample of mums [using modern cloth nappies] so the behaviour they were getting was quite elderly – people using old machines and terry squares – which coloured the overall thing.'

WRAP had been able to complete further work since then, Phillip Ward said, which he was confident would be reflected in the Environment Agency's follow-up report, which has since been taken over by Defra. 'If you look at the manufacturing, real nappies look better, but if you wash them at 90 degrees and tumble dry them and iron them [as some respondents were doing in the original study] they're not. However, if you look at washing them at 60 degrees using a modern, A-rated machine and not tumble drying or ironing them, then it's much better. It's all about how you use them. Hopefully, this will redress the balance and say that real nappies are better if you do these obvious things.'

It did, though Defra did nothing to publicise this. The updated lifecycle assessment was quietly published in October 2008 without a press release and, as predicted by Phillip Ward, it showed that a good laundry routine makes all the difference to the global warming impacts of reusable nappies. A 40 per cent saving in carbon emissions can be made if they are included in full loads, washed at 60 degrees in an energy-efficient machine and air-dried. And if they're reused on a second or subsequent children, that saving is even greater. According to WEN, using nappies made from organic cotton, bamboo or hemp ups the percentage even more. So reusable nappies can be *significantly* better than disposables. Given that the government is committed to making an 80 per cent cut in carbon emissions from 1990 levels by 2050, one wonders why it didn't trumpet this. The washing routine isn't unrealistic – we're all lowering our washing temperatures these days and money-gobbling tumble driers are falling out of favour in these cash-conscious times – so why bury the good news? And why is the issue of the pressure on landfill sites from the disposal of 690,000 tonnes of nappy waste each year glossed over?

A reprieve, then, for the cause of real nappies, though what's interesting is that, regardless of all this political wrangling, more parents will try real nappies simply if they are promoted to them positively in the first eleven days after giving birth, the critical window according to WRAP in a press release accompanying a

Real Nappy Resources Pack for health professionals.* I also know, from talking to nappy advisors, that being supported in this process makes all the difference to whether parents continue with real nappies or not. Hannah Tyzak, Mum to seven-month-old Leo, regularly attends a breastfeeding support group at Malton Hospital in North Yorkshire and says that 'a massive gang – half to three-quarters of the mums in the group' use real nappies. The fact that they meet up regularly and get the chance to 'moan together and support each other', be it over nipples or nappies, helped her to carry on when she was struggling. She said no health professionals mentioned cloth nappies to her and feels there's still a lack of publicity about them: 'People still think about the terry nappies. They don't realise how much real nappies have changed.'

To find some volunteers for my nappy challenge, I got in touch with a Sure Start centre in Selby, North Yorkshire. Sam Armstrong, who is a local advisor for Lollipop, a company that sells cloth nappies, has a regular stall there. Lollipop (www.teamlollipop. co.uk) sells many different makes and styles, from shaped nappies in fleece, hemp, bamboo and cotton through to one-size nappies (that work from birth to potty), pre-folds and pocket or 'stuffable' nappies, as well as the plastic pants and fleece liners. A lot of people in Selby are on low incomes, which was one of the reasons that I wanted to do the trial there. Being eco-smart can often mean having to spend more and I was keen to find out whether cloth nappies are a real option for families with less money. Lollipop and Sure Start kindly financed a set of nappies each and I got another UK nappy company, Tots Bots, to sponsor a third set. I also persuaded Lucy, a mum I know in York, to have another go with a set of Cotton Bottoms, reusable nappies that she'd bought from Boots for her first child and given up on.

*19 February 2007

Ellen, 29, is Mum to four-month-old Thomas. She tested Tots Bots organic cotton nappies and bamboo nappies ('Bamboozles'). Bamboo is the 'hip' fibre at the moment: it's highly absorbent with a soft, silky texture and natural antibacterial qualities and is good ecologically, having a short growing cycle and needing no fertilisers or pesticides, unlike cotton. Ellen found that 'being greeted by a wet nappy was a revelation' and that, as a consequence, she was changing Thomas more frequently. However, he had no problems with nappy rash or soreness and didn't seem distressed or unhappy about having a damper bum. I find this really interesting because all the mums said this and it dispels the myth that the big nappy companies constantly push that wetness is something to be avoided at all costs. (Huggies offer 'Up to 12 hours of dryness and SMILES' while Pampers Dry Nights have an 'extra sleep' layer.) Not only did the babies in the group not suffer redness or irritation or cry any more than previously, but the mothers expressed concerns about the over-drying effect of the absorbent chemicals that go into disposables. There is also a lot of anecdotal evidence to suggest that, because babies learn to tell the difference between wetness and dryness in cloth nappies – something they can't do with disposables – they potty train earlier, which is something that Lara also said to me.

Ellen was surprised and delighted at how well the cloth nappies she used contained the poo and had no problems with the changing or washing regime, incorporating the nappies with her regular washes. However, she did find the drying time inconvenient – 'Even on an airer in the kitchen with a Rayburn going they took at least twenty-four hours' – which is a particular problem with bamboo because the material is so absorbent. The other disadvantage she found, which most of the other mums concurred with, was that because the nappies tend to be bulkier she couldn't fit Thomas's clothes on so well. Sam's advice was to buy clothes a size larger than you would normally; also there are now companies such as Frugi (www.welovefrugi.com) that make organic cotton clothes especially to accommodate cloth nappy bottoms and give them 'room to wriggle'. Ellen was attracted to the idea of nappies that dry more quickly so Sam recommended the Lollipop 'Softee', micro polar fleece and pocket nappies (all-in-one nappies with a separate removable absorbency pad).

Like Ellen, Mandy, 31, had previously used Pampers and Huggies but had wanted to give reusable nappies a go. She tried Lollipop's own brand bamboo, and micro polar fleece 'Softee' nappies on six-month-old daughter Evie. Mandy's main concern was that the bulkier nappies restricted Evie's leg movement, so that she couldn't get her feet to her mouth as babies are wont to do. Sam assured her that this doesn't have any lasting effects – 'If you think about it, Linford Christie would have been in terry squares and he hasn't done too badly' – and that, for babies with 'clicky hips', it can be a positive advantage. Mandy also had drying problems with the nappies, partly because she didn't have the space at home to hang them up and partly because of the length of time they took to dry. She preferred the micro polar fleece nappies (very cute – they look like little hats and come in different colours) that dried more quickly and fitted more snugly, but has since switched to a different brand of reusables, Bambino Mio, passed on to her by her sister. Mandy plans to continue with these because they are slimmer fitting, so that's good news.

Lucy, who is 35, also has a six-month-old baby, Samuel. She originally bought the Cotton Bottoms reusable nappies from Boots for her first baby, Emily, but didn't continue with them once Emily outgrew that size, mostly because she never got round to buying the next size up. I was keen for her to go back to the Cotton Bottoms with Samuel and see how she got on with them this time. Again, having to air-dry them was a problem, this being winter –

everyone said they'd have no problem when the weather got warmer and they could be hung outside – but, possibly because the Cotton Bottoms, like the Bambino Mio, were 'pre-folds' – flat cotton nappies that you fold, with a separate waterproof wrap – they were less bulky and didn't restrict Samuel's movements. Lucy had no problems with leakage, provided she changed him regularly, and found them 'no more work than a disposable nappy, though getting into a routine with the washing is important'. Lucy is going to carry on using them now she's got back into the habit. Hooray!

My last tester was 17-year-old Acacia, who lives at home with her mum and three-month-old son, CJ (Charles Junior). Acacia hadn't heard about bamboo fibre before and neither had the baby's father, who spluttered, 'You're joking, aren't you? He's going to get poked in the arse by bamboo,' when she told him she was trialling them on CJ. Acacia tried a range of Lollipop nappies, though she used Huggies at night. CJ seemed to like them, even though 'he looked a bit like a sumo wrestler' in them, and apart from an incident in which Aracia's mum forgot to put on the waterproof wrap, the trial went without a hitch. I'm delighted to report that Acacia liked them too and plans to carry on using cloth nappies. 'People I've spoken to think they're all right. I think most teenage mums will like them because they're cheaper in the long run. That's a real benefit.' Acacia's mum, Angela, who does the laundry, said the fleece nappies dried very quickly and she loved them – having raised three children in terry squares, the revolution in cloth nappy technology astounded her – 'I was really surprised when I saw them. They're definitely better than the old days and much easier to clean.'

So where can you buy reusable nappies? Groups such as Sure Start and the National Childbirth Trust (NCT) have regular displays of Lollipop, Tots Bots and other cloth nappies at their meetings, and you can also buy online. Boots and Mothercare sell reusables

(Mothercare has launched its own Smart Nappy) and selected Waitrose stores sell the Modern Baby range of shaped terry nappies. At the time of writing, the other supermarkets do not sell reusable nappies – and one can hazard a guess why. A one-off sale of reusables, even if it is a substantial amount of money for the parents, does not nearly add up to the profits they reap from disposables. Furthermore, one suspects that the makers of the major brands wouldn't be best pleased to have to share lucrative shelf space with ethical alternatives. In an attempt to attract conscientious consumers, ethical incentives are being employed (for example, on jumbo packs of Pampers have '1 pack = 1 vaccine'). Other, more direct appeals to parents that are traditionally used include cartoon characters, such as Winnie-the-Pooh and Tigger on Huggies. Both brands also tap directly into the newborn market through the Bounty Newborn Packs that are given out in hospitals. These contain free samples and money-off coupons for Pampers and Huggies. I spoke to Bounty and asked why no information was included about real nappies and was told that any company could promote their product through Bounty if they bought into the scheme. This conflicted with what I'd been told from other sources, which was that cloth nappy companies were not allowed to promote their products through Bounty because they were made by private companies (which seems illogical if Pampers and Huggies can do it). Despite sending Bounty two follow-up emails, they declined to comment.

Even if your budget is tight, real nappies can still be an option. The Real Nappy Campaign is promoting washable nappies as a credit-crunch-busting measure. Pre-folds and flat nappies, such as the Bambino Mio, Lollipop terries and Weenee micro fibre nappies, are cheaper and particularly economical and many local authorities offer financial incentives (for example, if you spend £50 on reusables, you get £30 cash back). There is also a Real Nappy

Exchange (020 7481 9004) where you can buy used nappies more cheaply and a website, www.ukparentslounge.com, which offers a similar service.

Incidentally, I did have two other testers lined up, one who dropped out due to the pressure of starting a new job and the other a first-time mum who gave birth by Caesarean section and found the thought of washable nappies a bit too much to deal with on top of everything else. Both very common and under-standable reactions, but what's encouraging to me is that the testers all said that the biggest barrier to them starting on reusables had been 'psychological' and that they were amazed at how easy the process had been. 'It's no more work and no extra hassle – all you have to do is take the nappy bucket down with you to the washing machine,' said Lucy. 'I'm gob-smacked,' Mandy enthused. 'I think they're brilliant and Evie's just as happy.'

I'll leave the final word to Ellen: 'It's great not to be emptying the bathroom bin of disposable nappies. It was a daily activity for me. You can only imagine what landfill must look like.' Well, quite. Thank you, ladies, and thank you, babies. Let's hope this makes a difference.

Challenge 26:
Mother's milk or formula?

Oh, the lure of the baby aisle. I can still remember the first time I separated from my newborn daughter, which was to take advantage of a two-hour gap between feeds to dash out to Tesco while she was sleeping. It was about 8pm and the supermarket was relatively quiet. Strolling the baby aisles, packed with marvellous stuff – all of which I felt I simply must have to be a good mum – was like being in an SMA-sponsored wonderland. I was in the early days of breastfeeding, which, while it was encouraged on my maternity ward, definitely wasn't the norm, as the long shelves stacked with row upon row of tins of powdered baby milk seemed to spell out.

Breastfeeding may be natural but it isn't always easy. In the UK, nine out of ten women who stop breastfeeding before their baby is six weeks old would have liked to have gone on for longer according to the Breastfeeding Manifesto, which is endorsed by a coalition of over thirty UK organisations. The World Health Organization (WHO) recommends that babies should be exclusively breastfed during the first six months and that this continues up to age 2, but in reality only 2 per cent of babies in the UK are even breastfed to six months. I just about got there, but even if you only breastfeed for a short while it can still make a difference: in the first few days colostrum provides the baby with antibodies and immunity from infection and by six weeks a breastfed baby has only half the risk of getting chest infections before the age of 7. Breastfeeding for between two and six months helps lower the risk of the child developing food allergies, ear infections, asthma, eczema and gastroenteritis, while those that are breastfed for a year are less likely to become obese and have a lower risk of getting heart disease as adults. Those who continue to be breastfed for two years have higher average scores on intelligence tests.

There are benefits for the mother, too. Apart from the obvious convenience and physical benefits (I certainly found it helped with weight loss), breastfeeding mums should have less risk of osteo-porosis in the long term, though you need to breastfeed for longer than I did to get a significant reduction in the risk of developing breast cancer. Breastfeeding is also best for the environment (no carbon footprint!), so it's the eco-smart choice, too – if you can manage it. However, life doesn't always go how you plan it and that's more true when it comes to having babies than for just about anything else I can think of.

'It depends on your expectations of having a baby,' says Sam Armstrong, who helped me with the nappy trial and is also a qualified breastfeeding support peer. 'Because of celebrities, I think society believes it's OK to have a baby, get your figure back and go on *Jonathan Ross* a couple of weeks later. In reality, it's not so smooth. If people are more realistic, things like breastfeeding needn't be a problem, especially if you have help from advisors.' She invited me along to a baby café that the Sure Start Centre runs in Selby, and which provides an opportunity for mothers to get together and breastfeed their babies in a relaxed, comfortable setting. Chatting to the mums, it became clear to me how vital it was to have that help and support and, also, to have been set the example of other women doing it. Kathryn, who is 27 and has a five-week-old baby, said that on her maternity ward, breastfeeding was the norm. 'Of the ten women on my ward over the four days I was in, only two were bottle-feeding. Seeing other young mums doing it is a great example.' Rachel, 25, agreed: 'You see women breastfeeding much more than you used to.' Amanda, whose mother and sister both did it, said, 'It was never a consideration for me not to breastfeed.' She stressed how important it was to have other women with whom one could share experiences and ask questions, telling me about a time she'd been breastfeeding in Asda. 'I was in the café and a woman came over to me and asked, "Is it easy?" It turned out she was twelve weeks pregnant. None of her sisters had done it and she hadn't seen it before and wanted to know what it was like.' I thought breastfeeding in Asda was a pretty cool move – I got momentarily fired up by the idea of a posse of breastfeeding mums crowding the baby aisle in the Morrisons across the road to continue Amanda's excellent example – but decided it was too much to ask of them. They'd only come here for a coffee and a chat, after all. Denise, who is 40 and has an eight-month-old baby, remarked that breastfeeding in public is more acceptable now. She has two older children, aged 18 and 16, and found attitudes towards breastfeeding when they were small very different. 'I had some people frown and say, "Why are you doing that here?" I was breastfeeding my eldest on a bus once and got asked by the conductor to stop, otherwise he'd throw me off the bus. I told him that if I stopped the baby would scream, and he opted for the screaming.' This time around she's made a point of breastfeeding on a bus and has had no such trouble. 'The only criticism I get is from my 16-year-old!' There's gratitude for you.

I came away from the baby café feeling very positive about the take-up of breastfeeding compared to even ten years ago when I was doing it. True, it was just a snapshot, but it didn't seem to be reflected in the statistics relating to the UK generally. I asked Alison Baum, who speaks on behalf of the members of the Breastfeeding Manifesto coalition, about the disparity. 'There are pockets of excellence and Sure Start is doing amazing things, but there's still a huge amount to be done nationally,' she said, explaining that the coalition was about 'driving a cultural shift' to support breast-feeding through the manifesto's objectives.

The manifesto has seven objectives: to implement WHO's Global Strategy for Infant and Young Child Feeding; to implement NICE's postnatal care guidelines; to improve training for health profes-sionals; to create a more supportive environment for breastfeeding mothers at work, including legislating for breastfeeding breaks; to develop policy to support breastfeeding in public (in England, women can still legally be asked to stop); to include breastfeeding education on the curriculum; and to get the Government to adopt WHO's International Code of Marketing of Breast Milk Substitutes. The latter (which I naively assumed the UK had already adopted) has not been fully implemented, prompting groups such as Baby Milk Action to accuse the Government of 'bowing to industry pressure'. Alison Baum, who has expressed disappointment on behalf of the Breastfeeding Manifesto's coalition, stressed that the manifesto was not anti-formula: 'We're against the inappropriate marketing of formula. The branding and packaging of follow-on milk [which can be advertised, unlike infant formula] is so similar that 60 per cent of women think they've seen an advert for infant formula.' Statements on baby milk such as 'closest ever to breast milk' are also misleading, she said. 'A survey revealed that 30 per cent of women in the UK thought that formula was as good as, if not better than, breast milk. Which it isn't.'

It's a crucial point. According to WHO and UNICEF, 1.5 million babies die around the world every year because they are not breastfed. You can argue the case, as baby food manufacturers like Nestlé do, that it doesn't follow that the deaths are as a result of infant formula or bottle feeding (WHO's Global Strategy simply refers to 'inappropriate feeding practices') but it is undeniable that in developing countries, formula milk is all too often mixed with unclean water and fed in unsterilised bottles, resulting in fatal diarrhoeal diseases such as dysentery. It is also widely acknowledged that, because formula is expensive, it is either diluted to such an extent that it has no nutritional value or replaced with a potentially harmful substitute. It is shocking that people who have the least resources should be targeted by baby milk companies, but Baby Milk Action claims it is still going on. Despite WHO's International Code and a thirty-year boycotting campaign against Nestle, violations continue both at home and abroad.

Nestle, of course, refutes this. I spent two full days going through the allegations and denials from Baby Milk Action and Nestle and decided it was way too complicated to cover here. You can read the claims on their websites (see Directory) and make up your own mind. Suffice to say I made the family stop buying KitKats. Not much of a boycott, perhaps, but living in York, where Nestle makes them (our football ground is even called KitKat Crescent), I feel it's my duty to make a stand . . .

Challenge 27:
Which toys pass the toddler test?

It's blessedly easy to pick up toys along with the toilet rolls when you do the weekly shop. I've done my fair share of it: if there are birthday parties coming up you know you can get something for under a tenner without the bother of having to haul yourself out to Toys 'R' Us, which always makes my head spin. Then, of course, there is 'pester power' (if I'm silly enough to stray into the toy aisles of the supermarket when I'm out shopping with my daughter), which can be quite a challenge to resist. Fortunately, toys are usually in the 'extra' sections along with kettles, DVDs, mobile phones, crockery, towel bales and televisions, so if you're just in for the regular stuff you can avoid them. It's undeniably handy to have them there, though, and they're often discounted in super-markets, too. What more could you ask?

How about being assured of the safety of the toys, for starters? Never mind 2007 being China's Year of the Red Pig; it's more likely to be remembered as China's Year of the Great Toy Crisis. At the time of writing, Mattel has just announced what I make to be its fourth recall of toys made in China due to concerns about high levels of lead in paint. The original recall, back in August 2007, was for 1.5 million toys, including TV characters Big Bird and Elmo from *Sesame Street* and Dora the Explorer, all favourites with very young children. Less than a fortnight later came a massive recall of more than 18 million other toys, including play sets for Barbie and Tanner, Batman Magna, Doggie Daycare and Polly Pocket – in these cases, the safety concerns were about small magnets – and *Cars'* 'Sarge' character, which was a lead-paint concern. A third Mattel recall in September was for Barbie Accessory sets and Fisher-Price play sets, while the most recent announcement has Mattel pulling its Fisher-Price Go Diego Go! Animal Rescue Boat because the painted logo may be affected (go to www.mattel.com/Safety for more details).

Mattel has previously admitted that most of the toys recalled had 'design flaws' and that the Chinese manufacturers were not to blame, but this has not allayed consumers' fears about poor standards in Chinese factories, particularly since another company, Chicago-based RC2 Corp., was forced to recall 1.5 million Thomas the Tank Engine trains and parts after they were found to have been painted with lead paint. The Mattel recalls have already forced Argos and Woolworths to withdraw, best-selling products while Hamley's, the world's most famous toy shop, is now looking to source more UK toys for its Regent Street emporium. Meanwhile, the *Guardian* reported that fears over recalls could lead to Christmas shortages.* What, Santa's sack lighter of cheap, mass-produced Chinese toys? The *Emma Maersk*, the world's largest container ship, a few crates short of its 140,000-tonne load? Is that such a tragedy? A minor dent in the burgeoning Chinese economy perhaps, but it's a plus for the environment at least. The 400m-long *Emma Maersk* (dubbed the '*SS Santa*'), which made its maiden voyage from China to Felixstowe packed to the gunwhales and stacked as high as a couple of houses with containers of seasonal goods, was described as 'a microcosm of globalisation gone mad' by Green Party MEP Caroline Lucas. However, it's not just the

*30 August 2007

174

carbon footprint from shipping the stuff in that we should be considering. When you consider the greenhouse gases that China's coal-fired factories are pumping into the atmosphere, do you really want to keep feeding that great belching dragon?

Eco-smart shoppers may be having second thoughts, particularly in light of the safety concerns. Conditions for workers in Chinese factories can be brutal, too. United States workers' rights group, China Labor Watch, said in a report issued in August 2007 that manufacturers for Walt Disney Co., Bandai and Hasbro Inc. paid little heed to the most basic standards: 'Wages are low, benefits are non-existent, work environments are dangerous and living conditions are humiliating.' The answer, it would seem, is to search out toys made closer to home, preferably in the UK. Sounds simple enough, but believe me, it isn't. For a start, competition with supermarkets has forced many independent toyshops out of business, so outlets are few and far between. You can find traditional toys online, of course – thank heaven for the Internet – but if you want to touch and feel before you buy you'll have to seek them out at craft markets and festive fayres and in those boutiquey kinds of shops that tend to flourish in tourist areas.

Even then, there's no guarantee that, just because it's made of wood, a traditional toy will have been made in Britain. Far from it. I interviewed Steve Parker, who, with his partner Cathy Utley, owns Cusp, an independent toy and gift shop in York, and what he had to say surprised me. 'The China thing is something that affects everyone equally. From a wooden or soft toy point of view there isn't anything that isn't made in the Far East. Even in independent shops it all comes from the same places.' Pointing to a shelf of cute, hand-painted piggy banks, he emphasised that 'not all stuff made in China is bad' but acknowledged how hard it was to find accurate information on the origins of toys: 'It's amazing how little is known, even by the agents.' Cusp stocks a range of

Fairtrade toys by Lanka Kade, a company that uses locally sourced rubber-tree wood from sustainable forests and no child labour, but designs such as their wooden ark and the Jellicats soft toys are constantly being ripped off by supermarkets and sold much more cheaply. 'Supermarkets are shameless, absolutely shameless.' It is the supermarkets and the big companies that are pushing Chinese factory owners to squeeze their margins, resulting in the falling safety standards, he said. 'It comes from the top. They tell them customers want it cheaper. Personally, I'd rather have something that's a little more expensive and know where it comes from.' He paused. 'It's outrageous that you can actually buy toys for children that are made by children. We can't exist without sourcing things globally, but we can make sure we do it responsibly. Customers need to ask. That makes everyone ask.'

Cusp has been going for twelve years, managing to buck the trend of toyshop closures by specialising in personalised gifts and, when necessary, adapting. When I visited, it was having runaway success with a box of mesh balls (or 'haemorrhoid balls', as Steve's assistant called them), squishy balls which, when squeezed in the fist, squidge through their mesh cover in eyeball-popping-out style, changing colour as they do so, mutating into bunches like grapes. Or those other things. They are perfectly disgusting so I bought one for James, my 8-year-old nephew, whom I knew would love it. The mesh balls, being a novelty item, aren't representative of Cusp's core business, but unlike many of the shop's toys they are popular with kids. 'Most of the things we sell here are chosen by parents and grandparents,' Steve admitted, as I 'oohed' over the arks and animals, 'ahhed' over the dolls' houses and swooped on a humming spinning-top just like one I used to have when I was a girl. Meditatively turning the handle of a Tinkle Tonk wind-up toy, he continued, 'I honestly couldn't tell you whether a child alive actually likes them.'

This was something I wanted to test, since it doesn't matter how good the quality, how durable or how charming a classic British toy is, the question is whether it's going to capture the little darlings' attention in the way that an all-singing, all-dancing brightly coloured piece of plastic merchandising tied in with the latest Disney movie will do. Given the distractions available to modern children, the idea of introducing them to dolls' houses when you can dress a virtual family in whatever you want and have them burn pizza in 'The Sims' may seem like a non-starter. Still, I bought the humming spinning-top and a magnetic fishing set with wooden rods as a birthday present for another nephew, Nathan, who was about to turn 4, and a wooden popgun for my third nephew, Ben, who is 5.

The popgun was a big success; Ben was particularly impressed with the loud noise it made and reported back that he had had great fun playing Ninjas with it: 'You can hide behind corners and jump out and make a bang and scare people.' Apparently, he got Mummy several times this way. I hope my sister's still speaking to me, particularly since the mesh ball, which was equally popular with older brother James ('I liked the way the green bubbles came out'), got squeezed a bit too hard one day and the goo came out everywhere. The spinning-top was a hit with little Nathan, once he'd mastered how to make it whizz round and hum, so I'd say traditional toys came out well in this test.

I also took Nathan and my daughter, who is 10 and loftily above all that, to visit traditional toymaker Anthony Dew, who makes possibly the most exquisite hand-carved rocking horses in the world. They are exquisitely priced, too, but as Tony pointed out, you don't spend almost £2000 on something that's just a toy; a rocking horse is a beautiful piece of furniture. (Steve Parker said the same thing about a recent trend for home-knitted toys: 'They've become almost an interior design feature. The bigger toys are treated like cushions.') The Rocking Horse Shop also sells more affordable kits for people who want to make their own rocking horse or dolls' house or marionettes but it's clearly a pretty specialised business. We went home and played with the fishing game instead, which was holding Nathan's attention fairly well until a remote-controlled Mini Cooper made an appearance. (Interestingly, for all my daughter's snootiness about traditional toys, Miss Nintendo DS has spent a considerable amount of time this week lurking round the house with a wooden bow and arrow set, pretending to be Robin Hood escaping from the Sheriff of Nottingham.)

It's true that the cut-off age for traditional toys is low these days. Wooden bricks, pull-along toys, trucks, fire engines, shape-sorters, jigsaws and train sets are unlikely to go out of fashion with pre-schoolers, but even at that age the influence of children's television programmes is a powerful one. I speak as a parent whose child was raised with the *Teletubbies* and the *Tweenies*. A straw poll of mums at the park picnic mentioned earlier in this aisle revealed that, while wooden toys remained favourites with the parents, girls in particular get to about three-and-a-half and the pink plastic gene kicks in. Hobby-horses are dumped for My Little Pony and you've lost out to Hasbro for good. Or have you?

Robert Nathan, guild manager of the British Toymakers Guild (BTG), is breezily upbeat. There has been a definite revival of interest in traditional toys, he said. 'As a rule, we don't have any air miles. The supply chain is short – most of the companies are owner-drivers – which makes quality control easier. And toy safety in the UK is paramount.' The turnover in traditional toys in the UK is about £35m, a tiny proportion of the £1.2bn spent on toys annually. However, when you consider the small number of toymakers – the BTG has 150 members, though it's estimated there are about 2000 in the UK in total – the figure is impressive. As to whether traditional toys will continue to attract children, Robert Nathan is in no doubt. 'Children may be the end users but it's adults that buy the toys. Our toys directly appeal to the child in the adult.' He puts the age range for traditional toys at 0–6, picking up again as those children grow up and become parents, aunties and godparents themselves with a new generation to buy for. 'That's when they want to give those children what, in their warped imaginations, they think they had,' he said. 'Then we've got them for life.'

I've come to the conclusion that we overcomplicate things with children's toys. They don't need all that rubbishy plastic stuff (which, more often than not, breaks within a couple of weeks) with all its incumbent environmental problems. It's a brave parent who opts out of the merchandising racket entirely and I'm certainly not claiming we have, though it's heartening to discover that simplicity and imagination still have the power to entertain. Our daughter's best 'gadget' this year has been a long loop of multi-coloured string, which, after I taught her how to play Cat's Cradle, started a craze that took over her entire school, including the boys. Nathan's favourite 'toy' is a scrunched-up, dried-out baby wipe that he calls Scooby Doo. And Monica, a mum I know who comes from Papua New Guinea, told me how children there grow up playing with sticks and whatever comes to hand. Now she's settled in the UK, her family ask her to send back English toys as presents. She tells them she can't: they all come from China.

AISLE 10

Material Challenges:
Clothes, Cotton, Swapping and Shoes

Challenge 28:
Can a girl be eco-smart and still be stylish?

I was, in my former, less eco-sussed life, a bit of a shopaholic, as I believe I might have mentioned. I especially loved buying new clothes, both from the High Street chain stores and from supermarkets. Tesco Cherokee's cheaper-than-chips chic, George at Asda's cut-price catwalk clones and Sainsbury's affordable fashion range, Tu, were all such good value for money that I would pick up a skirt or a pair of trousers or a bag practically every time I did the weekly shop. With new ranges coming in all the time, I'd heap clothes into my trolley along with the washing powder and spuds without a second thought about the environmental and ethical implications of such disposable fashion. Then, when I realised that we simply can't go on consuming the way most of us do if the planet is to have a future, I made a conscious effort to rein in my shopping habit. The challenge I set myself was to resist the frivolity of fashion and step off the on-trend treadmill and, as far as possible, to stop buying new clothes altogether. Talk about going cold turkey!

To start with, I was rather pathetic about the whole business. If it wasn't for my daughter I might have succumbed, but whenever I popped into a shop to admire a dress or gravitated towards the clothing aisles to stroke a sweater I would be yanked back by my greener-than-thou 10-year-old. She became such a stickler for enforcing this challenge that at a secondary-school open evening, at an environmental stall in the geography department, she made me sign a pledge not to buy new clothes. 'I do practically everything else,' I grumbled, scanning the list of green promises. 'You're still buying clothes,' she said, thrusting a pen into my hand. The students on the stall, who recognised me from my newspaper column, said they'd be 'honoured' if I signed a pledge, so I did (flattery *and* arm-twisting: there was no get-out). I hope they will not take my recent shopping spree badly since I've found an eco-smart solution that allows me to purchase clothes with a clear conscience: buy Fairtrade.

Fairtrade fashion is a relatively new arrival to the High Street. We're familiar enough with Fairtrade tea (see Aisle 7) but it's Fairtrade tees that have taken the movement another giant leap forward. No longer the preserve of incense-scented shops full of hand-carved elephants and batik throws, Fairtrade clothing has gone mainstream. The ethical T-shirt is at the shapely forefront of this. I'm not talking about those baggy sloganising tees, as made famous by designer Katharine Hamnett back in the 1980s ('58 per cent don't want Pershing' – that's a cruise missile, if you're under 30). In my opinion, slogan T-shirts are all very well if you're a student but once you get to my age you are in danger of looking ridiculous in them. No matter: plain T-shirts don't need to carry a message because they *are* the message. If they're made of Fairtrade (and preferably organic) cotton, that is.

Fairtrade fashion isn't limited to T-shirts, thankfully, but that's where it really took off. Granted, you could buy expensive Fairtrade jeans from a few outlets and hand-blocked smock tops from the aforementioned hippy shops, but in March 2006 Marks & Spencer took the plunge into Fairtrade fashion retailing with a plain tee. The £7 price tag – a pound more than the regular T-shirt – was the only visible difference from the regular ones, but as the M&S campaign had it, it's what's Behind the Label that counts. How true. We're much better informed about where our food comes from and how it's produced, but when it comes to clothing it still tends to be 'the cheaper the better' and no questions asked. We know about sweatshops and exploitation in a vague kind of way, but the lure of jeans for under a tenner is greater. As for the T-shirt, it's always set a discount price benchmark in much the same way that a tin of supermarket baked beans has.

It's ironic, to put it mildly, that while battery eggs are now less popular than free-range, human beings are still being made to work in conditions that are almost as bad as those endured by poor caged hens. Yet only ten years ago it was a small minority of consumers prepared to pay extra for free-range eggs; but that's driven the change in the market and demand for organic food has gone up massively, despite the premium on the price. So why isn't it the same with clothing? Why, in October 2007, were children in a New Delhi factory working unpaid, for up to nineteen hours a day, in order to make clothes for High Street retailer Gap? This scandal was widely reported in the press and Gap withdrew a child's smock blouse from its shelves after it was revealed that children as young as ten had been forced to make it. The company stated that it had no knowledge of this and launched an investigation.* It's not the first time the company has been accused of exploiting sweatshop conditions to be sure, but

*See the report on the website at www.gapinc.com/public/SocialResponsibility/socialres.shtml

since the last outcry Gap has become a member of voluntary labour standards group the Ethical Trading Initiative. It's even earned itself a cautious commendation from campaign group Labour Behind the Label (LBL) for stepping up its efforts to address problems in its supply chains. So how can this happen?

Retailers like Gap do monitor their suppliers' factories and contracts are revoked if infringements are found, but investigators would have to go undercover to show up the sweatshops for what they are. Official figures show about 13 million children in forced labour in India. Unofficial figures put the figure between 60 and 100 million. It's something to think about the next time we pounce on a bargain. Fashion may be disposable but childhood surely isn't. Unfortunately it's impossible for auditors to keep tabs on all unethical practices and, while what matters most to consumers is low prices, the squeeze on margins further down the line means that suppliers will do what it takes to meet those costs. An excellent series called *Blood, Sweat and T-shirts* broadcast on BBC 3 in May and June 2008 followed six young British fashion addicts as they experienced life as factory workers and cotton-pickers in India. It showed the conditions the Indian workers experience more vividly than any amount of statistics can, especially the appalling state of the back-street factories of Dharivi in Mumbai, the largest slum in Asia, where clothes are made in a sprawling warren of stifling, stacked-up workrooms for export worldwide. The scale and problem of child labour was all too apparent: a child discovered hiding under a table at an embroidery factory was sent home and the owner fined. When Stacey, one of the team members, returned to check, she found that the young boy had simply been replaced by another one.

Even if forced child labour is eradicated – and most retailers claim to have a 'zero tolerance' attitude towards this – many garment workers still don't earn a living wage. Factory owners aren't necessarily to blame: suppliers are caught between a rock and a hard place according to Labour Behind the Label's report, 'Who Pays For Cheap Clothes: Five questions the low-cost retailer must answer'. While a compliance system requires better working conditions, retailers' own purchasing practices push working conditions down. The pursuit of leaner, cheaper clothes means the fast-fashion chains demand ever-shorter turnaround times for their catwalk copies. And the only way a supplier can guarantee that is to make their employees work longer hours, including night shifts and weekends (eighty-hour weeks are not uncommon). Workers are under more duress, without a living wage or any kind of permanency and often in very poor conditions, all the while denied the right to militate against all this. If they do attempt to complain or walk out, workers may be beaten, punished or lose their jobs.

The Ethical Trading Initiative was set up in 1998 and has a base code of labour practice that is supposed to protect workers from just this. However, even the ETI admits that adopting the base code 'doesn't mean they are perfect, or that their suppliers are perfect'. Indeed not: the 'Let's Clean Up Fashion 2008' update, produced by Labour Behind the Label, tracked the big fashion brands' performances for the third year running to see just how far they had gone towards improving wages for workers in their supply chains. It grades companies on a scale of 0–5, '0' being 'Does not accept the principle of a living wage' and '5' being 'sustained implementation of an effective living wage policy across the entire supply base'. Those it judged that had done 'no work to speak of on living wages' included Matalan, Clarks, French Connection, John Lewis, Laura Ashley, Mosaic Fashions (which owns Karen Millen, Oasis, Coast and Warehouse), River Island and Debenhams (the latter two are both ETI members). The worst offenders within this group were BhS, House of Fraser, Mk One,

Peacocks, Levi Strauss and Co and Burberry, which all scored 0. Four more ETI members were given 'one cheer' for 'mentioning work on living wages' albeit 'unconvincing so far' according to LBL: George at Asda (2.5), Sainsbury's (2), Tesco (2.5) and Primark (2). The Arcadia Group, which owns Burton, Dorothy Perkins, Evans, Topshop, Topman, Miss Selfridge and Wallis, isn't in the ETI but it got a 2.5. Along with Gap (3.5), the only brands to receive 'two cheers' from LBL for demonstrating 'work to increase wages, but not enough yet' were New Look (3), Next (3), M&S (3) and Monsoon Accessorize (3.5). All of these belong to the ETI, which just goes to show how wide the discrepancy among ETI members is.

It's important to talk about ethical trading because, as far as I'm concerned, being eco-smart means looking at the whole picture, not just the environmental impact, which is, anyway, inextricably connected. Concerned about the CO_2 India and China are pumping into the atmosphere from their coal-fired factories? Worried that, whatever you do at home, it won't make a scrap of difference to climate change because of rapidly growing Third World economies? Buying clothes whose materials may have travelled halfway round the world and back, made in far-flung cities so polluted that the air is toxic and the rivers run black? We're all part of this global geo-political system. I went to Tesco today to check out their clothing and they had the most gorgeous knits for £12. Or was it £8? Everything was labelled to encourage you to consume: 'wardrobe essential', 'fashion must-have', 'the ultimate dress' and so on. I walked the aisles, stroking and touching the fabric, overwhelmed by the sheer volume of clothes, their cheapness, the mind-boggling variety of styles. The difference was, this time I didn't get that old rush-of-blood-to-the-head or that knot of excitement in the stomach I used to get when I was about to buy something. This time I looked, I walked away and I had a cup of tea instead.

All very well for you, you might say, but some people can't afford to be picky. And why the hell should we, anyway? It's hardly a crime to buy from low-cost retailers. I had the Primark conversation with some girlfriends recently. They loved the choice, loved the fashionable look and unanimously agreed that the quality was rubbish. Still, they said, it's affordable and that's the main thing. Karen, my friend who is a student and single parent, was delighted to find a £3 dress for her daughter in Tesco. And my sister Claire, who is also a single parent and is on benefits, swears by George at Asda for her and the kids' clothes. Shopping with their consciences is a luxury they can't afford to indulge, and neither can I half the time. (You think most authors' advances, averaged out over a year, even hit the minimum wage? Think again. And don't even talk to me about long hours. It's 2.30am and I'm still working.)

I'm not here to guilt-trip people or make claims that I'm somehow better. The purpose of this book is to ask questions – of companies, of NGOs, of those in charge and of ourselves – and to address the larger questions, too. Karen went to Asda this week to look for a cheap outfit for her step-sister's wedding. While she was there, prompted by discussions we'd had about my book, she made a point of checking to see whether George stocked anything Fairtrade or organic. She found nothing apart from one lonely 'I love organic' T-shirt, which seems a tad ironic under the circumstances. She also asked at the till about George's 'Made in the UK' clothing range, introduced in March 2007. Neither of the assistants knew anything about it. A supervisor was called for. When the supervisor arrived, she said that there was a small amount of stock in store but that it was mixed in with the other clothes and that Karen would need to look for the Union Jack on the label. Karen, who wasn't prepared to rifle through every rack of clothing in George, even for me, gave up and came home. (I subsequently paid a visit to Asda and had no luck either.)

A survey commissioned by M&S revealed that 78 per cent of people would like to know more about conditions in the factory where clothes come from and what chemicals are used. So don't just wonder, ask. As the saying goes, 'If you think you are too small to have an impact, try going to bed with a mosquito.' Bite their ankles (metaphorically, of course). You will end up with a lot of T-shirts, if my short-but-sweet ethical shopping trip is anything to go by, but then it's going to get hotter anyway.

I did not, in a trawl of the High Street, find much in the way of Fairtrade clothes. You really have to go online to source a good selection. I love People Tree, which is one of the best known Fairtrade (and organic) brands. I first came across them in 2006 at an 'ethical fashion show' in the Slug and Lettuce, which was an odd place to find models slinking around but definitely hooked my interest, along with not a few beer drinkers. I didn't order anything then but mentally bookmarked it so that when this particular eco-challenge came up I knew I wanted to try their clothes. I went online (www.peopletree.co.uk) and ordered a couple of tops, a woollen cardigan, some fingerless Fair Isle gloves and a beret. The woollens are hand-knitted in Nepal by women who are paid 30–100 per cent more than they would earn locally. They also receive ongoing training and have the flexibility of working from their own homes. When the clothes arrived, the knitwear especially had that uniqueness that handmade pieces have. The puff-sleeved grey cardigan, which was fashionably cropped, was beautifully and professionally worked and you could see the care and attention that had gone into it. Call me a romantic, but I felt a real connection with the woman who had made it. It was rather like unwrapping a special parcel from your gran. I've bought more of People Tree's clothes since, because the prices are reasonable and I love the individual, designer-y look of them. People Tree has had a concession in Topshop's flagship Oxford Circus store since 2006 though it's not available in any other Topshop stores. Since doing this particular challenge I've noticed Fairtrade-certified clothes (usually tops) making more of an appearance in the High Street and in supermarkets, though a couple of rails does not a revolution make. Also, it should be noted that the Fairtrade cotton mark only certifies the cotton production stage, not the other stages of textile and garment manufacture, so it doesn't guarantee that the clothes are 'sweat-free'. Still, they are improving the image of ethical clothing, which has traditionally made far too much use of rainbow stripes in my opinion. I don't necessarily want to model my look on a Tibetan tribesperson, however much I want to support their community weaving programme.

A lot of ethical fashion is out of my price range – there's been a boom in eco-luxury, premium-quality sustainable womenswear with companies like Ciel, Katharine E Hamnett (the E stands for ethical and environmental), Junky Styling, Del Forte, Mumo, Stewart + Brown, to name but a few – but you can get affordable clothes if you know where to look. Marks & Spencer has an online 'Greener Living Shop' that sells organic, Fairtrade and recycled clothes, including menswear and children's clothes (www.marksand-spencer.com), and on the subject of school uniforms you can also get them from Clean Slate (www.cleanslateclothing.co.uk), a UK company set up by husband and wife entrepreneurs Mark Rogers and Carry Somers to make Fairtrade and organic school clothes that were Teflon-free (see Aisle 4). A good bet for ethical clothing at reasonable prices is Natural Collection (www.naturalcollection.com), the online 'eco department store', which has really branched out with its range of eco, organic and fairly traded fashion, including shoes and accessories, all reasonably priced.

Can you be eco-smart and sartorially stylish? Yes. You might not look like a dedicated follower of fashion but you'll be helping to promote a funky new and altogether more sustainable trend.

Challenge 29:
Can you find out where your fabrics come from?

Organic cotton is something I never made a special effort to buy until fairly recently. It was more expensive for a start and, not being clued up about cotton production, it was way down on my list of environmental priorities. I guess I saw it as something that would be nice to own – you see those newspaper ads for organic cotton bedding sets and they look absolutely gorgeous – but only if it ever came within my price range, which wasn't likely when you compare it with the cost of a duvet cover from Ikea.

So far in this Aisle I've concentrated on ethical rather than environmental reasons for eco-shopping. The two are linked – if you want to be 'greener' you're not going to say, 'I care about the environment but I don't give a stuff about people' – but I have separated the issues out here because textiles, be they tops or towels, often tend to be marketed as either Fairtrade or organic. Even if they are both, the two have different implications. Fairtrade tackles social issues, whereas organic cultivation is more about environmental impact, although in the case of cotton the exploitation of workers and effect of pesticides on their health is part of the whole sorry story. With cotton, the reason for buying organic is not because it's better for us, but because it's better for them. And for the planet, of course.

Here's why. Cotton is the most used fibre in the world and accounts for 16 per cent of global insecticide releases, according to the Environmental Justice Foundation. In India, which is home to over one third of the world's cotton farmers, cotton accounts for just over half of all pesticides used annually, despite occupying just 5 per cent of land under crops. Cotton production is an incredibly toxic process, which poisons the land and poisons the people who work on it. One million farmers need hospitalisation each year due to pesticide poisoning and 20,000 die from it. That's a general figure – the EJF says there are no specific figures for pesticide poisoning in relation to cotton growing per se – but I wanted to know more about what it really means for the people whose livelihoods depend on cotton growing.

I found an article in the *International Journal of Occupational and Environmental Health* (2005) that really put the dangers into perspective. A five-month study of acute pesticide poisoning in three rural villages in Andhra Pradesh, a major cotton-growing region of southern India, found 323 reported events, 39 per cent of which were for mild poisoning (headaches, dizziness, difficulty breathing), a further 38 per cent were for moderate poisoning (nausea, vomiting, tremors, staggering, blurred vision), and 6 per cent were for severe poisoning (seizures, loss of consciousness). And these were just the symptoms reported within twenty-four hours of pesticide application; the chronic effects of long-term neurotoxic/systemic poisoning by pesticides include impaired memory, confusion and severe depression. Some of the chemicals used were organophosphates classified as 'extremely hazardous' or 'highly hazardous' by WHO, and banned in other countries, yet the workers were barefoot and uncovered and wore no protective gear and many, being illiterate, could not read the instructions.

Women, it transpired, were just as vulnerable as the male farmers, since it is they who mix the concentrated chemicals, refill the spray tanks and follow in the fields behind the sprayer. There were no figures for children, but the study points out that 10–20 per cent of all pesticide poisoning cases are for children and that India uses thousands of 7–14-year-old girls to manually cross-pollinate the cottonseed plants. Children are also vulnerable because their homes are often close to cotton fields and because empty pesticide containers are reused. One pesticide, Monocrotophos, which accounted for 12 per cent of all pesticides used in the study, is known to cause paralysis in children and has been withdrawn from use in other countries for that reason. And if all that wasn't bad enough, pesticides find their way into rivers, polluting drinking water and having effects on wildlife and the general health of the human population which are incalculable.

The situation in India is compounded by the fact that the global market is weighted towards the US and the EU, where cotton is heavily subsidised so that producers receive prices that are effectively two to three times higher. Because of this, farmers in India get locked into an inescapable cycle of poverty and debt generated by using expensive pesticides and fertilisers in an attempt to increase their yields. Between 1993 and 2003, driven to despair, 100,248 cotton farmers committed suicide. Eighty per cent of them were indebted. Many of them took their lives with the very stuff that had killed their livelihoods: by swallowing pesticide.

These are the real, desperately sad facts about the cotton industry in India, but in Uzbekistan, where one third of the population is forced to work in cotton production by the government, there is a different problem. Uzbekistan is the second largest exporter of cotton around the world and the effect of the farming methods used has been catastrophic. The Aral Sea, which used to support a thriving fishing industry, has all but disappeared, having been diverted for irrigation purposes, while the arid land left behind is whipped into daily dust storms that spread the toxins left behind by pesticides, causing high rates of tuberculosis and cancer. However, the effect on Uzbekistan's children is, if anything, even more disturbing. An undercover report by the BBC's *Newsnight* correspondent Simon Ostrovsky on 30 October 2007 confirmed what the EJF had been saying and that Uzbekistan's President Karimov had been denying – that the use of forced child labour is widespread. Children as young as nine are routinely taken out of school, along with their teachers, marshalled by police onto buses and made to work picking cotton all day, with no protection and only water from dirty irrigation canals to drink. It is back-breaking work: they have to pick 60–70kg a day. They are paid just 2p per kilo.

The Environmental Justice Foundation is calling for Western countries to refuse to buy Uzbek cotton. Europe buys one third of it but since the cotton is shipped around the world and mixed with other fibres it's likely that everyone ends up wearing some of it. The EJF is asking people to 'pick your cotton carefully' and quiz retailers about where they buy their cotton from, so I thought I'd do this as the challenge for this section. Since I didn't have the time to ring round all the major High Street retailers, I decided to concentrate on the supermarkets that sell clothes and emailed a selection of girlfriends who like to shop, sent them the *Newsnight* link and asked them if they'd help out by contacting others.

Tesco said an immediate and firm 'No' when I rang and asked whether Uzbekistan cotton was used in any of their clothing ranges. 'We went back and checked,' said a spokesman. He was a little defensive when I asked if that was because of the *Newsnight* report – 'People always think, "Big bad Tesco's at it again"' – and when I told him I wasn't making any accusations, I just wanted to ask the question, he said there had been allegations that one of their suppliers in Bangladesh had been sourcing cotton from Uzbekistan but that the briefing was 'malicious and totally untrue'. Since then, Tesco has announced a total ban on raw cotton from Uzbekistan and declared its intention to implement a system to monitor its supply chain, a breakthrough decision that has immediately tipped the commercial scales (where the world's third largest retailer leads, the rest will surely follow). Asda, which issued a statement in response to *Newsnight*'s investigation saying it was 'extremely concerned' that child labour may have been used to pick cotton 'that ultimately . . . may have been used in making clothes sold by George', said it was 'calling on other retailers and the UK Government to join us in encouraging the authorities in Uzbekistan to take urgent action to improve working conditions in the cotton industry'. I rang their press office to follow this up and a spokesman told me that Asda was grateful *Newsnight* had brought the issue to their attention. 'We have a zero tolerance attitude towards child labour. Our policy is not to walk away from these things.' So far, so good. Sainsbury's, on the other hand, were far less clued up when I rang their customer care line. After several long minutes on hold I was informed that, 'All our garments are manufactured under the Ethical Trading Initiative code of conduct' and referred to the ETI's website. When I pressed the point about Uzbek cotton, I was simply told Sainsbury's clothes were manufactured 'throughout Asia and Eastern Europe'. I emailed the press office too, to see what they had to say. They didn't reply.

I've since emailed the Environmental Justice Foundation, whose director, Juliette Williams, confirmed their delight at Tesco's action. She said they had been told by Tesco that the supermarket was 'inundated' with consumer messages of concern after the *Newsnight* story, which once again goes to show the influence that ordinary people can have. More power to your elbows, eco-shoppers! Marks & Spencer, Matalan, Debenhams and H&M have also announced bans on Uzbek cotton, though ultimately, the real test will be whether Uzbek children get to go to school rather than being bussed out to work all day in the cotton fields.

Will all this make us think twice before buying a T-shirt and perhaps seek out an organic one instead? It has me. The good news is that retailers are (literally) cottoning on. I bought two organic tops in New Look, which is the only High Street chain I consistently find organic clothes in, though I have tried and failed to source any organic jeans on my High-Street trawl. And that continues to be an issue: 'eco-chic' and 'eco-couture' is very 'now' and many glossy mags and fashion designers have embraced it, but it's still way out of most consumers' league (I certainly can't afford to pay a couple of hundred pounds for jeans, however ethical they are). So, while at one end of the fashion scale it's all happening, change is much less visible on the High Street.

Katharine Hamnett, who is regarded as one of the fashion industry's most ethical and environmentally aware designers, concurs with this. She addressed a meeting with Defra saying, 'Sustainable clothing doesn't have to be more expensive. It can be more affordable and it should be more affordable.' It also needs to be out there, where consumers can see it and buy it. I'm encouraged that the Government is, finally, getting involved because ethical sourcing, designing and producing clothes and maintaining sustainability throughout the supply chain isn't going to be effective without high-level pressure. Could we end up with a sustainability rating on clothes like the energy ratings on fridges? That would take the eco-angst out of shopping. In the meantime, it's a question of looking behind the label. All of them.

Challenge 30:
Handmade and hand-me-downs

I have a confession to make (yes, another one): I have never been one for charity shops. I like the idea of them – they're a great way of recycling unwanted goods and providing an income stream for charities – I just don't enjoy shopping in them. Call me a snob but they have that distinctive worn-clothes smell that puts me off instantly and they always seem to be rather depressing inside. More to the point, I rarely find anything I like and, if I do, it's never in my size. I realise this isn't the best introduction to charity shops as an eco-smart alternative to High Street shopping, but I'm telling you this because it's where I started out. It is true that I used to wheel into a charity shop, turn around and wheel right out again, but since I've started trying to green my life I have lingered for longer, and it's paid dividends.

It has always infuriated me that other friends can find good stuff in charity shops. My friend Karen kits out herself and her kids from charity shops all the time and I'm forever going, 'Gosh, that's a nice coat/skirt/jumper. Where did you get that from?', only to be told, 'The 50p rail in St Leonard's Hospice shop.' My friend Lucy is not averse to buying from charity shops either, and also does well out of the hospice shop. The two of them were threatening to drag me round York's charity shops and purchase me an entire outfit when a brief encounter with the Sue Ryder shop changed my outlook completely.

I passed by and the dress in the window caught my eye. I stopped and went back, curious. It was white, with large polka dots in different shades of grey, and had a fitted bodice, shoulder straps and a flowing skirt, the sort of thing you might wear to a wedding or to the races. I could tell instantly the dress was 'me'. I went inside and checked the label. My size, too. Amazing. And it looked unworn. I tried it on. It was beautifully lined and fitted well, a little loose around the bust and shoulders perhaps, but nothing a tiny tuck wouldn't fix. The side zip didn't go all the way down, but I could still get it on and off. I bought it. The next time I saw Karen, I produced my purchase. 'It's Debut, the Debenhams label,' I said proudly. 'This season's. I looked it up online. They're £70 new.'

'How much did you pay for it?' she asked.

'Fifteen pounds,' I said, beaming.

Karen started laughing. 'Fifteen quid? I never buy anything from a charity shop for more than a fiver.' It seemed I had a little way to go before I became a seasoned charity-shop shopper. However, it did fire me up with a degree of enthusiasm I hadn't experienced for charity shops before – to me, £15 for a virtually new frock was still a bargain – and I started to go into them more after that and spend longer rifling through the rails. And that is when I found the Christian Lacroix top in the Woodlands Respite shop. It's a bit tight, if I'm brutally honest, but I'm keeping it for ever because it's the first and probably only designer item I've ever bought and I got it for £7.50. It is slightly outrageous and Madonna-ish, but I wore it to meet my publisher for this book and got the deal so I've already got more than my money's worth. Due to their eco-smart credentials and low prices – since the credit crunch began, charity shops have become so busy they are having trouble getting hold of stock to sell – charity shops are becoming the chicest places to buy your clothes these days. Oxfam has opened three boutiques in London (in Chelsea, Westbourne Grove and Chiswick) selling donated designer labels and items that have been refashioned by designers for their new Oxfam Reinvented range. Cancer Research has also got into this (at the shop on Marylebone High Street), joining up with designers Revamp to transform rags into inspired and beautiful clothes. I hope this spreads out across the country: since the Debut dress and the Lacroix top I'm in and out of charity shops all the time, though I've never had quite such good scoops again. My problem now is that if I find anything I remotely like I buy it because it's so cheap. But then I take it home and it hangs in my wardrobe for a few months and I forget to wear it, either because it doesn't have that 'new' cachet or because I didn't absolutely love it in the first place.

The charity shop thing raised an interesting ethical question: is it OK to buy labels you wouldn't normally buy if you find them in a charity shop? I was telling Pauline about a new George at Asda shirt I'd picked up from a charity shop that was brand new with tags and she pointed out that I wouldn't normally go to Asda (I have issues about Wal-Mart) and so what was the difference this time?

'It's second-hand,' I said. 'I'm recycling.'

'It's still from Asda,' she said.

Tricky. Still, it wouldn't have done to throw it away. Unbelievably, almost a million tonnes of textiles are thrown away each year – I find it unbelievable, at least, given the plethora of ways in which you can reuse, re-sell and recycle clothes – which is why charity shops, clothes collections (such as Bags 2 School), textile banks and appeals play such an important role in keeping clothing and shoes out of landfill.

Internet site eBay is, of course, another way to recycle your clothes and buy second-hand items cheaply. Some people have become so successful that they make a living out of it. My neighbour Yvonne does the eBay thing but I just can't buy clothes on eBay. I don't know why, since I'm happy enough to buy from a catalogue online, but it doesn't appeal. There are always car boot sales, of course, if you like that kind of thing, which I don't. I think it's because I'm not a rummager, which is why I don't join in with jumble-sale scrums. I don't have the necessary grit and determination and I like things laid out nice and neat. If you do have sharp elbows and a terrier-like tenacity, there is a way of getting clothes for free, which is even better. Ladies, let me introduce you to the not-so-gentle art of swishing.

Swishing parties, which started as a cult in London, have caught on elsewhere across the UK, especially since Twiggy popularised it on telly with *Twiggy's Frock Exchange* (October 2008, BBC2). I got invited to one at our school just the other day, at which the head teacher made us all line up and blew a whistle as if we were about to run 100 metres. Swishing is basically a clothes-swapping event that's being touted as green, glamorous and cool. The name came about from the dictionary definition ('to rustle, as silk') and has been redefined to mean 'to rustle clothes from friends' (ie, to rustle as in stealing cows or steers, to use proper cowboy parlance). At least, that's how I interpret it but you are bound to make a rustling noise in the process, if the frocks are of the rustly petticoat variety, that is. There's a website all about it (www.swishing.org) and you can download invitations from it, too. Basically, all you need to do is book a room, fix up some tables and clothes rails and invite as many girlfriends as possible to come along and bring at least one good-quality item, be it clothes, shoes, jewellery or other accessories. The swishing site doesn't say anything about men's or children's clothing, but I think it's pretty much a given that this is a girly free-for-all and not an NCT clothes sale and that kids will just be a liability and blokes a hindrance.

My friend Pauline, who knows about clothes (she teaches costume design for a living), was keen to help me organise a swish and offered her studio as a venue. We invited as many friends as we could think of and lots of people expressed an interest, but in the event only fifteen or so came. It still worked well though and everyone brought loads of good stuff. We hung it up on rails so that people could browse, drank coffee and ate fancy biscuits and at 12 noon I counted down to the swish and we all pounced. With greater numbers this could have become unseemly and, by all accounts, some of the London swishes are complete bun fights, but ours was really quite civilised. What was nice was that everyone went home pretty pleased with themselves having procured at least three new items. My friend Cindy, who got herself a gorgeous Hobbs dress and a skirt and a spotty top, hasn't stopped raving about it since. We're planning on doing another one this year in a more central location and inviting a lot more people because that way you get a better selection of sizes. Also, if you get more people to come, no one feels awkward that their clothes aren't shifting or worries about what their clothes say about their taste. It's also a great way to raise money for charity, since you can charge on the door or ask for donations, and with a few drinks inside you it could be a riot. Literally. The Swishing website carries a warning: 'Remember people: no scratching, spitting or biting.' Oh, really?

So much for shopping and swapping. But what about making your own clothes? After all, that's what people always used to do in days gone by and it's making a comeback. Sewing-machine sales are reportedly at their highest for years – Argos's cheapest model went up an extraordinary 500 per cent in 2006–7* – which is a reflection of how the 'make do and mend' ethos is returning to favour. Unfortunately, I'm a menace with a sewing machine, but Pauline made me a beautiful, floor-length evening gown *with a train* for a party we'd been invited to in return for me helping to promote her business, so it was a satisfying bit of skill-trading. If you've got a skill like that it's the sort of thing that would go down a bomb on a LETS scheme (it stands for Local Exchange Trading Systems), a local community-based mutual aid network in which people exchange all kinds of goods and services with one another without the need for money (www.letslinkuk.org).

I haven't tried a LETS scheme – ours was an informal agreement – but a couple of press releases in return for a frock felt like an excellent bargain. School 'promise auctions' are sometimes a useful way to get a bit of dress-making done, too, but in that case you'll have to cough up in the name of charity.

Independent, 21 April 2008

Knitting has also seen a boom in popularity, partly because celebrity endorsement (Julia Roberts, Sarah Jessica Parker, Uma Thurman, Madonna and Cameron Diaz are all knitters, to name a few) has made it cool. It's become so trendy that an entire network of 'Knit and Natter' and 'Stitch n Bitch' groups have sprung up and knitting has been described as 'the new yoga'. According to the website www.stitchnbitch.co.uk, it's good for you, too. 'Research has shown that your pulse rate slows and your blood pressure lowers when you knit.'

I can see the appeal of knitting because it makes you slow down. I just don't have time to do it! My neighbour, Sam, who knits, tried to get me interested. I borrowed a book from her and we had a yarn about yarns, as it were, but that was as far as I got. Incidentally, on the subject of making things, Sam made me a lovely bag out of some of her old cast-off clothes and cleverly stitched in the pocket of a pair of shorts as a mobile phone holder. This was another 'trade', though all we did was keep an eye on their house while they were on holiday so there wasn't much effort expended on our part. The very best bit was that she embroidered a quotation from *A Midsummer Night's Dream* inside it in gold thread, which makes it about the most perfect individually customised recycled gift a girl could have.

Thinking about it, and looking back over this section, it seems to me that sharing, swapping, making and recycling is the nicest way to source clothes. It's all about giving and receiving rather than labour and sweat and it gives the process a human face – and not the tired one toiling over a machine in a hot, dusty, noisy factory in some far-off country, whom we rarely, if ever, allow ourselves to think about.

Challenge 31:
Shoes and handbags: can a girl ever have enough?

The answer to this is no. The female consensus is that women need shoes for every occasion, and bags to match, and since fashion dictates that these have to be updated every season we require a non-stop supply. Now I'm a reformed character I haven't bought a new bag for a couple of years and keep everything in a dinky little rucksack that I've had for yonks. It's not the perfect bag but then the 'Perfect Bag' is an unattainable ideal that in all my years of searching I have never found. The point is, it doesn't matter to me any more. It's a bag. It holds my stuff. I can find my keys and phone without mad scrabbling, and it's big enough to take an umbrella, sunglasses, a notebook and emergency sweets. I can even stuff a bit of shopping in it, if necessary.

It's the same issue with cheap, mass-produced bags and shoes as it is with cheap, mass-produced clothing. If we really care about the environment we just can't keep buying things for the sake of buying them and acting as if we've got three planets' worth of resources. (At the other end of the scale, spending thousands of pounds on designer bags is, to me, morally abhorrent as well. The 'Let's Clean Up Fashion' 2007 update compares Coleen McLoughlin, the £1.5m spokesmodel for George at Asda, who spent £3000 on a Hermes Birkin bag, with Mohua, a Bangladeshi garment worker, who earns £300 a year sewing clothes for George.) I'm not saying we have to go around in hair shirts because, frankly, hemp is ever so much nicer and you don't need pesticides to cultivate it. However, we just can't carry on consuming so recklessly. You can be stylish without being a slave to fashion, either disposable or designer. I realise it's easier to say this as an older woman: now I'm in my forties, youthful trends to some extent pass me by. More significantly, I've got a confidence I never had in my teens and twenties and I've learned what suits me and how to disguise the other bits. Also – and this comes with having been around longer, too – if you hang on to the good stuff, it comes around again. I mean, how many variations on shoe styles can you get? I've got them all now, including a pair of old leopard-print cork wedges I must have bought fifteen years back and some snakeskin pointy-toed rock-chick ankle boots that have had to be resoled twice because I love them so much.

The quest for ethical shoes came about because of Crocs. Crocs – as if you didn't know – are those brightly coloured plasticky looking perforated clogs that give people disproportionately broad, clompy feet. Needless to say, they are everywhere. Crocs are like Marmite: you either love them or you hate them. Fans say they're wonderful and the most comfortable shoe they've ever worn; the anti-Crocs brigade (of which I'm a member) think they're gross. Some say they pose an accident risk on escalators; others that the soles build up static electricity that can blow electronic equipment in hospitals, but I worry about their environmental impact. People have a perfect right to wear ugly shoes but when I walk down the street and see Crocs *everywhere*, all I can think of is what our landfill is going to look like to the people of the future. Here in York, which was a Viking settlement, archaeologists are still digging up remnants of old leather shoes from Jorvik middens, buried a few feet below us. What are the archaeologists of the next millennium going to find? A great thick gaudy layer of Crocs. They're not actually made of plastic but a patented foam resin called Croslite, which means you're unlikely to be able to recycle them through your local authority and, while they can be washed and donated to charity, ultimately the same problem persists. A quick canter through Google has turned up suggestions that you can use them as bird scarers or planters. However, if you don't fancy decorating your garden with old Crocs, there's now a recycling programme, SolesUnited (www.solesunited.com). It currently only exists in the States, although I gather there are plans for a European service. At the time of writing I've only found one place where you can do this in the UK – the Fatshoesday shop in Edinburgh (see Directory) – but if you go to their website, www.fatshoesday.co.uk, you can order a 'return to recycle' bag for £2.50 which they'll send you to put your Crocs in and post back to them. The shoes are collected by Fatshoesday until they've got sufficient quantity to ship to the US, where they are reground and made into new Crocs for distribution to relief efforts and humanitarian programmes around the world.

Looking into the Crocs issue got me thinking about other types of shoes and how environmentally friendly – or not – they might be. Crocs, like almost all shoes these days, are made in China, so you've got the whole carbon footprint issue to factor in, but there are shoes that are made from recycled materials if you know where to look. Not on the High Street, unfortunately, though Clarks has its 'Soul of Africa' moccasin shoes that are hand-stitched by unemployed women in Kwa-Zulu Natal in South Africa, the proceeds of all sales going to help children orphaned by AIDS. Even my foot-healthy Think! sandals, although they use vegetable-tanned leather and are made in Austria, don't quite make it. Once again one has to turn to specialist 'ethical boutiques' or shop online, where you can find Terra Plana (www.terraplana. com), the market leader in the ethical shoe business, which produces some fabulously sexy, original shoes (though at £80 for a pair of pumps they are a little pricey). Terra Plana teamed up with environmental awareness group Anti-Apathy to create a range called Worn Again, unisex trainers made from 99 per cent recycled materials such as prison blankets, army jackets and coffee bags. These were worn by Conservative Party leader David Cameron in a number of photo shoots, but their green 'cred' was questioned after a journalistic investigation by the *Mail on Sunday* revealed that the eco shoe brand had shipped London fire brigade uniforms from the UK to China and then back again as trainers. Worn Again has confirmed that this was for a limited-edition range only. Their website (www.wornagain.co.uk) has a lot to say on the company's ethical policy and makes it clear that the recycled materials are now being sourced regionally, either in China, or Portugal where its other factory is based. It's also transporting most goods by land or sea rather than by air and is paying 15p from each pair of shoes into Climate Care to help offset CO_2 emissions. Anti-Apathy's Cyndi Rhoades even went to China and has written a long piece on the website about her visit to the factory. She says that pressure from NGOs and consumers in the West has played a 'big role' in improving working conditions, which is really encouraging to hear. Ultimately, Worn Again states that its long-term aim is to bring shoe manufacturing back to the UK. Do I spot a trend emerging?

Probably not, according to Mike Stables, who founded Soft-walker shoes (www.softwalker.co.uk) in Askam in Furness, Cumbria, in 2001. Mike and his wife Lynne took over a redundant K Shoes factory that had been closed down by Clarks, rehired some of the experienced Cumbrian staff and set up their own business making soft, springy ladies' sandals and shoes with a lightweight breathable foam footbed. They've even got into making shoes from environmentally friendly hemp (good news for vegans), which produces more fibre per acre than cotton and generates more oxygen into the atmosphere. I think the Softwalker shoes are reasonably priced at between £49 and £55 but Mike says that while people like the idea, 'They aren't prepared to pay a premium price for a green project.' He isn't terribly optimistic about the future – 'At the moment the cost of manufacturing in the West is too high' – but says consumers are being misled by the cheapness of Eastern imports. A genuine price, he believes, would include the cost of the environmental pollution generated in production and transportation from China, 'but the consumer isn't ready for that yet'. And, by the time the real environmental cost of coal-fired Asian factories comes home to us in terms of their contribution to climate change, it may be too late. 'We're all walking blindly towards the future,' he says.

At least, to put a positive spin on this, we can walk towards our uncertain future in a pair of eco-smart sandals the way Nature intended us to. Softwalker manufactures the revolutionary Kala-hari sandals that have a unique foot support which mimics walking barefoot in soft sand. They're designed to improve posture and alleviate foot problems and what's really cool is that you can have a pair individually made for you using your old jeans. Not only is this effective recycling but you'll end up with a new pair of shoes with probably the lowest carbon footprint on the planet (go to www.recycleyourjeans.com to order a pair). I was keen to do this as my 'eco-challenge', so I grabbed a pair of old jeans that decency won't let me wear any more and vanity won't let me give to the Oxfam shop because I like to think I can still squeeze into them, stuffed them into the pre-paid bag, and posted them off. Just over a week later they returned to me as a pair of sandals (and yes, they are the same jeans – if you send off paint-splodged jeans, you get paint-splodged sandals). They're really comfy to walk in and they look great.

It would be wonderful if this principle could be expanded and we could recycle more of our old clothes and textiles into new clothes and shoes and bags and things here in the UK. I'm going to be optimistic on Mike Stables' behalf, because there are a lot of enterprising people in this country and I think he's onto a winner with this concept. Think about how individual your fashion could be and compare that with being a Crocs clone. Ironically, it was the Crocs concept – or, rather, being approached to manufacture a 'recyclable Croc' – that led Mike to start his business. The recyclable Croc equivalent he was working on never happened – 'They can be ground up and melted but there is no manufacturing in the UK any more and it would have to have been made into something else' – but Softwalker did. Somewhere, in a Cumbrian valley, it's OK to be a woman who needs more shoes. Thank heavens for that.

AISLE 11

Checkout Challenges:
Bags, Packaging and Recycling

Challenge 32:
Kicking the plastic bag habit

I believe in making a statement about something if you care about it passionately. When all the hoo-ha about Sainsbury's cult Anya Hindmarch-designed 'I am NOT a plastic bag' carrier kicked off, I spent a week walking around with a sign pinned to my own 'Recycle for York' jute carrier that said, 'I am not a plastic bag either', with a smiley face drawn on it so that people didn't think I was a total weirdo. And guess what? No one, but no one, tried to buy it off me to flog on eBay for hundreds of pounds. In fact, no one has so much as commented, apart from a cashier at Sainsbury's, who laughed.

The Sainsbury's Hindmarch bag may be soo-o over but We Are What We Do (www.wearewhatwedo.org), which produced the shopper for Sainsbury's, continues to plug away with its campaign against plastic bags. It came up with a new reusable shopper – this time in organic cotton – that was given away free with the December 2007 issue of *Marie Claire* magazine (you can buy it from the website too). This one bore the slogan 'Plastic ain't my bag', repeating the movement's nationwide appeal to rid our stores of plastic carriers by Christmas. Stores were encouraged to display the logo in their windows in the hope that the sight of Christmas shoppers laden with plastic bags might become a thing of the past. I have to report that this didn't happen in my neck of the woods: I bag-watched throughout the festive season *and* the January sales and saw little discernible sign of anyone declining the proffered plastic at the till, though in the past year I have noticed it more. David Robinson, co-founder of We Are What We Do, has been quoted as saying, 'We are fast approaching a point where it is about as fashionable to carry plastic as it is to wear fur' and certainly in places such as Modbury in Devon, which introduced a town-wide ban on giving out plastic bags on 1 May 2007, this is true. Modbury's lead has since been taken up elsewhere: according to the *Independent*,* eighty towns, villages and cities throughout the UK have introduced or are considering a similar ban, while London's thirty-three councils have voted to recommend that the capital becomes a plastic-bag-free city. Since then, the *Daily Mail* took ownership of the campaign (though the *Independent* was behind it long before them), with the result that pressure about the scourge of plastic bags became so great that the Prime Minister, Gordon Brown, announced plans to introduce legislation into the Climate Change Bill. This would force supermarkets to charge a 'green levy' for single-use plastic bags if they do not sufficiently reduce their use voluntarily. The threat appears to be working: WRAP reported that shops gave out 3.5 billion fewer bags in 2008.**

It's about time. The UK is seriously lagging behind on this issue and all the while marine animals such as birds, seals, dolphins, whales and especially turtles are dying in large numbers. Thirteen

*14 November 2007
**Independent, 26 February 2009

billion plastic bags are issued in the UK each year and a proportion of them end up in rivers and streams and get washed out to sea where the turtles mistake them for jellyfish and eat them. One dead leatherback was found with twenty-four plastic bags tangled in its guts. Because plastic takes so long to break down – it's estimated it could be anything up to 1000 years, but since they've only been around since the 1970s, who knows? – the bags survive the animal's death and decomposition and are re-released into the environment to cause further damage. And they're not just deadly to marine animals. Plastic bags have been banned in Bangladesh since 2002 after it was discovered that storm drains clogged up with plastic bags were a major cause of flooding. In South Africa, the sight of plastic bags caught on fences and bushes had become so common that they became known as the 'national flower'. The bags were banned and stiff fines – and up to ten years' imprisonment – are awarded for anyone infringing the ban. Equally harsh penalties have also been introduced in parts of India, where it's estimated that around a hundred cows a day choke and die after foraging on wind-blown plastic bags.

Closer to home, Ireland introduced a 'plastax' on each new plastic bag in 2002 which brought about a 90 per cent reduction in use. Ninety per cent! Yet, until the *Daily Mail*'s campaign, the British Government refused to support such a move. A statement on Defra's website about disposable bags still reads: 'There is no clear evidence that such a tax would be beneficial on either broad environmental grounds or litter grounds.' This is ludicrous. On the one hand, the Government is working with the regional assemblies, WRAP and retailers towards achieving a 25 per cent reduction of carrier bags by the end of 2008 and Gordon Brown is calling for a total ban on single-use plastic bags. On the other hand, it's implying that reducing plastic-bag consumption may not be bene-ficial since 'the net overall environmental effect will depend on substitution by other products' (which, it hints, might be worse). So which is it?

Reading between the lines, I suspect that the Government knows a vote-winner when it sees one but didn't want the administrative headache of something that might be seen as a 'stealth tax', nor indeed the flack from the plastics industry, hence the voluntary route (until its hand was forced). Calculating the carbon footprint of anything has to account for its entire life cycle, and there are issues with the amount of energy it takes to produce and transport other types of bags. This is the case with paper, which is heavier, as is jute (for which you also have to factor in the resources that go into growing and harvesting the crop). People do reuse plastic bags as bin liners and dog-poop sacks but you can get cornstarch alternatives for those. Paper isn't great, unless it's made from recycled pulp, but it does biodegrade easily and is compostable and recyclable. Jute has a string of eco-credentials: it's a fast-growing crop with a much higher CO_2 assimilation rate than trees; it's abundantly available; it's completely renewable (compare that with plastic, which is a by-product of the oil industry); its cultivation creates employment in poorer regions of the world; and it's 100 per cent biodegradable. The only problem I have with jute and hemp bags is that they are often very boring, but you can get much funkier designs these days if you shop around, or just customise them yourself (I'm working on attaching a different green slogan every week on mine).

These days, when I do the food shopping locally, I take my stash of reusable bags with me. They can be a bit cumbersome and, if I've got lots to get, I take an empty rucksack too, which helps to distribute the load. I'm considering sourcing a sexy shopping trolley (it was so much easier when my daughter was in a pram) but in the meantime I only buy what I can carry, which can be irksome but is at least sustainable. If I do go to a supermarket, I take any plastic bags that we've somehow accumulated (not by me, honestly), reuse them for the shopping and deposit the rest in the plastic-bag recycling bin.

Supermarkets are making an effort with the whole bag issue, some more so than others. Tesco awards a green Clubcard point for every bag that's reused, which it says has saved giving out 1 billion bags, although it still gives out 3 billion annually. Tesco has also been making a big thing about its degradable bags, which is another whole issue in itself. Briefly, degradable bags are made of plastic and, although they will eventually break down if they're exposed to the correct conditions – sunlight, oxygen, water – they do not break down completely but into tiny pieces that remain in the environment. In landfill they tend to get compacted and buried and so may not break down at all or, if they do, the low levels of oxygen means the process gives off methane, a greenhouse gas twenty-three times more powerful than CO_2. Degradable bags are not compostable (unlike biodegradable bags such as kitchen caddy liners, which are usually made of cornstarch) but they can be recycled at carrier-bag recycling points. The environmental impact of degradable plastic bags is a concern, however. Not only can they survive intact for long enough to be a threat to wildlife, but, once broken down, the tiny pieces may be mistaken by animals for food. Degradable bags do have one advantage on the littering front, though: assuming they encounter the correct conditions to break down they should render 'witches' knickers' (bags fluttering from bushes and trees) a thing of the past. Sam Mendes, director of the film *American Beauty*, may have captured a haunting beauty in a plastic bag's airy dance but when 100,000 tonnes of them are thrown away in the UK every year, it's not the answer that's blowin' in the wind but a very serious plastic bag problem.

Tesco isn't the only supermarket to use degradable bags; the Co-op does too. Other supermarkets have pursued a different tack:

Sainsbury's distinctive orange bags are made from 33 per cent recycled material and it now 'hides' them at the tills so that customers have to request them specifically. Its 'bag for life' sales have gone up by more than 60 per cent and it's even texting customers to remind them to bring them with them when they go shopping. This operation seems to be working and it's on target to halve the overall total by April 2009. Marks & Spencer also uses recycled material in its bags and its Bags for Life are made from 100 per cent recycled plastic, as are Asda's and Tesco's. Indeed, all the supermarkets are taking positive steps on the plastic bag issue, though Marks & Spencer is probably being the most bullish. It's now charging shoppers 5p a bag for food bags after this brought about a 66 per cent reduction in bag use in a trial in Ireland and even better results in another trial in the south west (the proceeds go to an environmental charity, Groundwork, which invests in green spaces for neighbourhoods). Good luck to them, I say, because once M&S does it, the rest won't lag too far behind. The public has a handle on the issue now, if you'll pardon the pun, and it's the politicians who are having to play catch-up. I have high hopes that shoppers' arms are more likely to be laden with jute and cotton carriers this Christmas.

It's easy enough to change your bag habits, if you apply yourself. We keep our jute bags by the front door so that it's easier to remember to take them with us when we go out. I also keep a cotton bag and a Bag for Life folded up in my handbag because I get caught out by spontaneous purchases at the corner shop. They know me so well there now that they have stopped automatically stuffing my shopping into a plastic bag, though for a while they tried to do this even when I placed my jute carrier rather pointedly on the counter in front of them. There are other bag options you can carry on your person that allow you to SNUB (Say No to Unwanted Bags). Onya bags (www.onyabags.co.uk)

are made from parachute silk and pack up really small and attach to your keyring so you've always got them 'on ya' (I gave my husband one in black for Christmas, and it's cool enough that he actually uses it). There's also Turtle Bags (www.turtlebags.co.uk), string bags that are available in a variety of colours including lime green, hot pink and purple (they use eco-friendly dyes) and help raise awareness about the whole turtle-deaths-from-plastic-bags issue. Since I bought mine I have SNUBbed the greengrocer, the chemist, most of the cashiers in Costcutter and even a white-coated lady on a beauty counter in Fenwicks, which I thought was quite brave. I considered SNUBbing in M&S, but I'm not blasé enough to carry half a dozen pairs of panties around in an open-mesh bag. Luckily, it came in useful for the fish I got from the market. One really should keep knickers and kippers separate.

Challenge 33:
Packaging: can we get radical?

Packaging frustrates me. Either I can't remove it or I can't get rid of it, particularly plastic packaging. That's what clogs my bin up because we can't yet recycle mixed plastics where I live, though some local authorities seem to manage it. But it's not simply a local authority issue; supermarkets need to take a far more proactive stance. Having a few recycling banks at the far end of the car park isn't enough. We need a revolution in store so that customers don't have to leave the store with all that packaging in the first place. Changes are ongoing but as things stand now, at the start of 2009, there are still not enough signs of them on the shop floor.

I am staggered that supermarkets have been so slow on the uptake, given the level of public concern. According to WRAP,

50 per cent of household waste, which ultimately ends up in landfill, has originated from a purchase from the top five retail supermarket chains. As WRAP points out, 'supermarkets link massive supply chains with households' behaviour and are therefore well placed to influence change'. I would add that supermarkets have quite frightening powers to influence the livelihoods of farmers, the fortunes of manufacturers, the futures of small businesses and even the incomes of small countries. How can it be beyond their reach to minimise packaging at the point of sale?

Former Environment Minister Ben Bradshaw made the news in November 2006 when he urged customers to teach supermarkets a lesson about their profligate use of excess packaging by dumping it at the till. Nervous journalists, commissioned by their editors, sweated at checkouts and unwrapped their sausages while customers tutted in queues, but I've yet to see anyone do it in real life. Inspired by the WI's direct action in June 2006, when some of their members saved up a week's worth of packaging and returned it to supermarkets, I suggested in one of my press columns that a flash-mob-style packaging protest be coordinated by our local green groups. No one took the initiative at the time and I was too scared to do it by myself, so I assumed that was that. Several months later, I heard about a planned packaging protest from a friend of mine. It was all a bit secretive and, when I made inquiries, it became apparent that they weren't keen on publicity, so I didn't get involved.

It was when I got down to researching the packaging issue for this Aisle that I decided I'd better hit the stores again and find out for myself what supermarkets were doing about excess packaging and, if necessary, make my point at the checkout. Having read the claims on all the supermarkets' websites about what great strides they were making, it looked as if the situation was improving. Asda, Budgens, the Co-op Group, Londis, Iceland,

M&S, Morrisons, Sainsbury's, Tesco and Waitrose are all signatories to the Courtauld Commitment, an agreement between the major grocery retailers and WRAP drawn up in March 2005 to develop packaging solutions across the whole supply chain. The overall objectives were: to design out packaging waste by 2008; to deliver absolute reductions in packaging waste by 2010; and to identify ways to tackle the problem of food waste (more on that in the final Aisle). In addition, many of the supermarkets came up with their own waste reduction targets. 'At last!' I thought, expecting great things of my own personal 'supermarket sweep'. I couldn't face another trip to Tesco, having been there fairly recently on my research trip for clothes; I did, however, manage to hit Morrisons, Sainsbury's and Asda all in the space of about four hours, which is going some for me.

Once inside Morrisons you step immediately into their 'Market Street' where a fishmonger is all ready to greet you, the bakery wafts delicious home-baked aromas and fresh fruit and vegetables are piled up on 'barrows'. Well, some of them are. Some, predictably, are in polystyrene or moulded plastic trays and covered with film but if you want loose Conference pears, as opposed to fancy posh pears, you can avoid the packaging. Since the WI's concerns are about the over-packaging of fresh goods, in particular fruit and vegetables, that's what I focused on. It turned out to be a mixed bag (literally). The organic pears that I bought did come in a bag but it was compostable, which was fine. Swedes, whole or half, were only available shrink-wrapped, whereas turnips were loose, so I bought a turnip instead. Ordinary onions were loose, red onions (which I wanted) were in plastic bags. Fresh heads of 'naked' broccoli were banked up attractively but the organic broccoli, which was what I was seeking, was wrapped. Ordinary lemons, pick your own from a crate; unwaxed lemons, in plastic tray with wrapping. And so it went on. Morrisons has an on-pack labelling scheme for its own-brand produce that it calls its 'Recyclopedia' guide: a big grin means the packaging is 100 per cent recyclable or compostable (a speech bubble tells you which); a smiling face means that it is 'partly recyclable' and an unsmiling face means that the packaging is not yet recyclable ('but we're working on it'). I took my basket to the till and, after paying, politely informed the cashier that, although the packaging on several of my items stated that it was recyclable, albeit 'not in all areas', it certainly wasn't recyclable in our area yet and I didn't want to take it home with me. She seemed a little embarrassed but helped me remove the wrappings and plastic tray and discarded them in the bin under her desk. It was a relatively painless procedure, though had I had a huge volume of stuff and a big queue behind me I probably wouldn't have had the nerve to do it. My main problem with Morrisons is the same one I have with all the supermarkets: just saying something is recyclable is a cop-out if you're not going to provide the facilities on site to actually recycle it. Otherwise, it's simply the supermarkets awarding themselves a gold star for wrapping something in plastic (no change there) and then intimating that it's not their fault if you can't find anywhere to recycle it.

Sainsbury's, for all their PR about how much work they are doing to reduce packaging, seemed to me to be equally inconsistent. On their website it states that 'all ready meals, the majority of organic produce and some organic meat products' would move to compostable packaging by October 2007, yet when I visited, in November 2007, plastic trays and film were still much in evidence on ready meals. Beneath the organic mushrooms, which were in plastic trays and wrapped in plastic film, was a sign that read, '80% of all Sainsbury's SO Organic fresh produce is in compostable packaging and can be put straight on your compost heap'. It would be interesting to see that quantified, since besides the organic mushrooms, I found organic broccoli, organic dwarf beans, organic leaf spinach, organic celery, organic tender-stem broccoli, organic English apples and shrink-wrapped organic Savoy cabbage that were all in regular, non-compostable and currently non-recyclable, packaging. And that was only on a limited survey of the organic produce. I find the ethos of putting organic stuff in compostable packaging but not the non-organic fruit and veg frustrating: that's like saying that only people who buy organic produce care enough about the environment to do composting, which isn't true. Besides which, if the packaging for fresh produce was compostable across the entire range it might really boost interest in home composting, which would have a beneficial effect all round. At the checkout, I handed back the bag from my celery (it said 'return to store for recycling' so that seemed fair enough) and from my apples and tore the shrink-wrap off my organic cucumber after neither the cashier nor a supervisor was able to tell me whether it was compostable or not. It was at this point I began to feel like a professional pain in the butt, but they were ever so nice about it all and we ended up having a very interesting conversation, during which they told me that Sainsbury's was planning to have recycling points for other types of plastic in the future. I cannot confirm this because when I contacted Sainsbury's press office they never got back to me, despite my talking to two different press officers and sending several follow-up emails; neither did they get back to me on those targets mentioned above. Taste the difference? Hmm.

By the time I got to Asda I was running out of steam and bored with buying shrink-wrapped vegetables only to have to strip them of their plastic at the till. Asda is another supermarket that's made a lot of noise about how it's reducing packaging on loose produce and going back to 'the look and feel of a traditional green-grocer shop from the 1950s'. Asda's website states that it has launched a 'radical study' that could 'virtually eliminate the need for packaging on fresh fruit and vegetables', which I am delighted to hear, because when I visited the store almost all the organic produce was in packaging, as was a fair amount of the other fruit and vegetables. They do have a lot of loose produce too, but it didn't look significantly more than the other two supermarkets I went to that day. Asda says that it is redesigning the weight and volume of the packaging on its brands with the aim of reducing it by at least 10 per cent, and that it's already reduced the thickness of the plastic on its salad bags by 15 per cent. (I checked salads and found no mention of this on the bags so they're clearly being modest about this achievement.) I bought some fresh UK-grown coriander, a bag of oven chips and six tins of Heinz soup – they were on offer – and went home, shopped out.

Incidentally, the York Asda was one of two Asda stores piloting a 'Leave It With Us' scheme in May 2007 that invited customers to bring back examples of over-packaging so that the company could bring pressure to bear on their suppliers to reduce waste. Huge wheelie bins were placed in the foyer of each of the two stores (the other was in Dewsbury) for people to either return examples of over-packaging on their next visit or dump their excess packaging in after going through the checkout. Unfortunately, very few people actually used it and as a result the scheme, which Asda had considered rolling out nationwide, was withdrawn (though customers can still report over-packaging concerns on Asda's website). A spokesperson for Asda was quoted as saying, 'Customers weren't that keen on removing the packaging there and then.' Personally, I think it's a cultural thing. The Germans don't hesitate to make a fuss; they installed bins by the tills for customers to leave their excess packaging back in 1992 (that's right, 1992) because shoppers had become so militant about it. What is it with us Brits – are we just too polite? Repressed? Or not bovvered?

Of course, the fact that Asda was underwhelmed by returned packaging may just mean that customers are satisfied with the job it's doing. Research published by the Local Government Association (LGA)* revealed that Asda came out top of a packaging survey of all the main food retailers, while M&S, for all their green credentials, came bottom. Based on a shopping basket of twenty-nine common food items, M&S only had 60 per cent recyclable packaging, Tesco had 62 per cent, Morrisons, 68 per cent and Asda and Sainsbury's did the best of the supermarkets with 70 per cent recyclable packaging. Asda inched ahead overall among the big retailers because the weight of its packaging was slightly less. I checked the full report, which has illustrations of all the baskets and all the waste they produced, curious to see whether the 15 per cent-lighter salad bags had swung it, but they weren't on the shopping list. Credit where credit's due: even without playing their mixed-leaves trump card Asda outperformed the others; as for M&S, it needs to gear up its act, and smartish.

None of the big food retailers can afford to take it easy. The LGA has warned that supermarkets must take urgent action to reduce excess packaging or Britain will fail to meet its recycling targets. If we do not dramatically reduce the amount of waste sent to landfill, councils (and, ultimately, council-tax payers like you and me) will face fines of up to £3bn. The LGA concluded that supermarkets were beginning to think more ecologically, but its chair, Paul Bettison, emphasised that, 'It is important shoppers are actively encouraged to consider the environmental impact of their purchases.'

I couldn't agree more. Keep giving back that excess packaging, I say, until they produce the bins for it. Better still, shop locally.

*23 October 2007

Guess who the outright winners were in the LGA-commissioned packaging survey? Markets and local traders. They topped the chart with 79 per cent recyclable packaging. I confirmed this packaging reduction myself when I conducted my survey comparing prices of fruit and veg (see Aisle 1). Not only was market produce cheaper but the volume of packaging generated by the supermarket was shocking. Those 'old-fashioned' grocers' stores and 'market streets' are still out there in the real world, you know. But only as long as we keep using them.

Challenge 34:
Can the `Three Rs' solve the rubbish crisis?

You can't be an eco-shopper without being eco-smart about the waste your shopping inevitably produces, be it in packaging form or food waste. Once you've got your shopping home, sorted it, stowed it, eaten it or drunk it, worn it, applied it or used it, there's almost always something left to dispose of, however eco-freaky you are. That's the reason for this Aisle. Not that you need advice from me on taking your empties to the bottle bank or putting out the collectibles on the right day, but even with the best will in the world, basic recycling won't get rid of all your rubbish.

We are, belatedly, recycling more – figures for the year ending June 2008 show that the proportion of household waste being recycled or composted now stands at 35.5 per cent* – but the UK remains the 'landfill dustbin of Europe' according to the LGA. In contrast, Denmark and the Netherlands send almost nothing to municipal landfill. So what's happening?

*Defra, 12 February 2009

An examination of Defra's figures for 2003 reveals one (controversial) reason why other countries do better: incineration. Denmark uses incineration as the single main method of disposing of 53 per cent of its municipal waste; the Netherlands, Germany and France use it too, though to a lesser extent. Opinion is divided about incineration here, with environmental groups such as Friends of the Earth very much against it. However, the Austrians have proved that burning rubbish isn't the only way to go: they incinerate only a fraction more waste than we do in the UK (10.7 per cent compared with 8 per cent in the UK) but they recycle almost 60 per cent of their municipal waste on top of that, sending only 30 per cent to landfill. By contrast, we were recycling just 18 per cent in 2003 and sending 74 per cent of municipal waste to landfill.

Fortunately, there are councils in the UK that are setting a better example: St Edmundsbury in Suffolk was top of the league (just pipped by East Lindsey Council in 2007/8) for recycling or composting over 50 per cent. The secret of St Edmundsbury's success is its proactive approach to recycling: it introduced a three-bin system that involves the collection of recycled items from two bins one week with the rest of the rubbish the next. A brown bin takes compostable materials, including plain cardboard, while dry recyclables – paper and envelopes, directories, junk mail, plastic bottles, plastic packaging, cans and tins, foil and printed cardboard – all go in a blue bin. A black bin, put out the following week, is for the non-recyclable waste. St Edmundsbury has also joined forces with six other Suffolk councils and a commercial waste partner to invest in new technology at the Great Blakenham recycling plant, which has an optical sorter that can separate out PET and HDPE from other types of plastics. I'd heard that the plastics all went to China for reprocessing and, when I checked with St Edmundsbury, they confirmed this, stressing that it goes by container ship from nearby Felixstowe. 'If the facilities and the markets were available for plastics reprocessing in the UK or Europe we would of course use them,' their waste development officer, Kate McFarland, told me. 'As it stands at the moment the majority of our plastic products are imported from China, so there is no market anywhere else for reprocessing it.'

This doesn't apply to plastic bottles, as there is a good market in the UK for that particular grade of plastic, with new dedicated plants coming on stream to take advantage of the large demand for reprocessing at home (currently 70 per cent of the UK's waste bottles are shipped abroad). However, UK recycling companies don't take mixed plastics such as yogurt pots, margarine tubs, food trays and film, because it requires a lot of expensive sorting into the different polymers. This is why St Edmundsbury exports it to the Far East and why councils politically unwilling to take the 'slow boat to China' option are still sending it to landfill. Research into new technology is ongoing, but one of the other problems is that the 'end markets' – where the recycled plastic ends up – are equally underdeveloped in the UK and these are needed to 'close the loop'.

A new recycling plant which does just that opened this year in Dagenham. Operated by Closed Loop London, it turns UK PET from plastic bottles into food packaging. Marks & Spencer has already committed to sending the plastic from its London stores there. There are also some small companies recycling post-consumer and industrial plastic waste in innovative ways: here in Yorkshire, Huddersfield-based Revolve (By Cutouts) makes key rings from carrier bags, coasters from yogurt pots and rulers from plastic bottles. They can be ordered direct from Revolve's website, www.revolve-uk.com, and are also stocked in branches of John Lewis. There is also the Remarkable factory in Worcestershire that transforms car tyres into pencil cases, plastic boxes into notebooks

and plastic cups into funky pencils – go to www.remarkable.
co.uk. I gave their stationery to my niece and nephews at
Christmas and they thought they were 'well cool'. These days I
am never without a pen made from car parts. They're pink – very
Lady Penelope.

Reducing our waste mountain is doable, but only if local authorities, retailers and consumers all play their part and the recycling
facilities – and technologies – are in place. Under the EU Landfill
Directive the UK must cut the amount of biodegradable waste
sent to landfill in 2010 to 75 per cent of the amount we sent in
1995 (29 million tonnes). By 2020, that figure has to drop to 35
per cent of the baseline 1995 figure or we stand to pay massive
fines. Alternate collections of recyclables are one option; 'pay as
you throw' schemes, possibly involving prepaid sacks or
microchipped wheelie bins that can be weighed, are another. The
latter might not be such a bad thing – the more people recycled,
the less they'd have to pay in council tax – though opponents
argue that it would increase fly-tipping and that unscrupulous
householders would dump their trash in other people's bins.

I don't know what you do about this. All I know is that I thought
I was 'doing my bit', sending our drinks cans to be turned into
planes or cars or yet more drinks cans, washing out our jam jars
and taking our phone books to the designated skip. And yet my
best efforts at recycling alone weren't reducing our own household
waste enough. Why wasn't it working? Frustrated by putting out
a full dustbin every week, I decided it was time to go back to
basics. I needed help with our recycling and at a local primary
school I found someone with all the answers, even if he did talk
a bit funny: Recycler, the rapping robot.

Recycler (go to www.recyclezone.org.uk) is a big proper robot
with swivelling blue eyes, a red flashing mouth, jointed arms and
some natty, Peter Crouch-style dance moves. A spokesbot for Waste

Watch, he's made from recovered waste materials and has the very important job of touring UK primary schools and educating the children about the new 'Three Rs': reduce, reuse and recycle. According to Recycler, every family fills the equivalent of 100 baths of rubbish every year, which is enough to fill a classroom up to the ceiling. Yuck. Recycler's mission is to tell children – who are under strict instructions to then rein in their parents' excesses – that reducing what we buy is the first step ('It's naughty grown-ups who buy things with lots of packaging'). Next comes reusing things (Recycler is good on junk modelling) and only after that option has been exhausted comes recycling. Having exhorted the kids to make sure Mum bought loose mushrooms in a paper bag instead of packaged ones in a tray, Recycler left us with a catchy little rap that we all had to sing at least twice. It's been lodged somewhat annoyingly in my brain ever since. Whenever I baulk at washing out a baked-bean tin, I hear Recycler's electronic voice. 'Re-re-recycle. Got to recycle. Yeah, yeah, yeah, yeah-yeah.' Get that robot patrolling the aisles in supermarkets. He's worth his weight in recycled plastic bottles – and more.

In fact, I'm beginning to think every home should have a Recycler on hand for help and advice and perhaps a little light can-crushing. My daughter's made a start – building robots out of the contents of the recycling box is a popular pastime – but they're just not the same without the song-and-dance routine. Recycler's right to remind us about those other two 'Rs': we may have improved our recycling rates but we're not so hot on reducing the stuff we buy and we're still too quick to throw things out rather than reuse them.

I suspect that's my problem, particularly the buying things, so I thought I'd set myself an eco-challenge to participate in Buy Nothing Day on 24 November 2007. This is a day when people are urged to 'switch off from shopping and tune in to life' and 'detox from consumerism'. I had to go into town, which was heaving, because my daughter has a Saturday-morning drama class. Normally I'd buy a large latté, get a paper and do some shopping while I wait. This time I still bought a coffee (and a croissant – I hadn't had breakfast and this wasn't Faint from Low Blood Sugar Day) but after that I went to the library and did some work. It was very restful, plus it was free, and I didn't miss the hurly burly of the crowds one little bit. By contrast, 'Buy Nothing Day' 2008 was barely mentioned anywhere – largely because, with a recession biting, it was becoming a public duty to buy *something* to keep shops open.

Ironically of course, the trend of 'reduce', 'reuse' is becoming more popular from the credit-crunch angle. Sustainability isn't just ethical, it's the right thing for all of us. My friend Harriet, has been experimenting with buying nothing new apart from food, toiletries and underwear for a year. This, I've since learned, has a name and a movement – Compacting – and a growing number of people worldwide are doing it. I asked Harriet for a report on how she was getting on and whether she was sticking to it. She told me she was buying Christmas presents from charity shops, which is allowed because they're second-hand, but that there had been a few slip-ups. To date she has bought: one straw hat, by accident (she had a voucher from Accessorize but the hat came to more than the voucher), although it's since been inadvertently recycled as she left it behind in a café in Spain; a Spanish ceramic ('It was a local, artisan-made piece – it would have been rude not to') and a dog lead, but since her boyfriend bought this she's hoping it doesn't count.

Harriet has joined Freecycle and the last I heard she was scouring it for wellies. Freecycle is a good bet for just about anything: I heard of a young couple who had furnished their entire house for nothing using it. If you're not already familiar with Freecycle (go to www.uk.freecycle.org), then let me introduce you to what must be the best way of re-homing stuff you don't want and finding stuff you do want, and all for free. It's a grassroots movement that has spread worldwide but operates at a local level. You don't swap things; you offer things or ask for things or you reply to a posting to take something. 'Our goal is to keep usable items out of landfill,' the Freecycle website states. 'By using what we already have we reduce consumerism, manufacture fewer goods and lessen the impact on the earth.' So that's reducing, reusing and recycling, all in one. Hooray! I joined Freecycle about six months ago and on the first day I got about eighty separate emails, so do opt for the updated digests if you don't want your inbox to fill up. Even the bulletins come through five times a day, but at least they make you feel as though somebody out there loves you. Until recently I had only tried, unsuccessfully, to secure guinea-pig hutches (they're very popular) though I did get rid of the hamster cage I bought from Oxfam because we never got round to purchasing the hamster to go with it. Spurred on by writing this piece, I have just advertised an ancient Bontempi keyboard that we inherited from a relative. I received several inquiries and it's now found a new and grateful owner. I also advertised a broken kettle, but that wasn't so popular. Still, it seems there's little that won't go on Freecycle: from a random selection of Freecycle postings I've noticed pond weed, a pink fluffy singing unicorn, organ pedals, fifteen ovulation tests, eight old concrete posts, three dusty demi-johns, two Playboy handmade duvet sets and a partridge in a pear tree. Okay, so I made that last one up. But for all I know it's been on twice already.

AISLE 12

Rubbish Challenges:
Composting, Wormeries and Magic Microbes

Challenge 35:
Is composting the answer?

Composting was the very first eco-challenge I took up, back in September 2005. It was after I'd written a column about recycling and I was contacted by Keely Mellor on behalf of Rotters, a home-composting support group, who asked me if I'd like to take part in a Weigh Your Waste trial. You got a free kitchen caddy and a bucket, plus optional hand-holding, and a small compost bin for the discounted price of £8. In return, you had to log every caddy and bucket of waste that you composted and return the results once a month. As an incentive, randomly drawn Rotters could win a box of organic chocolates. If you completed the trial you got a free jute shopping bag. I signed up for it.

To start with it was fun and I piled apple cores, banana skins, wilted lettuce leaves and potato peelings into my new compost bin with abandon, feeling extremely virtuous. This initial enthusiasm waned, however, when clouds of apparently malevolent flies rose out of the bin and swarmed around my face every time

I opened the lid. I resorted to doing this at arm's length, flipping the top open with a long stick, while keeping my lips tightly sealed. My husband did it once and returned to the house trau-matised. I persevered, unwilling to lose face. This became harder once the wasps joined in. Plus, the thing stank.

Panicking, I called up Keely, who came to investigate. She was shocked at the state of my fly-blown bin, declaring it 'the worst case I've ever seen', and offered to remove it and help me start afresh. I was relieved; by now my husband was issuing dire threats. A couple of days later, Keely returned with another Rotter, John, a tall, bearded man with a ponytail who had been instrumental in setting up the group. Donning a pair of rubber gloves he got stuck in, tipping the contents of my teeming bin out onto a plastic sheet. The stench was awful, just like sewage. I had to retreat but John, undeterred, had a good riffle through and told me things weren't as bad as all that.

'It's just got too wet and compacted, which encourages anaerobic bacteria. We need to add more fibrous stuff to it, like scrunched-up cardboard,' he said confidently. 'Ideally, you want more of the drier, tougher, carbon-rich brown materials – stuff like straw, hedge trimmings, waste paper, cardboard, sawdust and older plant material – than you do the wetter nitrogen-rich green stuff like fruit and vegetable peelings and grass cuttings. The mix you're aiming for is roughly 60:40.'

'Oh,' I said, surprised both at the proportion of fibre the compost required and at the fact that John seemed to think I was going to continue with that particular pile of poo-smelling muck. 'Aren't you going to take it away?'

'No, it's your bin, your compost. You've got to own it,' he replied. I would have laid down and drummed my heels but the ground was too disgustingly mucky.

'What about the flies?' I demanded, batting at a wasp.

'It's been a bad year for fruit flies,' he said philosophically. 'It's global warming.' He straightened up. 'Think of them as spider food, or food for blue tits. All part of the food chain. Wrap your fruit peelings up in newspaper or tear out pages from old Yellow Pages. It'll help keep them away and add fibre to the compost.'

He tossed the smelly mess back in, wrapping some of it up in newspaper and supplementing the heap with plenty of cardboard, which he and Keely scrunched and twisted. This, I was told, helped to add texture and aerate the mix by creating air pockets and would rebalance the activity of the anaerobes. 'Keep your cardboard packaging in an open bin bag by the compost bin. The rain will get in and dampen it, which, together with the moisture from the fruit and veg, is all you need.' (I had committed the sin of watering my compost which, being entirely slimy kitchen waste, had contributed to the problem.)

I retired the compost bin two or three weeks later. It was almost full anyway and the flies were still awful, so I rolled it round the corner – it was one of those smaller, flexible fabric bins that are useful if you've got a back yard rather than a garden – and propped it behind the shed. Starting off a new bin was easier: a good layer of woody garden material went in first to allow air to circulate at the bottom (I was warned not to add dead leaves because they are very slow to rot and are better off composted separately) and I kept my cardboard, mostly packaging waste such as pizza boxes, cereal packets, kitchen roll tubes, etc, in a bin liner, as directed, by the heap, adding some each time I emptied a caddy. 'Feeding' the compost with strips of twisted cardboard made it slightly more of an effort, since you couldn't just chuck a load of peelings in and put the lid back on, but I applied myself virtuously. Once I'd got the hang of it I discovered that composting could be a strangely meditative experience. It's not that it takes that long, but while I'm sorting the heap and turning it and scrunching up the cardboard the birds come down to wait, bright-eyed, for the opportunity to grab a worm and I get to take a little time out from all the rushing about and appreciate the stillness and solitude. (Once, when I was standing there quietly going about my composting, I surprised an intruder in my next-door neighbour's garden, which was a slightly more unnerving kind of encounter with the local wildlife.)

Autumn progressed and the days grew shorter and colder and with the drop in temperature there was little discernible activity in the heap. While this made a pleasant change from the swarming mass of insect life that had invaded the first bin, it meant that the second bin was filling up quickly. (You can 'lag' your bin with old blankets to help retain warmth and speed up the microbes.) Christmas came and upped the compost level to the top, what with all the Brussels sprout leaves, parsnip peelings, envelopes from Christmas cards and wrapping paper – you can compost it so long as it's not the shiny metallic kind and pick the sticky tape out when it's all rotted down. A leaflet from the Rotters extolling us to recycle as much of our Christmas packaging as possible had me stripping crackers to their cardboard inner tube, crunching them up and composting the jokes which, frankly, was the best thing for them.

By New Year, I could fit nothing more into bin no. 2 and had to find a solution. Having first donned my Marigolds, I cautiously unzipped bin no. 1. This had been living quietly behind the shed all this time and, to my surprise, it had rotted down to less than half its volume. With some difficulty I tipped its contents out onto a groundsheet. It was still claggy and a bit slimy but didn't smell as bad as the first time. I attacked it with a garden fork, shaking up the clods of congealed cardboard and unidentifiable brown matter, and speared a worm. It was hard not to. The compost was alive with worms, for whom Christmas was clearly an all-year-round event. Apologising to it, I slung the worm back and called the family over. Predictably, they reacted with indifference (him) and horror (her). As for me, I felt something rather different. Seeing the results of my initial composting trial provoked an unexpected fascination with the biological process of decay. In a way, composting is like conducting an experiment: you put the waste in, subject it to various influences – warmth, wetness, worms – and chemical reactions take place resulting in something entirely different coming out. Observing those changes, even though I was really only halfway through the experiment, made me glad that John had made me stick with it. In a peculiar sort of way it was quite comforting to witness the process of physical breakdown of organic matter, to see how our bodies too will someday return to and nourish the soil. Not that I'm advocating adding deceased relatives to your compost heap, though John (whom you may have seen on *Newsnight*'s Ethical Man series) occasionally supplements his heaps – he has many – with any roadkill he comes across when he's cycling around town.

Well, each to his – or her – own. My school friend, Spit, who lives in the wilds of Tasmania, advocates adding urine to one's compost. It's well known that the nitrogen makes a good compost activator, and I guess if you live quietly in ten acres of your own land, nipping out with a potty is pretty easy. I fear that the jungle drums would start up pretty soon if I did it, what with being overlooked on both sides of our mid-terraced property, besides which I'dve heard that male urine is supposed to work better (something to do with female hormones, I think). I did try to get my husband to sneak out in the dark and tend to it, but he flatly refused. In the end, in the name of research, my 16-year-old nephew, who was staying with us for the weekend, volunteered to do the job. He seemed to quite enjoy communing with Nature and offered to do it again the following night; either that or he was having a sneaky fag out the back. I didn't notice a discernible difference in my compost but I suspect a regular application is what's called for.

On the subject of compost activators, you can also add comfrey leaves and nettles to your heap, which will speed things up. My top tip, though, is to make sure you site your bin in a warm, sunny spot (preferably not next to your back door or you'll be invaded by fruit flies). Also, place it on soil so that worms can get in from underneath. If you can't see much evidence of wormy activity, ask a fellow composter for some well-rotted, worm-dense compost to augment yours with, or buy some brandling worms – also called tiger worms – from a fishing tackle shop or online from somewhere like Wiggly Wigglers (www.wigglywigglers.co.uk). You'll definitely need to do this if you're composting in a back yard, in which case the bin should be on cardboard to soak up the leachate.

By this time, I'd completed the 'Weigh Your Waste' trial with the Rotters and my results were in. I had composted an incredible 172kg of kitchen waste, more than twice as much as most people in the trial, mainly because I do a lot of home cooking. (Some of the other volunteers barely filled a caddy a week; I was filling a caddy every two days.) I wasn't too sure if that was good or bad. On the plus side, if I carried on composting, I would save more than half a tonne of methane-producing biodegradable waste from going into landfill over the year. On the bad side, my high average suggested I got rid of a lot of wasted food. I thought guiltily of the rotting aubergine and three-week-old cabbage in the back of the fridge, a home they shared with some withered parsnips, two-month-old beets and a rock-hard lime. My weekly supermarket shopping blitz did not tend to be very focused. Still, at least the uneaten stuff wasn't being thrown in the bin any more. In fact, as a direct result of composting the kitchen waste, we had halved our rubbish output from the outset, putting out one bin bag a week instead of our usual two.

Eventually, I was able to fork the contents of that first, disastrous bin onto the flowerbed as a mulch. By now it smelt almost acceptable, though it wasn't the soft crumbly mixture I'd been hoping for – the claggy brown lumps still predominated – and I could pick out pieces of coloured cardboard. But you know what? The honeysuckle took off like crazy, so I must have done something right. By the time the compost from the second bin was ready – it can take anything from six to eighteen months, depending on where you site the bin and a variety of other factors – I'd honed my rotting skills and the end result was a dark, soft, crumbly material that was just like proper compost (because it was proper compost). I couldn't have been more proud.

I am now the owner of three compost bins – two 'Daleks' (the big black compost converters) and a Komp, which is cuboid in shape and has removable slatted sides – and become something of a composting queen. I've made a *Video Nation* film for the BBC about it and have become a Rotter myself, helping out with stalls and roadshows, writing about the subject for magazines and joining in compost-bin drumming publicity stunts to promote the cause. I've composted my next-door neighbour Lindsay's kitchen waste, too, and I've converted my mate Karen, who only has a small concrete back yard, and she now composts her kitchen waste using my old textile bin. It's been a steep learning curve at times but I'm so glad I stuck with it. I honestly think it's the most practical, efficient and productive action I've taken out of all my eco-challenges because of the reduction it's made to what we throw away and because I personally get a great sense of pleasure from turning waste into this wonderful, fertile stuff. And don't be put off, thinking you're going to be overwhelmed with compost; it's surprising what a small quantity a whole bin produces (about a sixth of its volume). Once the compost is ready it can be used as a mulch, soil improver, or lawn feed, in pots and tubs, around trees and to grow fruit and vegetables. We've got a raised bed now and lots of the compost has gone in there to condition the soil. I can't wait to be able to eat our own homegrown vegetables in the summer. It completes the cycle from soil to living plant to food to compost to growing something again, which is incredibly rewarding. Most of all, in a small but important way, it gives you a sense that you can do something real and relevant to help stop the madness.

Challenge 36:
Worms: charming or alarming?

I think worms are kind of cute but a lot of people are positively phobic about them. If you are such a person, then a wormery probably isn't for you. Wormeries are a great alternative for composting your kitchen waste if you don't generate that much, or if you've got very little outside space or if you live in a flat. They are self-contained systems that you can keep in a back yard or on a balcony and you can even keep them indoors (they should, anyway, be brought inside during winter months to stop the worms getting too cold). They're a constructive kind of pet, being 'working worms', and very educational if you've got kids. You may even find them good company (they are excellent listeners) and have little chats with them. Um . . . or is that just me?

I confess that the worm thing may have gone a bit too far. The thought struck me when I found myself dancing around our local park in a pair of high-heeled shoes trying to attract worms to the surface live on air for local radio to promote a worm-charming competition I was involved with. However, it was too late by then. There was Compost John, twanging the ground with a garden fork and trying to coax them forth with his chant of 'Wormy wormy wormies!', me dancing a kind of frenetic salsa in my best going-out shoes (now ruined) and another Rotter doing a bit of African drumming, all in the hope that the vibrations would bring the little fellas up to see us. The presenter was cracking up so much he could hardly do his commentary and then, miracle of miracles, my stamping produced a worm, which only narrowly avoided being spiked by one of my heels.

The reason for holding these events, other than to have a bit of fun in the fresh air, was to get people a little bit more familiar with worms and to promote composting. We had a composting display set up and a wormery for people to look at, which was going to have been mine before I managed to commit wormicide and kill the lot of them. As you can tell, I didn't do very well with my wormery. In fact, this eco-challenge turned out to be an eco-disaster. I was trialling a new wormery on behalf of the Rotters and was quite excited at the prospect of producing what the instruction leaflet described as the 'caviar of compost'. Vermicomposting, as it's called, produces particularly fine, dark, rich, soil-like compost that's very high in nutrients because it has passed through the worms' bodies and been turned into 'casts'. The process is relatively slow, at least initially, so it can't take a huge volume of waste but the amount of compost you get is enough to pot up some herbs or a trough or maybe a hanging basket or two if you don't have a garden to put the compost on.

One of the other advantages is that, unlike regular composting, you can recycle some cooked food waste, although if you add meat or fish it will attract houseflies and there may be a problem with odour until the food has been consumed. Worms are best fed small quantities of foods such as fruit and vegetable peelings, teabags, coffee grounds, crushed eggshells, cooked food scraps, including pasta, potatoes and rice, hair and nail clippings, torn up or shredded paper or soaked card and baked beans. Yes, really. They go down a treat with the toe nails. You'd think, with a diet like that, worms wouldn't be fussy creatures but they don't like anything too acidic so don't give them onions or citrus.

Wormeries come in different shapes and sizes and prices, or you can make your own. Of the ones I've seen in use, I like the Can-O-Worms the best, which is a system of stacking trays that sit on top of each other and allow easy access to the finished compost. I was trialling one that looked like a large, square-sided kitchen bin or a scaled-down wheelie bin with a tap at the bottom. Inside, it had a perforated plastic tray that you slotted uprights into and which holds the worm bedding and allows the leachate to drain through. You would normally get a colony of special compost worms with your wormery, or an order card to send off for some when you're ready, but I got mine from Keely. She suggested I take some of the worms' bedding with them to give them something familiar. 'They get upset when they move wormeries,' she confided.

'How can you tell if a worm's upset?' I asked, intrigued at this need for a wormy comforter.

'They try to escape,' she replied.

When I got the worms home, a bit worried about having cooked them in the boot of my car (it was a boiling hot day and they don't like extremes of heat any more than they like the cold), I tipped the worms in their 'familiar' compost carefully onto dampened shredded newspaper in the wormery and added some new worm bedding compost to bolster their old bedding. They seemed a bit subdued but they were definitely moving, albeit in a lackadaisical fashion. It seemed fair enough. You wouldn't expect them to start a house-warming party before I'd even got the food in. I tipped in half the contents of the kitchen caddy, minus the remains of the trout we'd had the night before; in the extreme heat that would have been starting off a bit too optimistically. After that, the instructions said to leave the bin open for ten minutes (sunlight prompts the worms to burrow) and then seal them in. Extra lockdown precautions need to be taken in the first seven days, during which the wormery must be left undisturbed. There were additional catches on both sides of the lid to prevent any worms going AWOL.

A week later I opened the wormery, excited to see how the lads had settled in. (Actually, all worms are both lads and ladettes at the same time because they're hermaphrodites, which – parents be warned – can trigger some interesting questions about sex when you're least expecting them.) I was met by a scene of post-apocalyptic desolation. A bloom of white mould covered every-thing. It was more than a bloom. It was a mouldscape. Impressive white fluffy afros covered the bin's contents like disco wigs. From what I could see, the food waste underneath was undisturbed. There were no signs of life, no flashes of wriggly red tails, no indications that the worms had been doing their stuff. I assumed that the heat had proved too much for them but when I gently probed the surface with a garden fork I saw a couple of worms moving. OK, so they weren't getting much of a wriggle on, but they were definitely alive. I picked one up, wearing rubber gloves to protect it. It lay draped across my palm, playing dead again. I poked it gently. It recoiled, but slowly. It was quite a pale, pinky-grey fattish worm. I wondered if I had the wrong type: weren't they supposed to be thin, red little whiplashes? Perhaps it had just stuffed itself silly and was now too full to do anything much except lie about groaning, like you do after Christmas dinner? I replaced it, puzzled, and forked the bedding over some more. The worms were there all right. Heartened by this, I added four more handfuls of carefully selected kitchen waste (nothing too indigestible: strawberry hulls, carrot peelings, chopped leeks and wrinkled apples cut up into quarters), sealed the lid again and crossed my fingers.

Unfortunately, my worms never did get really stuck into their composting job. I tried a number of things: adding lots more dry shredded newspaper, as recommended; calcified seaweed (this is usually supplied with a wormery and is added to prevent conditions becoming too acidic); letting it rest; adding different food. Nothing seemed to get them going, even though, in theory, they should have been able to handle most of our kitchen waste after three weeks or so. Also, the compost seemed to be getting damper and damper and started to make vaguely squelchy noises despite the fact that when I turned the tap on at the bottom, nothing drained out, even when I tipped it forward (you should tap off the wormery regularly; the diluted leachate can be used as a plant feed). A combination of warm weather and water-rich foods such as lettuce and fruit peelings can encourage a release of moisture into the compost and, on Keely's instructions, I ended up adding balls and sheets of newspaper to help dry out the waterlogged compost. However, it seems there may have been a problem with that particular tap because, when Keely and I got round to taking the wormery apart, the leachate had built up in the sump, saturating the compost and effectively drowning the worms. When we poured it out it stank, the absolute worst smell I've ever smelt, plus there were what looked suspiciously like maggots in it.

A new tap was ordered, but after that I really didn't have the heart to give it another go. A website I visited on vermiculture says of raising your red wrigglers (as *Eisenia foetida* are colloquially called), 'Don't worry if you murder them all.' Apparently this is not uncommon, especially on a first go. But I did worry, because

I felt a responsibility to my worms and I'd failed them. I composted what I could salvage in my Dalek bin. It seemed only fitting. That's not to say I wouldn't recommend getting a wormery, because I've seen others that work perfectly and are teeming with happy, healthy worms producing wonderful compost. Perhaps they just didn't like being relocated to a new home. Or maybe they didn't like me. You never can tell with worms.

Challenge 37:
Do Bokashis and magic microbes do the business?

Once you start to become eco-smart about shopping, it's easy to develop a bit of a bee in your bonnet about things like plastic bags and packaging and recycling. I've seen these obsessive types and, were it not for my husband's cynicism providing a check to my (occasional) imbalances, I would be in danger of becoming one myself and then I'd never get invited to dinner parties. Hang on a minute, we *don't* get invited to dinner parties. Damn. However, I have been known to entertain here once in a while and I do find that the cooking and clearing away procedures intrigue our guests. Plate scrapings go into a kitchen caddy lined with newspaper. Raw fruit and vegetable peelings go into a lidded bucket by the bin. My mother-in-law gets so confused as to what goes where that she's given up on the grounds that she might put cooked spaghetti in the compost bucket and ruin the system. Our last guests made the mistake of showing a genuine interest and got taken down to the bottom of the garden to see the whole Bokashi-composting system in all its mucky glory. Now there's a new twist on the *Abigail's Party* theme. They left while I was still emptying a fermented chicken carcass into the composter. I can't think why.

Food waste is pretty revolting to look at, especially when it's all jumbled up together, and our natural instinct is to shove it in the bin. Out of sight, out of mind, end of story. Except that it isn't. An estimated 6.7 million tonnes of household food waste is produced each year in the UK which, to get that figure in perspective, makes up about 30 per cent of the waste collected by local authorities that goes to landfill. Most of it could have been eaten and the rest of it could, with the right equipment, be safely home composted. This is far more than packaging waste, which we tend to be more concerned about. Yet not only is all that chucked-away food a massive waste of money, it's also a massive squandering of energy. When we throw out a piece of cheese, we rarely think about all the physical and fossil energy that went into producing it, from rearing the cow, feeding it, milking it and making the cheese to packaging it, transporting it and refrigerating it. WRAP, the Waste Resources Action Programme, estimates that 20 per cent of the UK's greenhouse gas emissions are associated with food production, distribution and storage. According to WRAP's Love Food, Hate Waste campaign, if we stopped wasting food it would have the same impact in terms of CO_2 emissions as taking one in five cars off the road. And that's just from the embedded energy; once the food ends up in landfill its breakdown produces methane. In 2005, landfill sites accounted for 40 per cent of the total UK methane emissions so that's a double whammy of greenhouse gases as a result of our wasteful shopping, cooking and eating habits.

Top of the food waste pops are fresh fruit and vegetables, including potatoes, which account for 40 per cent by weight of food thrown away. The top five 'most wanted' foods after that are meat, fish, bread and bakery products, rice and pasta. WRAP says the fault lies in us cooking too much food and not using food up in time, both of which I'm certainly guilty of. From experience, I'd add that the doing-it-all-in-one-swoop method of supermarket shopping, with all its inducements and special offers and opportunities to impulse buy, also makes us over-consume. The Love Food, Hate Waste campaign has a website, www.lovefoodhatewaste.com, designed like a recipe book, with practical help and advice on calculating portions, planning meals, and storing food, and tons of recipes for using up leftovers, which is really useful. However, there are times when things are too far gone to make into soup or pasta bakes or slap between tortilla wraps with cheese and fry, and if you don't fancy eating up everyone else's plate scrapings then I'd recommend a Bokashi. Or a dog. But the Bokashi is less work, believe me.

While home composting allows you to get rid of fruit and vegetable peelings and things like teabags and coffee grounds and eggshells (but only if they're well crushed), you are not advised to compost meat, fish, dairy, bread, cereals or cooked food in a compost heap because of the risk of attracting rats. We managed to reduce the amount of rubbish we put out each week by half by simply doing basic composting, but I still found I was putting a lot of food in the bin. I might have persevered with the wormery, which provides one solution to the cooked food problem, had I not, by then, been introduced to Bokashis. For my money, they do the job much more efficiently and comprehensively than a wormery. Bokashis require virtually no maintenance, other than periodic draining and a regular wash out and they also improve the activity in your compost bin. Furthermore, they do not die on you, which is much better for morale.

So what are they? A Bokashi is a kitchen composter, basically a squat lidded bin that, used with a special bran-based activator, effectively neutralises odours and renders food waste unattractive to vermin, thus making it safe to compost. You can order kitchen composters and Bokashi bran from websites such as www.recyclenow.com and some councils are also doing special offers for residents, so check with your local authority. And if they don't, lobby them!

I admit, I was sceptical about their efficacy at first. Bunging in a chicken carcass, some festering feta, toast crusts, soggy cereal, uneaten spaghetti and mashed potato, as well as the usual vegetable peelings and apple cores that I'd collected in my kitchen caddy, I didn't see how this lot could not whiff after a fortnight. To this I added two scoops of Bokashi bran as instructed, sprinkling it over the entire surface so that all the food was covered. The bran is the magic ingredient. 'Bokashi' is a Japanese term meaning 'fermented organic matter' but the bran looks just like regular bran except that it contains friendly bacteria called EM or 'effective micro-organisms' that aid fermentation. It's important to squash the material down as far as it will go, because the system is anaerobic – the opposite of normal composting – and you need to get as much air out as possible. Once you've done that, the lid goes on and you can leave it in the kitchen or wherever is convenient, adding to it whenever the kitchen caddy is full and sprinkling on more Bokashi bran each time. You need two bins, as a full Bokashi needs to stand for a further two weeks to allow fermentation, and during that time you can start filling your second bucket.

Bokashi bins have a perforated separating tray over a sump in the bottom, just like a smaller version of my wormery. This allows liquid to drip through. As with the wormery, you need to drain off the excess liquid regularly by using the tap at the bottom. This can be collected in an old jug or plastic milk carton. The first time I did it, I made the mistake of leaving it a bit too long – about ten days – before collecting it, with the result that I drained off half a litre of straw-coloured liquid that smelled like – well, not to put too fine a point on it, baby sick. If you do it more regularly it doesn't pong, it just smells a bit cheesy. This liquid is actually full of nutrients and can be used in a variety of ways, either diluted as plant food or down drains and toilets to prevent algae build up and control odours. I was dubious that pouring it down the loo would actually improve things, but the kitchen sink is definitely less whiffy and my houseplants are loving it.

After the kitchen waste had fermented for a fortnight, I opened the Bokashi bucket with some trepidation. There was some white mould on top, which is normal, but no maggots or nasty surprises. In fact, nothing looked as if it had changed at all. If you leave a bucket of cooked chicken, fish bones, Weetabix mush, leftover chips, slimy lettuce and mouldy baked beans for two weeks, you kind of expect something to happen. I wouldn't be surprised if one of those toilet monsters, so beloved of loo-cleaner commercials, didn't crawl out snarling from the depths. You don't expect it to look just the same. It doesn't seem natural. You would also expect it to smell rank, but it really didn't smell. Well, not nasty, anyway. There is an ever-so-slightly pickled smell, but it's completely inoffensive.

The Bokashi is an in-between process; you still need to dispose of its contents either in your regular garden composter or by burying it if you really like digging. I put it into our Dalek bin, forking it in and covering each couple of forkfuls with drier material. It came out in a sort of jellified wodge, which needed breaking up and spreading around a bit. The advice is to layer it, so alternate it with twists of cardboard, screwed-up envelopes, fruit and veg peelings, straw, even vacuum cleaner dust or a little soil. It can be a bit yucky but there is no point in being squeamish about this; composting has its yucky side so you've just got to get over yourself. Once you've got used to it, the yuck factor won't bother you any more.

The benefits of using the Bokashis have been far greater than I'd anticipated. The first thing I noticed was that my compost converter was working extra-efficiently due to the EM, which carries on the fermenting process inside your bin. After you've added a Bokashi-load you'll find the level in your bin drops quite dramatically after a few days because it speeds up the composting rate, and it can really get quite hot in summer. If you put your hand in, you can feel the warmth coming off it and sometimes I've actually seen steam. Considering mine is a 'cold heap' (the usual, low-maintenance system; hot heaps require careful construction and frequent turning but rot down much more quickly) it can really get cooking in there. It also, I think, improves the quality of the compost you get at the end. Best of all though, by composting all of our kitchen waste through the Bokashi and regular compost heap, as well as recycling, we've reduced our rubbish still further to roughly half a bin bag a week (which is almost all non-recyclable plastic). That's an overall reduction of three-quarters from where I first started and I think it's a real achievement. What with that and all the WI recipes I've been exploring, no food waste goes to landfill from our house. There are, I admit, three extra helpers who assist with this. Our guinea-pig recycling team, Bubbles, Ginger and Pepper, aka 'the Spice Pigs', were bought mainly because I didn't like to see good stuff like broccoli stalks, cabbage leaves and carrot tops going into the compost bin. (Pepper has since been re-homed with Karen after creative differences set in: basically, he took the back-biting too literally.) Their bedding improves the fibre-moisture balance of the compost, too (but just add hay or straw; not sawdust, it takes forever to rot down).

There's another, unlooked-for advantage: the little chaps keep me entertained now that the worms have gone and I have no one to talk to when I'm at home writing all day. Yes, you're right, I should be getting out more. And now that I've finished this alternative supermarket trip, seen you back home and got rid of the rubbish I just might. Happy eco-shopping!

Conclusion

I wondered, when I set out to write this book, whether there was really a need for it any more. The situation has changed so rapidly over the past two to three years and environmental issues are finally setting the agenda. It may be twenty-five years behind schedule – much of this was being talked about in the early 1980s – but at least people are listening now. Or, at least, most of us are, though there are still some who cling determinedly to the notion that climate change is nothing to do with us. I chaired a debate recently in which a fervent global warming sceptic made just this argument. He won the DVD of Al Gore's film *An Inconvenient Truth* in the raffle.

I suspect that there are those with fixed opinions whom one can never reach, even when Bangladesh has disappeared completely under water and clothing retailers are forced to source cheap labour from higher ground. It's safer to cling to the minority view that it's all a big con or a conspiracy to raise stealth taxes; it's a much scarier prospect to accept that what more than 90 per cent of the world's scientists are saying is right. Still, the Pope and Rupert Murdoch have come on side now, Britain has a new Climate

Bill, and the USA has a new president, Barack Obama, who has put climate change at the top of his political agenda and is determined, like Britain, to cut CO_2 emissions by 80% of 1990 levels by 2050. Maybe we're not as doomed as we thought.

I was talking to someone at a party the other day, telling them about my attempts to live a greener lifestyle, and they asked me whether I was optimistic about the future. I admit the question set me back a bit. Whatever I do as an individual can feel utterly futile at times, especially when I read the headlines in the *Independent*. Then I pick up the *Sun* and realise people are far more into *The X-Factor* than the destruction of humanity and I can't blame them (apart from their taste in TV reality shows). Even if the Intergovernmental Panel on Climate Change believes we've got less than ten years to forestall global catastrophe, it still doesn't seem real. As Homer J Simpson says on my favourite tea mug: 'No catastrophes today'. The words are printed inside a big green radioactive mushroom cloud, giving the lie to this. Happy Homer is giving us the thumbs-up in the midst of a meltdown.

I wouldn't be bothering with all of this, and doing these (occasionally nutty) eco-challenges, if I didn't think there was hope. To me, there's no alternative: I have a daughter and I want her to have the best future she can. It's taken just a couple of hundred years to trash the planet and now we're going to dump it on our kids' doorsteps and say, 'You deal with it'? I don't think so. It's our problem and it's happening now. Although I'm a fan of Obama, I don't trust governments to act out of any sense of moral duty, though economic expediency may yet save the day. As to large corporations, their first duty is to their shareholders, although even investors are beginning to revolt against the obscenity of the system. (On 30 June 2007, the *Guardian* reported that almost 20 per cent of Tesco's shareholders at the company's London AGM voted against an executive pay deal and called on the supermarket to pay workers in the developing world a better wage instead.) Typically, the supermarkets' response is that we can buy our way out of environmental crisis. Tesco's chief executive Sir Terry Leahy has called for 'a mass movement in green consumption', a kind of 'When the going gets tough, the tough go shopping' approach. But while I agree with him that ethical consumerism can make a difference – I wouldn't be writing this book if I didn't – being an eco-shopper isn't just about buying stuff. The concept of 'enoughness', as espoused by E. F. Schumacher in *Small is Beautiful*, appears to have been lost by us.

David Cameron made a speech in May 2006 in which he called much of modern consumer culture 'unsatisfactory', adding, 'It's time we focused not just on GDP but on GWB – general well-being', which gave me a glimmer of hope. I haven't heard him repeat this assertion since, though perhaps it's for the best: a Tory Ministry for Happiness is a scary prospect. The main thing is to buy less and make what you do buy count. Reuse things. Make things. Share things. Love things. Keep things. But know when not to buy things, too.

So is Tesco boss Leahy right about green shopping being 'the new revolution' in sustainability? I was making Sunday lunch and half-listening to the radio when I caught Professor Tim Lang, the man who invented 'food miles', on *The Food Programme*. Tim Lang has campaigned on food policy issues for many years and wrote about how supermarkets were crushing wholesalers and markets back in the mid-1990s. He told the interviewer, Simon Parkes, that more than ten years on, little had changed. 'You cannot have a cornucopia in a supermarket of 26,000 items of food and not be raping and pillaging the earth. It is not possible.' Asked whether consumers can change things, he said that it came down to a 'big fight' between two structural issues: choice-led individualism – the single-handed purchases we make at a personal level, also called the 'choice ethic' (ie, me dithering over whether to buy Fairtrade or Yorkshire Tea), the impact of which he called 'piddly' at a global level – and 'choice editing', which is where someone with a system you can trust delivers it for us.

Ah, trust. There's the rub. Throughout the course of writing this book I have come up against the trust issue again and again. First of all, there's the matter of our own sense of trust and whether it is, at times, misplaced. Just because a company or a retailer or an organisation is a big one, are we right to trust it automatically? Or is our unquestioning trust in it little more than wilful ignorance? Trust removes complications and difficult choices, but trust has to be earned. How many of us – myself included – have said, 'Don't tell me, I don't want to know' when someone tries to tell us how chickens are slaughtered or reveals that there's lead in our favourite lipstick? Don't tell me that dairy farmers are losing their livelihood; I only come here because the milk's cheap. Don't tell me about the coffee growers who can't afford medicine for their children; I always drink that brand. We don't want to know about the cotton growers who've committed suicide or the citrus growers poisoned with pesticides or the fish that have changed sex due to household chemicals. It's easier just to trust. Knowledge is a nuisance. Knowledge compels you to act. That, or it condemns you to indifference.

Our acceptance of the status quo is something that manufacturers and retailers rely on; once we ask them to validate our trust it puts the heat on them. *Can* we find a system we can trust to deliver the goods? When you start asking questions and pursue a subject beyond the corporate spin, you start to discover that things are not always as clear-cut as they would have us believe. When I began this journey I never expected to be examining some of the subjects in the depth that I have done. It wasn't my intention, but that is where the questions led me, like following that white rabbit of Alice's down the deep, dark rabbit hole into a place where perspectives are unexpectedly different.

I'm not saying that retailers are all out to deceive us: on balance, most people's decision to trust a store or a supplier is reasonably well founded, most of the time. There are, after all, laws and regulations to keep the system in place and reputations to be upheld. But trust is a complicated equation: it requires credibility, reliability and a degree of intimacy to acquire that status, things that the supermarkets, especially, work hard to promote with their loyalty cards and special offers, clubs and coupons, marketing and sponsorship, computers for kids and corporate responsibility statements. For all that meticulous reputation-building, trust can evaporate in a moment when a scandal breaks (eg, the milk price-fixing allegations) and self-interest shows its hand. Self-interest, for which read 'profit', is what really drives business; the warm, green fuzzy stuff is great PR and it does achieve some good but never forget that it's part of the battle for your trust and your cash. That is why 'the system' works best when there is genuine competition – and not just from other supermarkets. And that is why we must continue to ask questions. If you don't like the answer, don't buy the product – and make sure you tell them why.

As consumers, we have extraordinary powers to initiate change. But if it were up to us, and us alone, to force the pace, we'd never do it. The choice ethic is valuable because it's a catalyst for change; if enough people choose to buy Fairtrade bananas or Fairtrade coffee, say, choice editing – in this case, Sainsbury's deciding to sell only Fairtrade bananas and M&S deciding to sell only Fairtrade tea and coffee – will follow. But choice-led individualism is still largely a luxury of the middle classes; it certainly isn't an option for people on low incomes. We're constantly being told we ought to be paying more for our food and, being Mrs Eco-Shopper, I do. But there's not a lot over for extras. We can't afford holidays and our house is tatty. You can see why people go for cheap chicken and cheaper flights. It's an awful lot easier.

Joel, my dance teacher, and I had this conversation when we were taking a break between tangos. I'd brought up Socrates, the Ancient Greek philosopher who believed that, if we know the right thing to do, we will do it. Not out of a sense of moral obligation, but because to do anything less ultimately damages ourselves. It's common sense, or at least you'd think it would be: if we know what to do to save the planet, we'll take whatever steps are necessary. If we don't, we are in danger of losing everything we hold dear. It may be logical but, as Joel pointed out, that doesn't make it human nature. Cigarette packs carry stark warnings that 'Smoking Kills' and people still smoke. They get drunk even though it's bad for their liver and they take short-haul flights even though it's bad for the environment. Taking personal responsibility for something you feel you have no control over, particularly when it involves changing your behaviour, is not a great motivation. Easier to shrug your shoulders and say, 'If we're all going to fry, we might as well have fun.'

This is where we look to our leaders to put those 'systems you can trust' in place to help us to do what's necessary. In July 2007, I went to lobby my MP, Hugh Bayley, about climate change. I cycled round to the Labour Party office in the rain, risking life and limb (I'm still terrified in traffic and dismount rather than turn right, but I'm wobbling less now) with the bike stuck in third gear. I guess if you're going to make a point about the need to take personal responsibility for the environment, arriving sweaty and dishevelled with smudged mascara and helmet hair shows you're trying. I asked Hugh Bayley whether he thought people – including politicians – were aware of how little time we have to take action before it's too late. 'I honestly don't think Parliament and the public have recognised just how critically important climate change is,' he said. How depressing is that? If those in power still don't get it, what hope is there? We talked about Kyoto and Tony Blair and the G8 and China and all the 'Earth in Imminent Peril' headlines and whether they prompted people to act or simply made them too depressed and fearful to do anything. He said: 'I'm not sure that scaring the pants off people is the wrong thing to do, providing you can convince them there is something they can do.' He was flattering about my list of eco-challenges – 'it's a wonderful prompt for action' – and said he'd look into doing home composting. We have corresponded since over the Climate Bill, with the result that he invited me to several public consultation meetings about it. At least a hundred other people came to the meetings – ordinary people, concerned that not enough was being done, who spoke passionately about the need for change. Mr Bayley listened to us and, together with a group of other MPs, pushed the Government to set higher emissions targets. It did, partly because lots of ordinary people did the same and signed petitions such as The Big Ask, Friends of the Earth's campaign. This is democracy in action. Take part.

I'm not making any great claims for myself, but at least I've used the system. It wasn't difficult. In fact, there's nothing earth-shattering about any of the challenges I've attempted. But, you know, that's the point. The challenges I set myself are about making lots of little changes, rather than investing in expensive kit. Besides which, like most people, we simply can't afford to. It would be nice to be able to generate enough electricity to heat our hot water, say, but until the Government provides serious financial support for greening our homes (discounts for home insulation are a good start but it ought to be free for everybody) then draught-proofing the doors, turning down the thermostat and putting foil behind the radiators is, at least, a step in the right direction. I agreed to make a Video Nation film for the BBC recently, but when it came to it, I thought, 'Well, what is there to show people? We haven't got a wind turbine or chickens in the back garden or solar panels on the roof.' So I told my composting story and showed off my Bokashi bins and filmed the vegebox being delivered instead (http://www.bbc.co.uk/northyorkshire/content/articles/2007/10/05/kate_lock_composting_videonation_video_feature.shtml). Quentin Tarantino it isn't, but when I got choked up at the end the emotion was real.

Most of the challenges I succeeded in doing; some of them I failed. Still, you can learn as much from failure as from success and I hope my experiences will be useful to other people. The situation is changing all the time and I've no doubt that, in the months between updating this book and it being published some issues, particularly regarding packaging and waste, will have moved on yet again. I hope so. As for the challenges themselves, they've forced me to reassess how I live my life. I've made real changes, and not just for the sake of the book – although I'll admit I might not have got around to some of them without the pressure of a deadline. Our carbon footprint is now down to under 5 tonnes of CO_2, which is more than three tonnes less than before and less than half the UK average. This year, our big step has been to get rid of the car. We've also improved our home insulation, which stretched us financially but will pay dividends in terms of lower heating bills. After that, who knows? Perhaps I will get a goat, after all.

It's been a life-altering experience, in a humble way. I'm not the magazine-reading, beauty-product-addicted shopaholic I was and I've discovered a more radical side to my nature, too. I've also discovered that you can't do everything. There isn't the time and you'll end up having a nervous breakdown over a saucepan of greasy homemade gravy wailing, 'Why did I listen to Janet Street-Porter?' Believe me, I've been there.

But we can all do something, and probably a lot more than we think, as the friends and family and strangers that have joined me in these challenges have proved. I'd like to thank everyone who helped – it really feels like a communal effort – and I'd especially like to thank all the people who took that extra step and made changes to their lifestyles. Will all this stop the polar ice caps melting? No. As Al Gore says, 'Along with changing the light bulbs, we need to change the laws.' And we need presidents and prime ministers to do that. But they answer to us and that's what keeps me motivated because all around me I see and hear people asking questions, people altering their own behaviour, people demanding green and ethical alternatives. The tide is changing. What started out as a ripple has become a groundswell and that groundswell is rapidly becoming a great wave of public support for a more sustainable future.

So, to return to the question I was asked at that party: am I optimistic? Yes. Becoming an eco-shopper isn't difficult or, necessarily, expensive. As I've demonstrated, a greener lifestyle is very often a cheaper and more rewarding lifestyle that can save families money (up to a thousand pounds a year if you make lots of small but significant changes, according to Marks and Spencer's Plan A). And, before you know it, all those little changes bring about bigger changes, including your own mindset. OK, my husband still won't do the composting, but he is now helping to shape green IT strategy in government departments, which could cut considerably more carbon. My daughter is no longer Miss Nintendo DS but a bike-riding junior eco-warrior. As for me, I'm going to keep writing, lobbying and speaking out. And making soup. See you by the organic veg . . .

Acknowledgements

Lots of people have helped with the research for this book and most of them didn't even get a free drink (with the exception of the scientists, who had to drink so that we could rate their headaches the morning after). So to all those friends, family and neighbours who tested everything from homemade moisturisers to Mooncups or who joined me in my experiments with worm-charming and swishing, or who emailed me links or read the manuscript or just gave me moral support, a big thank you (and apologies if I've missed anyone out). They are, in no particular order: Pauline, Karen, Lucy, Michael, Cath, Keely, Ivana, Joel, Yvonne, Sam, Spit, Deborah, Cindy, Patricia, Helen, Anastasia, Steve, Compost John, Janet and Dave, Harriet, Adrian, Lara (and Arlo), Naomi, Margaret, my sisters Debby and Claire, nephews Nathan, Ben, James and Dan, mother-in-law Pam and my Auntie Maggie. Also, my daughter's friends Jack, Jenny, Coral, Grace, Niall, Martha, Alice, Amy and Sarah.

Thanks are also due to: the mums and children of the Very Young Friends of Rowntree Park; Andy and Bernie at Bike Rescue; the teachers at Scarcroft Primary School; the gardening team at

Brunswick Organic Nursery; Ebor Brass Band; Goosemoor Organics; Kat and Denise of ecoathome; John B and the team at York Environment Centre; York Rotters; Gary and the team at the Stockholm Environment Institute; breastfeeding café mums Kathryn, Rachel, Amanda and Denise; Hannah Tyzack; the real nappy testers – Lucy and Samuel, Ellen and Thomas, Mandy and Evie and Acacia, her mum and baby CJ – not forgetting Sam Armstrong, who did a wonderful job of project managing, as well as Maria Knight, Lindsey Green and Lollipop, Sure Start and TotsBots for providing the nappies.

I also appreciate the time and trouble that the following people gave me: Dr Chris Exley, Dr Gareth Morgan of Oinoudidasko Wine Education, Jem Gardener of Vinceremos, Peter Fawcett of Field & Fawcett, Mark Dawson of York Fairtrade Forum, Jane Holroyd of Mother Earth, Steve Parker of Cusp, Anthony Dew of the Rocking Horse Shop, Robert Nathan of the British Toymakers Guild, Mike Stables of Softwalker and Hugh Bayley MP.

Finally – well, almost – I'd like to thank my editor, Judith Longman, her assistant Cecilia Moore and the team at Hodder; my agent, Sheila Ableman and Chris Titley, who gave me the column on *The Press* from which sprouted the germ of this book.

Last but not least, undying love and gratitude to my husband, who prefers to remain a man of mystery, and my daughter Isis, for their patience, good humour and belief in me and for almost never leaving the TV on standby now.

Web Directory

Aisle 1: Fresh Challenges

Supermarkets:

Tescopoly is an alliance of organisations concerned about the negative impacts of supermarket power. It has information on local campaigns and how you can get involved. www.tescopoly.org

Friends of the Earth (www.foe.co.uk) is running campaigns to 'Say no to monster supermarkets' and stop supermarket bullying. Go to www.foe.co.uk /campaigns/real_food/press_for_change/

Competition Commission inquiry into supermarkets: www.competition-commission.org.uk/inquiries/ref2006/grocery/index.htm

Organic box schemes:

I use Goosemoor Organics near Wetherby which delivers throughout the north of England – www. goosemoor.co.uk. To find your nearest organic box scheme go to the Soil Association's website, www.soilassociation.org/ directory. For useful recipes and much more, go to www.vegboxrecipes. co.uk (they even have a 'rogues gallery' for identifying mystery veg!)

Local shopping:

FARMA (www.farma.org.uk) is a co-operative of farmers and producers selling on a local scale and farmers' markets organisations.

www.farmersmarkets.net is the only directory of inspected and certified farmers' markets in the UK.

www.farmshopping.net lists farm shops that are members of FARMA.
www.pickyourown.info lists 'PYO' farms throughout the UK and highlights what's in season.

Allotments and veg gardening:
www.allotments-uk.com has a directory of allotment sites and heaps of advice. To find out about allotment availability in your area contact your local authority or go to their website.
The BBC has a great gardening site that's very beginner-friendly and has all the links to the networks' TV and radio gardening programmes: www.bbc.co.uk/gardening/

Aisle 2: Homemade Challenges
TV Chefs & links:
www.jamieoliver.com will take you to *Jamie's School Dinners, Jamie's Fowl Dinners, Jamie at Home* and all other things Jamie.
www.chickenout.tv is the website for River Cottage's Chicken Out campaign.

WI:
The Women's Institute www.womens-institute.co.uk/ is 'the modern voice of today's woman' and a fantastic campaigning body, fighting to promote sustainable consumption and working to reduce food waste through its Love Food Champions.

Aisle 3: Chiller Challenges
Milk:
www.findmeamilkman.net should help do the job.

Vegetarianism/Veganism:
The Vegetarian Society: www.vegsoc.org/
The Vegan Society: www.vegansociety.com
Compassion in World Farming: www.ciwf.org.uk/

Fish:
www.fishonline.org tells you which fish you should and should not eat. It's a website of the Marine Conservation Society (www.mcsuk.org/).
The Marine Stewardship Council (www.msc.org/) is an independent non-profit organisation that promotes responsible fishing practices.
Freedom Food is an RSPCA-monitored UK farm assurance scheme. Go to www.rspca.org.uk/ and click on Freedom Food.
Loch Fyne restaurants: www.lochfyne.com

Aisle 4: Household Challenges
Chemicals:
www.chemtrust.org.uk is a charity that works to protect humans and wildlife from harmful chemicals.

Environmentally friendly cleaning and laundry products:
Ecover (www.ecover.com); Bio-D (www.biodegradable.biz); E-cloths (www.e-cloth.com); Dryer balls (www.dryerballs.co.uk). If you can't source the above products locally (Lakeland shops sell Ecoballs and cryerballs or go to www.lakeland.co.uk) you can buy them online at sites such as Natural Collection (www.naturalcollection.com). Others to try include Ethical Superstore (www.ethicalsuperstore.com), which sells the Soapods soap nuts and Ecoballs, as do Alternative Stores (www.alternativestores.com) and Ecozone (www.ecozone.com).

Food storage:
Natural Collection (see above) stocks the silicone food covers (called Eco food covers) and a whole lot else besides. Onya Weigh bags for food storage from www.onyabags.co.uk

Aisle 5: Healthy Challenges 1
Toxins in cosmetics:
The Women's Environmental Network campaigns on environment and health issues from a female perspective (www.wen.org.uk).
There's also lots of helpful info on the Channel 4 website for *Beauty Addicts: How Toxic Are You?* www.channel4.com/health/microsites/T/toxic/

The excellent US Campaign For Safe Cosmetics website allows you to check out the chemicals in your beauty products. Go to www.safecos metics.org and click on The Skin Deep Report.

Beauty products:
Lush beauty products: www.lush.co.uk
Udderly SMOOth Udder Cream is available in the UK from selected stockists and on line. Go to www.udderlysmooth.co.uk for details.
Green People: www.greenpeople.co.uk
Mother Earth: www.motherearth.co.uk
Shea Alchemy: www.sheaalchemy.co.uk

Making your own beauty products:
Culpeper (www.culpeper.co.uk); Neal's Yard (www.nealsyardremedies. com) and G Baldwin & Co, the UK's leading herbalist and supplier of natural products and remedies (www.baldwins.co.uk). And try your local pharmacy, too!

Aisle 6: Healthy Challenges 2
Deodorant:
PitRok natural deodorant: www.pitrok.co.uk

Sanpro:
Mooncups (menstrual cups) are now available at larger branches of Boots, or buy them online at www.mooncup.co.uk
Menstrual pads: Moonrabbits: www.moonrabbits.co.uk; Lunapads (from www.twinkleontheweb.co.uk).
Or make your own menstrual pads: (http://www.wen.org.uk/sanpro/reports/makeyourown_web.pdf)
Natracare sanitary products: www.natracare.com

Aisle 7: Liquid Challenges 1
Relevant Organisations:
Fairtrade Foundation: www.fairtrade.org.uk
Ethical Tea Partnership: www.ethicalteapartnership.org
Rainforest Alliance: www.rainforestalliance.org

Tea and coffee:

Teadirect information is on the Café Direct site: www.cafedirect.co.uk
Clipper: www.clipper-teas.com
Yorkshire Tea: www.yorkshiretea.co.uk
Good African Coffee: www.goodafrican.com
Fair Instant Coffee: www.fair-instant.co.uk

Aisle 8: Liquid Challenges 2

Wine:

Vinceremos is the UK's leading organic wine specialists www.vinceremos.
co.uk
Field and Fawcett (delicatessen and wine merchants, based in York)
www.fieldandfawcett.co.uk
Oinoudidasko Wine Education: www.oinoudidasko.co.uk/

Juices:

Tetrapak sustainability: www.tetrapakrecycling.co.uk
Innocent smoothies and juices, etc: www.innocentdrinks.co.uk

Water:

Belu water: www.belu.org
Water Aid: www.wateraid.org/uk/
Brita: www.brita.net/uk and click on the recycling locator which will give
you the nearest participating retailer.
Tap bottles: www.wewanttap.com

Aisle 9: Baby Challenges

Nappies:

Real Nappy Campaign: www.realnappycampaign.com
The Real Nappy Exchange is a service run by WEN. Go to
http://www.wen.org.uk/nappies/parents.htm
www.ukparentslounge.com has a directory of small and independent
nappy sellers.
Real nappy companies mentioned in the book:
Lollipop (www.teamlollipop.co.uk)

TotsBots (www.totsbots.com)
Bambino Mio cotton nappies (www.bambinomio.com)
Frugi (was Cut4Cloth) makes organic cotton clothes to fit over cloth nappies: www.welovefrugi.com

Breastfeeding & Baby Milk
The Breastfeeding Manifesto: www.breastfeedingmanifesto.org.uk
NCT (National Childbirth Trust): www.nctpregnancyandbabycare.com
Baby Milk Action: www.babymilkaction.org
Nestle: Baby Milk Issue Facts: www.babymilk.nestle.com/
For legislation: www.babyfeedinglawgroup.org.uk

Toys
Toy recalls: www.mattel.com/safety
British Toymakers Guild: www.toymakersguild.co.uk

Aisle 10: Material Challenges
Campaign groups:
Labour Behind the Label (www.labourbehindthelabel.org). See also www.cleanupfashion.co.uk/
Environmental Justice Foundation: www.ejfoundation.org

Organisations:
The Ethical Trading Initiative: www.ethicaltrade.org

TV links:
The BBC has an online fashion magazine, *Thread*, devoted to eco-friendly style: www.bbc.co.uk/thread/. There's also a link to the four-part BBC Three series, *Blood, Sweat and T-Shirts* (www.bbc.co.uk/thread/blood-sweat-tshirts/)

Fairtrade & Organic Clothing:
People Tree (www.peopletree.co.uk)
Natural Collection (www.naturalcollection.com)
Adili (www.adili.com)

Ciel (www.ciel.ltd.uk/)
Katharine E Hamnett (www.katharinehamnett.com)
Junky Styling (www.junkystyling.co.uk)
Stewart+Brown (www.stewartbrown.com)
Mumo (www.mumo-uk.com)
Del Forte Denim (www.delforte.com)
Clean Slate Clothing (www.cleanslateclothing.co.uk): Fairtrade and organic school uniforms.

Shoes:

Crocs recycling: www.solesunited.com (US); also through www.fatshoes day.co.uk (UK).
Terraplana: www.terraplana.com. See also Worn Again's website: www.wornagain.co.uk
Softwalker Shoes: www.softwalker.co.uk
Turn your jeans into funky eco sandals at www.recycleyourjeans.com

Aisle 11: Checkout Challenges
Alternatives to plastic bags

www.wearewhatwedo.org is a movement inspiring people to use their everyday actions to change the world. Declining plastic bags is no. 1 on their list.
www.onyabags.co.uk practical, stylish bags that attach to your own bag with a clip so that you've always got it 'on ya'.
www.turtlebags.co.uk colourful string shopping bags that help to save the turtle!

Reduce, reuse, recycle

Revolve (By Cutouts) makes environmentally responsible giftware out of post-consumer waste: www.revolve-uk.com
Remarkable gives new life to recyclables from car tyres to plastic cups by turning them into stationery: www.remarkable.co.uk
Find Recycler the robot at www.recyclezone.org.uk, the site for schools, children and teachers.
www.recyclenow.com has information and help on everything you need to know about recycling and composting. Also, www.letsrecycle.com is

the UK's leading news and information service on recycling and waste management.

Buy Nothing Day (www.buynothingday.co.uk/).

The Compact (http://groups.yahoo.com/group/thecompact/) is a group committed to a 12-month flight from the consumer grid (calendar year 2008). More on the blog: http://sfcompact.blogspot.com/

Freecycle (www.uk.freecycle.org) is a grassroots movement who are giving (and getting) stuff for free in their own towns.

Aisle 12: Rubbish Challenges

Composting

The RecycleNow website has loads of information and links on home composting: www.recyclenow.com/compost/

York Rotters: www.stnicksfield.org.uk

Worms and wormeries

www.wigglywigglers.co.uk has worms, wormeries (including the Can-o-Worms) and a whole lot more.

Home composters/Bokashi

Available from Recycle Now (see composting) or try www.evengreener. com, part of Straight plc, the UK's leading recycling products and services group.

General:

Non-Government Organisations

The Soil Association (www.soilassociation.org/)

Waste Online (www.wasteonline.org.uk/)

World Wildlife Fund (www.wwf.org.uk). To calculate your carbon footprint go to http://footprint.wwf.org.uk

The Fairtrade Foundation (www.fairtrade.org.uk)

Sustain (www.sustainweb.org)

www.together.com: 'easy ways to help combat climate change'.

The Stockholm Environment Institute: www.york.ac.uk/inst/sei/

WRAP (www.wrap.org.uk), the Waste and Resources Action Programme, helps individuals, businesses and local authorities to reduce waste and recycle more.

RecycleNow (www.recyclenow.com)

Government Organisations

Defra (Department for Environment, Food and Rural Affairs): www.defra.gov.uk

CEFAS (Centre for Environment, Fisheries and Aquaculture Science, an agency of Defra): www.cefas.co.uk

National Office for Statistics: www.statistics.gov.uk

The Food Standards Agency: www.foodstandards.gov.uk/

The Environment Agency: www.environment-agency.gov.uk

And finally . . . Me!

www.ecosmartshopper.co.uk is the website for this book, which will continue to chart my progress and will aim to keep you updated as things (inevitably) change on the eco-shopping scene. It's part of my blog, http://blog.klockworks.co.uk

To see my Video Nation film, 'Compost Crazy', go to www.bbc. co.uk/northyorkshire/contents/articles/2007/10/05/kate_lock_composting _videonation_video_feature_shtml